Political Education in the Southern Farmers' Alliance, *1887–1900*

Theodore R. Mitchell

Political Education in the Southern Farmers' Alliance, *1887–1900*

The University of Wisconsin Press

Published 1987

The University of Wisconsin Press
114 North Murray Street
Madison, Wisconsin 53715

The University of Wisconsin Press, Ltd.
1 Gower Street
London WC1E 6HA, England

First Printing

Printed in the United States of America

For LC CIP information see p. 242

ISBN 0-299-11470-8 cloth, 0-299-11474-0 paper

For My Parents

Who helped me see and hear and ask

Contents

viii   Contents

Illustrations

Tables

Acknowledgments

This is the fun part. While it has been a joy to live for several years with the members and leaders of the Farmers' Alliance, it is a greater pleasure still to acknowledge publicly the help and support of friends. That friendship, often manifest at critical junctures, has made this project possible and has more surely improved its quality.

David Tyack—teacher, scholar, and friend—played the central role in the development of this book. His strong but gentle guidance has and will continue to be a model.

Carl Degler led me to the Farmers' Alliance and, once there, insisted that I learn from the mistakes of those who preceded me.

Mark Mancall taught me to look at the world in ways that were new and unfamiliar. That teaching, which continues in profound ways, has informed every step of this work.

In addition to these three, several people have read all or part of the book and have provided valuable insight and assistance: Nelson Kasfir, Joel Levine, W. Richard Scott, Harvey Kantor, Faith Dunne, Bill Spencer, Peter Gunn, and Dru van Hengel.

Librarians at Dartmouth, Stanford, UNC—Chapel Hill, and archivists at the Southern Historical Collection, the Rockefeller Archive Center, and the Library of Congress have taken me under their wing and with consummate skill and good humor have unlocked treasures that have enriched this work in untold ways.

The editors at the University of Wisconsin Press, Gordon Lester-Massman, Nancy Brower, and Jack Kirshbaum, sped the production of this book along and made valuable contributions, always with professionalism and good humor.

xiii

Stanford University, the National Institute of Mental Health, the State of California, the Charles Culpeper Foundation, and Dartmouth College have all provided generously for the funding of this project. To each of these organizations I owe a great debt.

To four individuals go special thanks for their friendship. Beginning in graduate school, Harvey Kantor and Bob Lowe learned much more about the Alliance than they wanted to, but their thoughtful comments and our long conversations over the years are deeply embedded in the argument of this book. Dru van Hengel became a part of this project as an undergraduate research assistant. She transcended that role early on and has logged long hours working and reworking the text and footnotes and keeping me on track amidst a flurry of distractions.

Completing a manuscript requires sacrifices of various kinds, but the brunt of these fall not on the author, but on those she or he loves. It has been so in this case. Jane Ackerman has lived with this project from its beginnings, as an unavoidable consequence of living with me. She knows the Alliance at least as well as I do now, and is at least as good a writer. I should probably have turned the project over to her years ago. As my friend, as my severest critic, as my staunchest defender, Jane has had a hand in every word. Quite simply, her support, her patience, and her encouragement are responsible for the completion of this manuscript.

The responsibility for what follows is, of course, mine. I am grateful to all these friends, old and new, for saving me from some errors and I lay claim alone to those that remain.

Political Education in the Southern Farmers' Alliance, *1887–1900*

Prologue

The Farmers' Alliance and Political Education

*The Alliance movement, during its brief existence, has done
more to educate the great mass of people in the principles of
government than all the schools and colleges have in the past
century. The people are, through the methods made use of by
the Alliance, learning the rights and duties of citizenship with a
rapidity and clearness truly alarming to the chronic politician.*
—Col. R. J. Sledge, Alliance organizer, 1891[1]

We educate to contend for universal right and justice!
—Nelson Dunning, Alliance historian, 1888[2]

1

At 1:30 P.M. on October 12, 1887, Texan Charles Macune walked to
the podium at the convention hall in Shreveport, Louisiana, to open
the first annual meeting of the National Farmers' Alliance and Cooperative Union. "This is indeed an auspicious occasion," he began.
"It is the first session of this body; and this body is the first organization of real cotton growers inaugurated on a plan calculated to assist
the poor man."[3] The meeting was a personal triumph for Macune. His
efforts and persistent negotiation over a one-year period brought together under a single banner several independent agrarian organizations, each working to reverse the rapidly deteriorating economic position of farmers and rural producers in the South. Although 'national'
overstated the scope of the organized movement for most of its history, the National Alliance brought together the Texas Farmers'
Alliance, the Louisiana Farmers' Union, the Arkansas Agricultural
Wheel, and several smaller farmers' organizations around a single
rallying point: to "assist the poor man."[4] While members of earlier

1. R. J. Sledge, "The Duties of Membership," in *Farmers' Alliance History and
Agricultural Digest,* ed. N. A. Dunning (Washington, D.C.: Alliance Publishing Company, 1892), 330.
2. Dunning, *Farmers' Alliance History,* 260.
3. Macune's address is reported in Dunning, *Farmers' Alliance History,* 67–69, and
in W. L. Garvin and S. O. Daws, *The History of the National Farmers' Alliance and
Cooperative Union* (Jacksboro, Tex.: J. N. Rogers & Co.: 1887), 63–64, and in the
Dallas, Texas, *Southern Mercury,* October 15, 1887.
4. Histories of the National Alliance abound. From contemporaries and participants

organizations of working people, the Workingmen's party of the 1830s for example, might quibble with Macune's claim to uniqueness, neither they nor we can deny the importance of the Alliance. For a decade, between 1888 and 1898, the Farmers' Alliance challenged politics as usual in the South "with a rapidity and clarity" that did indeed alarm the "chronic politician." In its challenge, the Alliance broadened the scope of political discourse in ways that still demand attention.

First, the Alliance played an important oppositional role in the realignment and redefinition of American electoral politics that took place in the last decades of the nineteenth century. In the face of growing professionalism in politics, the Alliance demanded a political culture that was Jacksonian in its scope, drawing Macune's "poor man" into political debate. In the face of government support of concentrated industrial and financial capital, the Alliance demanded a political system that was Jeffersonian in its purpose, using government to serve the interests of the small independent producer. The Alliance most often defined these interests by negation, specifically by opposing its aims to those of urban-based political professionals on one hand and to the growing hegemony of industrial and financial interests on the other. Their voice stood out against the very assumptions of progress that predominated in the Gilded Age.

Second, Alliance opposition to what it saw as the shifting of political power from the people to the experts, from the countryside to the city, and from the farm to the corporate boardroom, brought into momentary but sharp focus the major tensions in the emergent American polity. In highlighting the growing polarization of interest, power, and wealth in America the Alliance and its partners in the agrarian movement identified—even if they did not fully understand, appreciate, or come to terms with—the major dichotomies and oppositions that define us still today. More to the point, Alliance efforts to define itself, define what it stood for and what it stood against, raised the major social, economic, and political questions of their generation and our own.

Third, and most important here, Alliance leaders offered the move-

---

in the movement we have Dunning's *Farmers' Alliance History,* Garvin and Daws, *History of the National Farmers' Alliance;* and a partial autobiographical history by Charles Macune, "The Farmers Alliance," in the Eugene C. Barker Texas History Collection (University of Texas Archives, Austin). Secondary histories exist for the National Alliance and for state alliances throughout the South. See Appendix A for specific histories.

ment as a remedy to the drift toward centralized power and wealth, as the last chance for the mass of common people to gain power over the government and its laws. To leaders like Macune, both the problem and the solution boiled down to one issue, political education. The farmers had allowed political power to slip from their grasp because they lacked education in politics. The movement called upon education as the most important weapon in its struggle to restore that power, to revive democratic citizenship, and to equalize access to wealth. Alliance lecturer Harry Tracy summed up the movement's faith in and dependence upon education:

> The only remedy visible or possible is to educate the masses upon the sciences of social, financial, and political economy . . . to the teaching of these indispensible fundamental principles of popular government the [Alliance] is bending its every effort, with the firm belief that every citizen in the U.S. who loves freedom, justice, and law will rally to its support.[5]

For Macune, the relationship between the Alliance and education was even more fundamental: "the Alliance (was) founded on education. All it is," he continued, "and all it will ever be must emanate from that source."[6]

This is the story of that education, it is a history of the political educating defined and carried out by the Alliance. It is a history of the self-conscious attempt by the leaders of the agrarian movement to educate farmers and their families in "the science of economical government" and of their efforts, through education, to give farmers a clear and united voice in political and economic debate.[7] These were substantial tasks, and by 1891, leaders like R. J. Sledge could point with pride to an organization engaging nearly one million members across the South in the Alliance's project of mass political education.

The experience of Sledge, Macune, and thousands of Alliance lecturers throughout the South constitutes an important story for those interested in the ways education proceeds outside schools. It is also an important story for those interested in the ways oppositional move-

5. *National Economist,* June 29, 1889.
6. *National Economist,* September 5, 1891.
7. Throughout, I have relied on Lawrence Cremin's definition of education as "the deliberate, systematic, and sustained effort to transmit, evoke, or acquire knowledge, attitudes, values, skills, or sensibilities." Cremin, *American Education: The Colonial Experience, 1607–1783* (New York: Harper and Row, 1970), xiii.

Colonel R. J. Sledge, 1891, an Alliance organizer

Dr. C. W. Macune, 1891, President of the National Farmers' Alliance, and editor of the National *Economist*

ments generate support and understanding within the culture they oppose. Finally, it is a story that, despite Macune's claims of the importance of education to the Alliance, remains largely untold.[8]

2

As he looked out at his audience, Macune could see representatives of the "poor man" from nearly every state in the South, all hoping that the Alliance would free them and the farmers they represented from the grip of political and economic forces that drew them, in increasing numbers, into poverty and powerlessness.[9] Following Macune's welcome, the delegates broke into committees, working through the day to hammer out a formal constitution for the Alliance.

In the early evening of October 12, the Committee on Resolutions presented to the delegates a draft of the Declaration of Purposes of the National Farmers' Alliance and Cooperative Union. The "strength and permanency" of the government of the United States, read the preamble, depends upon "the prosperity and success of agriculture and labor . . . pure and elevated public sentiment . . . [and] the intelligence of its citizens." The Alliance "view[ed] with alarm the tendency in this government to reverse these cardinal conditions . . . by the concentration of wealth and power in the hands of a few, to the impoverishment and bondage of so many." The "overthrow and certain destruction of the growing and menacing dangers to the institutions of the country and the liberties of the people depends on agitation, education, and cooperation, carried on by the means of thorough organization of the masses."[10] The Alliance pledged to

> encourage and strive to increase the facilities among ourselves for a closer study and better understanding of the organisms,

8. Rush Welter's underused *Popular Education and Democratic Thought in America* (New York: Columbia University Press, 1962) was the first work to take the Alliance leaders at their word. More recently Lawrence Goodwyn has examined one aspect of the Alliance's educative efforts, its efforts to fashion a culture that in itself educated members. See Goodwyn's *Democratic Promise* (New York: Oxford University Press, 1976).

9. Represented were farmers' organizations from Mississippi, Missouri, Tennessee, Alabama, Florida, Arkansas, Louisiana, and, of course, from Macune's Texas. Texans took the lead and were elected to the principal offices of the new national organization. It is probably not the case that the delegates to the convention were themselves "poor men."

10. Garvin and Daws, *History of the National Farmers' Alliance,* 72-73.

powers, and purposes of government; more attention to the laws of the country, local and general, the better to understand their scope and meaning, their influence on society, and the public good and thus educate ourselves in the science of economical government [and] elevate the standard of citizenship.[11]

The committee, and the Alliance movement, understood education to mean several things, each consistent with the Alliance's opposition to the "menacing dangers" encroaching on the individual liberty of American farmers.

Urbanization and industrialization threatened traditional social and economic relations, undermined a yeoman farm economy, and shifted the nation's cultural self-definition from the countryside to the city. These broad realignments changed the way rural southerners lived and the way they thought about their lives. Some experienced these changes directly, some only indirectly. For future Alliance president Leonidas Polk "[c]entralized capital, allied to irresponsible corporate power, stands to-day as a formidable menace to individual rights and popular government."[12] For a contributor to the Raleigh, North Carolina, *Progressive Farmer,* the issue was more specific: "banks have never done a better or more profitable business, yet agriculture languishes."[13] And for farmers throughout the South, the issue was not just specific, but personal; their understanding, or their confusion, was fashioned from direct experiences. Wrote one farmer, whose bankruptcy led to the public auction of his farm and equipment, "I could not keep from crying when I read today where everything else we have is to be sold."[14] From whatever vantage point, southern farmers and their supporters saw their way of life and their system of values threatened by change. An anonymous writer looking back at the significance of the Alliance said simply:

We had the best of reasons for joining. Our rights and liberties were being taken from us, our tax burden made heavier each year, while money was being made scarcer and through it the

11. Garvin and Daws, *History of the National Farmers' Alliance,* 75.

12. L. L. Polk, "Presidential Address to the National Farmers' Alliance and Industrial Union," in Dunning, *Farmers' Alliance History,* 139–151. Polk's address is also reprinted in *National Economist,* December 13, 1890.

13. Raleigh, North Carolina, *Progressive Farmer,* April 28, 1887.

14. Quoted in Burton Shaw, *The Wool Hat Boys* (Baton Rouge: Louisiana State University Press, 1984), 15.

price of our produce and our labor was being reduced all the time.[15]

Education, at the most basic level, meant understanding what had happened in the political economy to change the nature of agriculture as an enterprise. In 1890, Alliance president Polk told his listeners that the first goal of the movement was to "educate those who now feel the agricultural and other depression but who do not fully understand its cause."[16] Chapter 1 of this book attempts to trace the material and cultural changes in the southern political economy that altered farm life and that prompted hundreds of thousands of rock-ribbed southerners to seek unity, understanding, and self-defense through the Farmers' Alliance.

Education, in Alliance terms, also meant participation in a culture consciously fashioned by the movement to "educate in the mutual relations and reciprocal duties between each other, as brethren, as neighbors, as members of society," to educate "for higher thought, higher aspiration, and higher manhood among the masses."[17] To create this culture of cooperation and mutual improvement, the Alliance brought farmers together "by our frequent meetings," and by so doing began to "break up the isolated habits of farmers, improve their social condition, increase their social pleasures, and strengthen their confidence in and friendship for each other."[18]

Specifically, the Alliance aimed at uniting farmers and rural producers around a recognition of the commonality of their circumstances and the identity of their interests. In other words, the Alliance "curriculum" struggled to strengthen "class" identification and to make class conflict the center of the political debate. Alliance leaders thus cast themselves not only as the apostles of the political creed of Jefferson but as stewards of a true Christian moralism based on the

15. Anonymous pamphlet in the *Louisiana Populist*, February 19, 1897.
16. Polk, "Presidential Address, 1890," 142.
17. Polk, "Presidential Address, 1890," 142.
18. "Declaration of Purposes," Garvin and Daws, *History of the National Farmers' Alliance*, 76. We have virtually no models of this kind of organization today. Certainly political party membership does not carry with it either the depth or breadth of involvement inherent in Alliance membership. Fraternal lodges are closer to the mark, but their purpose is social, not political, leaving lodges without either the sense of purpose or the sense of unity that marked Alliance groups. In our dispersed culture, we simply do not have the kinds of extrafamilial organizations of the kind represented by the Alliance. This makes the reconstruction of Alliance culture and Alliance education at once exciting and strange. In order to understand the experience of the million or so members of the Alliance, such a reconstruction is essential.

sanctity of labor. In these ways, the movement's culture and its educational themes drew upon deeply held southern traditions.[19] In other ways, though, as in overtures made to black farmers and farm laborers, the movement's pursuit of class consciousness mired the movement in conflict with tradition and with the southern culture of which the movement was a part.[20]

The tension in the Alliance between tradition and change became a major point of internal conflict as the movement grew. While programs of collective action such as joint marketing arrangements and cooperative buying plans reinforced the message of unity and class cohesiveness, divisions in the broader culture, like those of race, section (North versus South), and party, worked against the Alliance goal of a united agrarian force. Chapter 2 examines the way Alliance leaders

19. In particular, the Alliance drew upon, in modified form, the religious heritage of the South. Recent works that explore the individualistic orientation of southern religious teaching include Frederick A. Bode, *Protestantism and the New South* (Charlottesville: University Press of Virginia, 1975); David Edwin Harrell, Jr., ed., *Varieties of Southern Evangelicalism* (Macon, Ga.: Mercer University Press, 1981); Samuel S. Hill, Jr., *The South and the North in American Religion* (Athens: University of Georgia Press, 1980); and Charles Reagan Wilson, *Baptized in Blood: The Religion of the Lost Cause, 1865-1920* (Athens: University of Georgia Press, 1980). Secondary work on the Alliance and religion is limited to Bode's "Religion and Class Hegemony: A Populist Critique," *Journal of Southern History* 37 (August 1971).

20. Within the movement, Tom Watson, the Georgia Populist, saw more clearly than many of his peers the dilemma the Alliance faced in living up to its promises to black farmers. Watson's "The Negro Question in the South," *Arena* 6 (October 1982), 540-550 is the most eloquent statement of that dilemma. Histories of the Colored Farmers' Alliance begin with R. M. Humphrey's, "The History of the Colored Farmers' National Alliance and Cooperative Union," in Dunning, *Farmers' Alliance History,* 288-293. Humphrey, a white man, was appointed head of the black Alliance by the Supreme Council of the National Alliance and served as head of the organization throughout its existence. Gerald Gaither has written the best history of the relations between blacks and whites in the farmers' movement. His *Blacks in the Populist Revolt* (Baton Rouge: Louisiana State University Press, 1974) is critical of the actual benefits accruing to blacks either as members of the movement or in general. See also the work of William Holmes: "The Arkansas Cotton Pickers' Strike and the Demise of the Colored Farmers' Alliance," *Arkansas Historical Quarterly* 32, no. 2 (1973): 107-119; "The Demise of the Colored Farmers' Alliance," *Journal of Southern History* 61, no. 3 (May 1975): 187-200. Holmes emphasizes the independent action of the Colored Alliance that drew it away from the interests and actions of the white organization. Finally, the work of Jack Abramovitz explores the nature of the Colored Farmers' Alliance in the context of the white movement. See his "The Negro in the Populist Revolt," *Journal of Negro History* 38, no. 3 (July 1953): 257-289; "The Negro in the Agrarian Revolt," *Agricultural History* 24, no. 2 (April 1950): 89-96; "Agrarian Reformers and the Negro Question," *The Negro History Bulletin* 11 (March 1948): 138-139.

organized the culture of the movement to be educational in social, cultural, and political ways, amidst prevailing educational underdevelopment in the rural South. Chapter 3 explores the ideological foundations of the Alliance curriculum in detail, particularly at the way Alliance lecturers and the movement's leaders attempted to steer a steady course between the Scylla of tradition and the Charybdis of radical change, taking direction from both but fighting to stay clear of either.

The Alliance took up the challenge of political education even more directly, offering a program of education in "the science of economical government" aimed specifically at demystifying politics and giving farmers basic intellectual tools, such as literacy and numeracy in the context of building skills in political analysis. This was implicit in the Declaration of Purpose written in Shreveport:

> we shall boldly enter into the discussion and investigation of all laws, public measures, and governmental policies that have a direct or remote bearing on the productive industries . . . approving the good and condemning the bad.[21]

Charles Macune and other editors of Alliance newspapers made this kind of skill training explicit and used the press as a means of conveying an Alliance "text" to the small local suballiances where tutorials in reading, writing, and calculating focused on current political and economic affairs. After a tour of suballiances in Texas, Macune reported happily that "hard financial and economic questions are being discussed in the suballiances now, with an ability and a calmness that would be truly astonishing to those who are accustomed to speak of the ignorant farmers."[22] This formal program of political education addressed both instrumental and general needs.

On the general side, Alliance leaders genuinely wanted to elevate the standard of citizenship, to lead rural producers to a more active participation in the affairs of the polity based on a familiarity with and understanding of the issues facing them. On the instrumental side, the leadership proposed a view of politics and political action that supported the specific reform program of the Alliance. In its baldest terms, this view of politics weighed candidates and "public measures" according to their ability or willingness to ameliorate what the leadership perceived to be the ills facing the nation's "productive industries." Chapter 4 examines the formal pedagogy of the Alliance. This

21. Garvin and Daws, *History of the National Farmers' Alliance,* 73, 75.
22. *National Economist,* November 14, 1891.

explicit "campaign of education" aimed at teaching intellectual and political skills together through the mechanisms of the reform press and the suballiance. In the process of establishing this structure, the leadership not only educated but emphasized new "configurations" of learning and teaching.

Perhaps most fundamentally, the Alliance educated about education. Alliance leaders believed that "knowledge is power," and saw in education the restoration of the Republic.[23] The education "of the people," the Declaration of Purposes stated, was "fundamental to good government in sustaining its institutions and multiplying its blessings."[24] In support of informed citizenship, the Alliance promised "at all times [to] advance and encourage [education] in the highest possible degree among farmers and laborers and their children by every means in our power." In general this encouragement meant the support of expanded opportunities for public education, for adults and children alike. Alliance declarations echoed nearly universal rhetorical support for expanded schooling. But from the beginning, that support was not uncritical, and the determination of the Alliance to fashion a school system congruent with its goals to empower the farmer and rural laborer made the Order a different kind of public school supporter. "Through the means of investigation and discussion in our Alliance meetings, our press and public speakers," continued the Declaration of Purposes,

> we propose to examine the various methods and systems of education in use, with the view to determine the best adopted to the wants and conditions of the agricultural and laboring classes.[25]

At times the leaders of the Alliance and the public school establishment differed in their opinion of what kind of schooling was "best adopted to the wants and conditions of the agricultural classes."

The political purpose of Alliance education made school professionals uncomfortable. The movement's "curriculum" spoke in the language of liens and mortgages, of power and privilege. Its values often conflicted dramatically with the values of public school texts. In vocational and agricultural training, in particular, the political vision of the Alliance came into direct conflict with the more technical cast

23. Evan Jones, "Presidential Address: 1889," in Dunning, *Farmers' Alliance History,* 100.
24. Garvin and Daws, *History of the National Farmers' Alliance,* 73.
25. Garvin and Daws, *History of the National Farmers' Alliance,* 74.

of publicly supported child and adult education. Chapter 5 examines this philosophical difference through the problematic relationship between the Alliance and the public school.

Finally, chapter 6 explores the legacies of the Southern Alliance's educational efforts as those efforts waned and gave way to a very different kind of educational movement: the Crusade for Education in the South. The Crusade, as its participants called it, was a well-funded, well-organized effort by John D. Rockefeller's General Education Board to empower educational professionals in the South and to create universal public schooling in the region. The success of the Crusade meant the end of the Alliance educational campaign and the defeat of the ideas about education that had motivated the movement's efforts for a decade. In the Crusade, immense private fortunes controlled the development of public schools through hand-picked professionals: it embodied all that the Alliance opposed. And yet the very success of the Alliance in articulating the importance of education to southern farmers contributed to the ultimate success of the crusaders. Such was the ironic legacy of the Alliance in education, a legacy that was shaped in significant measure by the history of the larger agrarian movement.

3

In the broadest sense, the very existence of the Alliance movement educated a generation of Americans. In its political oppositions to the dominant culture—drawn quickly and surely, in black and white with little grey—the movement painted the major tensions of a modernizing nation on a canvas large enough to be seen by all. To those closer to it, the Alliance offered an alternative to the dire future it feared; it advanced, through its culture, its rhetoric, and its electoral efforts, an image of an America in which wealth accrued to those who produced it with their hands and power accrued to those who best served the interests of all the people. Their educational aims were to transmit this ideology and to train individual farmers to act in ways that would make this future real. In its efforts to build a reformed nation, the history of the Alliance is a history of both spectacular success and catastrophic failure.

In setting a national agenda, the Alliance and the People's party were perhaps most successful. Newspapers, magazines, lecturers, preachers, and politicians from New York to California all attended to the Alliance's growth, some with approval, some with fear, and some, maybe most, with scorn. Whatever the reaction, for ten years the nation's leaders and would-be leaders struggled to answer the questions fired off by the farmers and their supporters: Why are cotton prices so low and freight rates so high? How can one man, John D. Rockefeller, command so many of the nation's resources when so many are poor? Is it fair to burden farmers with killing mortgages when railroads get free money from the government? Why cannot the government own the railroads and subsidize their continued use rather than just their construction? Why cannot the people elect senators directly? These were questions that the Alliance leaders distilled from the experiences of the membership and made the central issues in their analysis of Gilded Age capitalism. In uniting farmers and others within the membership, the Alliance scored a second success.

The Southern Alliance, the organizational heart of the national movement, claimed a membership of one million by 1890. Although that claim is unsubstantiated by hard evidence (only scattered membership data exist) it was not challenged by contemporary critics. Somewhere near a million southern yeomen, tenants, teachers, preachers, and some plantation owners took the secret oath of membership and became a part of this complex and multifaceted movement.[26] Membership meant participation in a whole "culture" that included social, intellectual, and economic dimensions. The Alliance's breadth as an organization deepened its educational role in all areas of farmers' lives. That breadth also reflected the necessity for internal cohesion and external security, for despite its size, the Alliance was not a movement with a large body of support outside its boundaries. Where opposition to the Alliance was strong, membership often isolated Alliance members from the normal web of social relations.

The Alliance, and its partisan offspring, the People's party, won significant victories in the state elections of 1890 and 1892. In 1890 candidates tapped by the Alliance were victorious in four gubernatorial races, forty-four congressional races, and three senate contests. As important, pro-Alliance candidates emerged as a majority in eight state legislatures. In 1892 the results were again striking. Four more governorships were added to the populist ranks, along with ten representatives and five senators. At the national level, the People's party candidate, Union General James Weaver of Iowa, received 8.5 percent of the popular vote and twenty-two electoral votes. It remained the

26. Alliance members tended to be landowners rather than tenants, but among the poorer quartile of all landowners. For more on membership, see Appendix A.

best showing by a third-party candidate until Robert La Follette's loss to Calvin Coolidge in 1924.[27]

Many inside the movement saw these successes as the first pebbles in an avalanche of popular support for Alliance ideals, an avalanche that would bring Macune's "poor man" into power in America. Unfortunately, too many leaders of the movement gloated that victory was near and in so doing began to define the success or failure of the Alliance, the People's party, and the larger movement in terms of electoral success. For them, and for the rank and file, victory at the polls became the only kind of victory that counted, and electoral defeat the only defeat that mattered.

In party politics the Populists suffered stinging defeats, made catastrophic by this exclusive identification of the movement's success with electoral success. By 1895, internal and external forces tore at the strength of the Alliance and the People's party and led to their rapid decline.

First, after 1892, the Democratic party in the South began taking concerted action against the populists. Supporters of the Populist/Alliance platform were summarily ejected from Democratic party councils. Members of the Alliance were banned from membership in the Democracy in Texas, Georgia, and Alabama. The pressure on individual voters and their families became intense; intimidation was frequent and often brutal.

The more they became focused on partisan politics, on winning elections, the less the movement's leaders concerned themselves with the maintenance of the Order and its culture. This neglect left former Alliance members disenchanted and left former populist leaders, now candidates, with a constituency instead of a movement. Most of all, it left the cultural and social dimensions of the movement without real energy or focus, at precisely the moment members of the Order needed a sense of cultural and social connection.

Some Alliance leaders, Macune being the most important, withdrew support from the People's party, arguing precisely that the movement was larger and ultimately more important than elections and that the populist surge deflected attention from the real economic and political tasks of the Alliance, which were to build a self-conscious class of rural producers. Alliance membership and People's party membership appear to have declined after 1892, perhaps in part because it became more costly, in personal terms, to be a populist, and in part because the growing strategic division between Macune on the one hand, and

27. Sheldon Hackney, *Populism: The Critical Issues* (Boston: Little, Brown & Company, 1971), xv.

people like Georgia Congressman Tom Watson on the other, robbed the movement of a single focus.

The politicking required of Populist candidates also sapped the strength of the underlying movement. In several states, fusion by the People's party with one or another of the major parties in 1894 and 1896 blunted the oppositional edge of Populist politics. For years Alliance lecturers, editors, and Populist candidates had told audiences that the major parties were morally and politically bankrupt. After asking farmers and their families to risk becoming outcasts in their own communities by leaving the Democracy, the sudden alliance struck some as the same brand of bankruptcy they had organized to oppose in the first place. Agrarian leaders came to resemble too closely the "chronic politicians" at whom Col. R. J. Sledge had pointed an accusing finger in 1891.

Second, exogenous to the strategic moves or mismoves of the organization, a small but sharp increase in the price of cotton and the gradual recovery of the nation's financial markets after the recession of 1888–1892 and the depression of 1893 alleviated some of the pressure on the budgets of small-hold farmers, especially in the South. The economic exigencies that ushered in a decade of agrarian protest waned, and as they did, so did the fortunes of the Alliance. Moreover, as the economic prospects, if not the actual conditions, for farmers improved, Alliance arguments about the inevitable conflict between capital and labor, between city and country, between farm and factory, began to ring hollow. The Alliance "programs" for the rural economy—including the establishment of cooperatives, the instigation of legislation supporting low-interest loans to farmers, and opposition to crop liens and usurious and restrictive mortgages—seemed to have borne little fruit. At the same time, the opponents of the Alliance argued with some legitimacy that eventually economic development would benefit all.

In 1896, the Populists were anxious for a good showing in the national elections and eager to make inroads at the state level. Neither happened. Populist candidates were swamped across the nation. William Jennings Bryan's defeat by William McKinley reflected the fortunes of the third party and fusion candidates even in former Alliance strongholds. The defeat embittered as scarred a fighter for the Populist cause as Tom Watson, who proclaimed sadly, "our party, as a party is finished . . ."[28] The 1896 election destroyed the effectiveness of the national agrarian organizations. The People's party, the Na-

28. Quoted in C. Vann Woodward, *Tom Watson: Agrarian Rebel* (New York: Oxford University Press, 1975), 285.

tional Alliance, and the Colored Farmers' Alliance ceased to play important roles in politics and, more important, in the daily lives of members and former members. In local areas, leaders tried to keep the flame of opposition alive, lighting their own particular brand of populism. In Texas, Milton Park, longtime editor of the *Southern Mercury,* the official newspaper of the Southern Alliance, turned from broad reform to more specific demands for low-interest loans to farmers.[29] Marion Butler, Populist senator from North Carolina, remained a Bryan Democrat and a currency reformer until his last days in the Senate in 1908. But these and other leaders of the farmers' movement were dispirited and disillusioned. In one particularly downcast editorial, Park referred to his fellow Texans as "cattle" and argued that it was no wonder the reform movement had failed.

While the defeat of the Populists at the polls and the disintegration of the Alliance disillusioned some, it embittered others. Tom Watson and Jim "Cyclone" Davis continued their political careers, but after 1896 they were careers defined by bitterness and hatred. Both men blamed blacks for the demise of the agrarian movement, maintaining that Alliance involvement with blacks had caused a white backlash too strong to overcome. Both men blamed immigrants for providing the cheap labor that fueled America's industrial growth and hastened the decline of agriculture. Both men blamed foreign investors and foreign capital for centralizing control of American business enterprises. Davis carried his zeal for reform and his talent for oratory to the Ku Klux Klan, where he quickly rose in the ranks. Watson took his rhetorical might and his white supremacist agenda to Congress. In 1920, Watson made his platform of hatred, isolation, and exclusion the basis of a presidential campaign.[30]

If some of the old cadre of Alliance leaders fought on, if some just fought, others simply folded their tents and surrendered the field to a new generation, a new set of ideas, and a new struggle. Charles Macune was one of these. In many ways his personal history mirrored the history of the movement he did so much to build and to lead.

Macune was born in Kenosha, Wisconsin, in 1851. His father, who worked as blacksmith and Methodist preacher in Kenosha, died when

29. See Park's editorials in the *Southern Mercury,* during 1897. Perhaps because of the disillusionment that came with the failure of the Alliance reform efforts, Park became, in his later years, a socialist organizer in his home state.

30. For a brief assessment of the post-Alliance careers of the leaders of the movement, see Goodwyn, *Democratic Promise,* 557–564. At least one contemporary account places some of the Populist leaders after the 1896 election: William Peffer, "The Passing of the People's Party," *North American Review* (January 1898): 12–23.

Macune was still an infant. Mary Macune moved with her son to Freeport, Illinois. Times there were hard for the widow. Straitened circumstance forced Charles to drop out of school at age ten in order to begin full-time farm labor. He worked as a farmhand through the Civil War.

When the war ended, Macune left Illinois and farming behind, although he never left behind his memories of the struggles of farm life or its essential nobility. Macune moved first to California where he worked on a cattle ranch. After a year, he abandoned the West for Kansas and found work there in a circus and later as a cattle driver. In 1874, Macune's odyssey landed him in Barnett, Texas.

In Barnett, Macune tried one enterprise after another. First he tried the newspaper business. Failing at that, he bought a local hotel. That, too, failed. While business was bleak, Macune's personal life was bright. He won the heart of a Barnett woman, Sally Vickery. Macune and Vickery were married and soon moved to San Saba, Texas. There Macune painted houses, studied medicine with a local doctor, and read law during his spare time. The Macunes moved once more, to Milam County, where they settled in. Charles practiced law and medicine and in 1886 became involved with the nascent farmers' organization there.[31]

Macune's talents for public speaking and for generating ideas rocketed him to the chairmanship of the Texas Farmers' Alliance Executive Committee that same year. Within a year, Macune was at work organizing an ambitious cooperative marketing and purchasing program under the organizational title of the Alliance Exchange. Through the Exchange Macune attempted to centralize the purchasing power of farmers to secure lower prices for seed, cloth, and other necessities. It was the first of several important initiatives by Macune that galvanized the farmers' movement. The Exchange also gave Macune a national reputation inside agrarian circles that propelled him to national leadership.

. As Chairman of the National Alliance Supreme Council, Macune again and again set the agenda for the movement. He pressed the cause of education, and as editor of the *National Economist* took a central role in articulating the educational agenda of the movement. His plans to increase the flow of low-cost funds to farmers by decentralizing the functions of the U.S. Treasury by placing a subtreasury in

31. Biographical information on Macune is scarce. The best is Theodore Saluotos, "Charles W. Macune," in *Great American Cooperators,* ed. Joseph Knapp and associates (Washington D.C., American Institute of Cooperation, 1967), 10–13.

every congressional district became the centerpiece of the Alliance demands in 1890. Perhaps more than any other leader, Macune was able to translate the farmers' problems into concrete proposals for reform.

He was only thirty-six when he stood in front of the Shreveport convention and only forty-one when he withdrew from the Alliance, alienated and angered by the leadership's uncritical support of the Peoples' party. When he resigned from the Alliance in 1892, Macune retired from public life and slipped from public view.

For eight years he practiced law in Cameron, Texas. In 1900 he received an appointment from the Central Methodist Conference as a preacher. For eighteen years, Macune traveled through the small towns of Texas ministering to the spiritual needs of the same agrarian poor he had once helped galvanize politically, economically, and educationally. Macune spent his last years doing volunteer medical work among the poor near his home in Fort Worth. He died in 1940 at the age of eighty-nine.

Macune's retreat from social, political, and economic struggle against the dominance of "monied interests" into spirituality, or at least into a mission of spiritual uplift, is symbolic of the retreat by rank-and-file Alliance members. When the Populist experiment failed, many turned inward to the traditions of hard work, faith, party loyalty, and racial solidarity that had been their ideological heritage in the years before the Alliance.

For others, though, membership in the Alliance proved a turning point in their personal histories. Agrarian radicalism, especially in the South, owes its persistence to the seeds planted by the Alliance in the 1880s and 1890s.[32]

4

This study seeks to build upon a growing tradition among historians of populism that explores the cultural history of the organization by integrating the intellectual, political, and social currents of the movement from within.[33] In focusing on education, this analysis sets out to examine the Alliance in terms that its members and leaders would

32. James Green's argument in his *Grass Roots Socialism* (Baton Rouge: Louisiana State University Press, 1978), esp. 12–53, suggest broad Alliance involvement.

33. For a more detailed discussion of this and other historiographical trends, see Appendix A.

recognize as important. It aims, as well, at reintegrating education into our shared historical view of the Alliance.[34]

Within a different historiographical tradition, the Alliance and its campaign of political education serve as a "case study" addressing the ideas of Bernard Bailyn and Lawrence Cremin, who have insisted that historians attempt to understand the many ways that education takes place outside schools.[35] Bailyn's call for "a broader definition of education" issued at the Conference on Early American Education in 1959, urged historians to "think of education not only as formal pedagogy but as the entire process by which a culture transmits itself across generations."[36] Cremin's essays on American education and his massive *American Education* trilogy work to establish both a substance and a method in exploring the complex historical process of cultural transmission. Central to Cremin's work is the idea of "configurations" of educational apparatuses operating at any point in time. Looking at the nineteenth century, for example, Cremin finds families, churches, popular press, and voluntary organizations all operating in various ways alongside schools in educating Americans. The relation

34. There are two exceptions. Homer Clevenger discusses suballiances as sites of political debate and discussion in his article "The Teaching Techniques of the Farmers Alliance," *Journal of Southern History* 11 (February 1945): 504–518, and Goodwyn makes much of the educative force of Alliance culture, particularly the importance of cooperative business ventures in radicalizing farmers. This argument is weakened by evidence that few farmers, even in counties where People's party candidates were popular, were involved in the Alliance's economic endeavors. See Stanley B. Parsons, Karen T. Parsons, Walter Killiae, and Beverly Borgers, "The Role of Cooperatives in the Development of the Movement Culture of Populism," *Journal of American History* 69, no. 4 (March 1983): 866–885.

35. Nonschool education has both a descriptive and prescriptive literature. Historians have generally followed the lead of Lawrence Cremin, working with schools as only one element of complex "configurations" of educational forces operating simultaneously in society at any time. Other elements of Cremin's configurations include the press, organized religion, and the family. See Lawrence A. Cremin, *Traditions of American Education* (New York: Basic Books, 1977) for the basic explanation of educational configurations. Thomas L. Webber, *Deep Like the Rivers* (New York: W. W. Norton, 1978), explores the educational configuration of the slave quarter community in which there were no formal schools. In prescriptive terms, the work of Paolo Freiri has been influential in building an intellectual and practical model of pedagogy for oppressed peoples. Freiri's *Pedagogy of the Oppressed* (New York: Seabury Press, 1970) broke new ground in arguing that education in support of radical social reform must take place outside the walls of state-sponsored schools and must be based on the life-experiences of the "students."

36. Bernard Bailyn, *Education in the Forming of American Society* (New York: W. W. Norton, 1972), 14.

between the various elements of the configuration is obviously dialectical and just as obviously complex. At any moment, different elements might conflict—for instance, the family and the school, or the press and churches. But, Cremin argues, taken as a whole and in combination, the often colliding interests of these elements ultimately perform the function of cultural transmission. The different elements, then, represent for Cremin expressions of a broadly shared cultural view that differ only in form from one another.

Cremin refers to this broad consensus as an American *paideia*, borrowing a term that Werner Jaeger used to describe Greek culture. For Jaeger and Cremin, *paideia* captures the set of cultural mechanisms that teach successive generations about that culture. Homeric legend, the plays of Aeschylus and Sophocles, the actions of government in Athens: these are elements of Jaeger's *paideia*, and they correspond to Cremin's examination of schools, clubs, newspapers, and religious organizations.

The Alliance fit only imperfectly into the American *paidea* of the late nineteenth century. What makes the movement and its educational history different from the configurations described by Cremin is the Alliance's self-described opposition to the dynamic of cultural and economic change.

Once again, its deliberate and self-conscious educational efforts make the Farmers' Alliance an exciting source in furthering our understanding of how education takes place in systematic ways outside schools. Uncovering and examining the "curriculum" and the "pedagogy" of the Alliance in their historical context will help us to better understand both the historical and contemporary processes of nonschool education.[37] In particular, if we are to know more about the ways in which social movements educate, then the reliance of the farmers' movement on education offers an excellent starting point.[38]

There are, of course, limitations to this portrait of education within the Farmers' Alliance. Like so much of our understanding of the educational past, this is a history of what was taught more than a history of what was learned. It is a history of the attempts of Macune and other Alliance leaders to create a "curriculum" and then spread that

37. In this way, if not in others, Charles Macune would have felt an intellectual and political kinship with the leaders of the social movements of the 1960s. The "teach-ins" of that generation would have been familiar in form and content to the cotton farmers of the nineteenth-century South.

38. The movements of the 1960s have suffered a fate similar to that of the Alliance. Historians have not considered the educational aims or processes of these attempts to galvanize a generation of young people around political and social issues.

curriculum to farmers and their families in the most underdeveloped and undereducated region in the nation. The movement's rank and file have left few traces, and those speak only symbolically—in terms of membership numbers or subscription rolls—of the transformation wrought by the Alliance's efforts. What they have left though, are the outlines of the structure of their daily lives, of the forces that influenced their decisions to join their friends and their neighbors in seeking the kind of education that would "give them the power to right existing wrongs."[39]

We begin, then, where the Alliance began, by tracing and trying to understand the changes in southern agriculture that altered the way farmers in the region made their living and that tore at the fabric of traditional southern rural life.

39. *Southern Mercury,* October 15, 1891.

1 The Hard Lessons

. . . Lend us not into temptation, but deliver us from hungriness
For thine shall be the crop, the mules, and the land forever
and ever,
IF WE DON'T PAY!.

—The Storekeepers prayer[1]

Almost persuaded facts to believe;
Almost persuaded truth to receive;
Starve us a little more,
Masters we thee implore;
Closer the lines you draw
Sooner we'll see.

—Alliance song[2]

1

From the first, the Alliance's educational effort responded to the changes in southern economics and politics that produced confusion, poverty, and powerlessness among the farming population of the region. The Alliance can be best understood as an organization created by men and women searching for explanations of these changes and for the means to control the direction of social change.

Samuel Beard, an Arkansas cotton farmer, was one of the many farmers who sought help from the Alliance.[3] In the fall of 1891, Beard signed a lien with his local merchant for forty-three dollars to cover his household expenses until harvest time. Beard put up as collateral his entire crop and his stock, one horse and a milk cow, despite the fact that the stock alone was worth much more than the balance of the loan. In early December, Beard's wife fell ill and a local doctor told

1. Quoted in Thomas Clark, *Pills, Petticoats, and Plows* (New York: Columbia University Press, 1949), 155. See also Michael Schwartz, *Radical Protest and Social Structure: The Southern Farmers' Alliance and Cotton Tenancy, 1880–1890* (San Francisco: Academic Press, 1976), 55.

2. Leopold Vincent, *Alliance and Labor Songster* (New York: Arno Reprints, 1975), 18.

3. How it is that social movements emerge, develop, and then deteriorate forms a fascinating body of scholarship that cannot be summarized here. In general, I have adopted the view that protest comes from perceived economic or political dislocation mediated by both a traditional ideology and an emerging ideology of protest. In the case of the Alliance, the connections between the traditional ideology and the emerging ideology were those exploited by the educational campaign in its more informal manifestations. See chapter 3 and Appendix A.

the farmer that unless Beard could provide a steady diet of beef broth, his wife would die. Beard returned to the merchant to ask for more credit, with which he would buy beef. The merchant ignored Beard's entreaties. Unable to win over his creditor and desperate to help his wife, Beard signed another lien, this time for just seventy pounds of cotton, with a nearby planter. In return Beard received a side of beef and enough lumber to make a door for his shack and shutters to keep the winter winds from his wife's sickbed.

The same January storm wiped out Beard's crop and hastened his wife's decline and ultimate death, leaving Beard alone to face two creditors, both with current claims on his chattels. The merchant took possession of Beard's shack, his stock, and the few pounds of cotton that survived the winter. The planter, with whom Beard had contracted an illegal second mortgage, informed the authorities, who tried Beard and found him guilty of violating Arkansas' Landlord Tenant Law. Farmer Beard served his one year sentence and returned to cotton farming, but as a wage laborer rather than as owner of his own farm.[4]

Beard's story is not unique. Changes in the structure of southern politics and southern economics shattered the traditional nexus between hard work and economic progress for individual farmers and for farmers as a class. These changes established a new environment in the region, an environment outwardly both hostile and bewildering to farmers like Beard. Squeezed by sagging prices, mounting interest, and unfavorable laws, farmers began searching for explanations and remedies. The Alliance grew out of this new environment and responded to its challenges not only in political and economic ways but, overwhelmingly, in ways that were educational.[5]

2

Even so uncritical a supporter of southern economic development as Henry Grady had to admit that there was something seriously amiss among the yeomen farms of the region. For Grady and for others, the dynamics of the agricultural crisis were easy to see if not to understand:

4. W. S. Morgan, *History of the Wheel and Alliance* (Fort Scott, Kans., 1889), 58; "State of Arkansas v. Beard," 43 Arkansas, 1891.

5. U.S. Department of the Interior, Bureau of the Census, *Report on Farms and Homes: Property and Indebtedness at the Eleventh Census* (Washington, D.C.: Government Printing Office, 1894), 24–25. Hereafter cited as *Eleventh Census: Farms and Homes*. Also Schwartz, *Radical Protest*, 76-80.

Having once mortgaged his crop for supplies to his merchant, the farmer was practically the slave to that merchant. Under the prevailing price of cotton his crop would barely pay his lien. He was thus left dependent for next year's supplies on his merchant, who charged him what he pleased.[6]

Grady was close to the mark. The history of farming during the period is one of decreasing self-sufficiency in the production of food crops, increasing dependency on market mechanisms for credit, and perhaps most significant of all, ever greater reliance on cotton as a staple.[7] For many small-tract farmers in the region, the changes toward specialization led to the kind of dependent relations described by Grady and experienced by men like Beard.

Reporting to the Senate Committee on Forestry and Agriculture, in 1895, S. L. Benham, a Wise County, Texas, farmer, stated that the condition of those who raised cotton in his county was "fair," but that farm operators "were generally in debt to some extent." This indebtedness was so general that Benham, when asked to be specific, reported, "most of them [are] insolvent, under your definition, say ten to one."[8] Other testimony showed a similar state of affairs throughout the South. Tenancy, a sound measure of dependency, rose by ten percent for each census year between 1870 and 1900. Absolute rates of tenancy in the South were higher than for any other region in the nation.[9] For Benham, it was a simple matter: "There is a depression among cotton raisers . . . due not to want of energy."[10]

Basic to the problems facing southern farmers was the destruction

6. Henry Grady, in *The New South,* ed. Oliver Dyer (New York: Robert Bonner's Sons, 1890), 178.

7. Indicators of this specialization have been noted by, among others, Robert P. Brooks, *The Agrarian Revolution in Georgia, 1865-1912* (Madison: Bulletin of the University of Wisconsin, 1914), passim; Roger Shugg, "Survival of the Plantation System in Louisiana," *Journal of Southern History* 3 (August 1937): 235-36; Stephen Hahn, *The Roots of Southern Populism* (New York: Oxford University Press, 1984), 134-141; Jonathan Wiener, "Class Structure and Economic Development in the American South 1865-1955," *American Historical Review* 84, no. 4 (October 1979): 971-973; Harold Woodman, *King Cotton and His Retainers* (Lexington: University of Kentucky Press, 1968); U.S. Congress, *Report on the Condition of Cotton Growers in the U.S.,* Senate Report 986, 53d Cong., 3d sess., 2 vols. (1895), hereafter cited as *George Committee.*

8. *George Committee* 1:359.

9. *Eleventh Census: Farms and Homes,* 25-27. Also Roger Ransom and Richard Sutch, "Debt-Peonage in the Cotton South," *Journal of Economic History* (Spring 1972): 649; and U.S. Comptroller of the Currency, *Annual Report for 1901* (Washington, D.C.: Government Printing Office, 1902), xvi.

10. *George Committee* 1:360.

of the traditional economic structure of the antebellum southern community. As Steven Hahn describes the Georgia up-country, "the physical destruction, economic hardship, short crops, and dramatic decline in livestock brought about by the war . . . underminded the general self-sufficiency of many yeoman households."[11] Moreover, the traditional and reciprocal economic relations that existed between planters and yeomen in the slave South disappeared with the destruction of the slave economy.

The market in which antebellum planters and yeomen participated was, in Hahn's words "local in character and regulated by custom."[12] Small-tract farmers raised grain and livestock and a few bales of cotton. They marketed this cotton individually through factors or had their crop sold with the larger crops of their planter neighbors. Yeomen who were short on grain one year often borrowed grain from their more prosperous neighbors. Planters also served as a source of cheap labor at harvest time, renting slaves to yeomen in the community. Credit—and Hahn's work shows that borrowing was common— was administered in a similarly personal way and debts were often retired in return for payment in kind or services rendered.[13] This economy bound by custom was replaced by an economy bound to the national and international markets for cotton and credit, an economy that had little place in it for the small, self-sufficient southern producer. Several structural features of the southern economy and several exogenous changes in the functioning of that economy combined to plunge yeomen into what Hahn calls the "vortex of the cotton economy."[14]

First, outside the major trading centers, formal credit and banking facilities developed slowly in the South. Informal mechanisms upon which farmers depended failed to keep pace with credit needs. Much antebellum trade was handled on a semibarter basis, particularly in local markets and in transactions between neighbors. Many farmers financed the current year's purchases by borrowing against next year's crop from the local planter or from a cotton "factor." These factors

11. Hahn, *Roots,* 180.
12. Hahn, *Roots,* 33.
13. See Hahn, *Roots,* chaps. 1 and 2; Robert Gallman "Self-Sufficiency in the Cotton Economy of the Post-Bellum South," *Agricultural History* 44, no. 1 (January 1970); 7–12; Eugene Genovese, "Yeoman Farmers in a Slaveholders' Democracy," *Agricultural History* 49, no. 3 (April 1975); 331–333; Gavin Wright, *The Political Economy of the Cotton South* (New York: W. W. Norton, 1978), chap. 2; James Henretta, "Families and Farms: Mentalité in Pre-Industrial America," *William and Mary Quarterly,* 3d series, 35, no. 1 (January 1978): 3–32.
14. Hahn, *Roots,* chap. 4.

represented large cotton mills or international trading companies. They worked through large landowners to purchase crops from yeomen in a particular area, advancing money to farmers during the growing season in return for the eventual delivery of the mature cotton crop.

During the war, the Union blockade disrupted trade in cotton. International traders opened markets in Egypt. Those who remained worried that the southern cotton economy could not survive without the labor power of an enslaved population.[15] Crop failures in 1866 and 1867 drove most of the factorage houses from business, dramatically reducing available capital in the region. Both because of custom and law, banking institutions were unprepared to fill the void.

During the Civil War, the Union legislature had passed the National Banking Act. As a result of the timing of the legislation, and a vindictive spirit among influential Republican legislators, the southern states received almost none of the allotted $80 million in start-up money for the national banks. In 1869, there were only 26 national banks in the states of the exconfederacy, compared to 829 national banks in New York, Massachusetts, Pennsylvania, and Ohio alone.[16]

As late as 1895, the South lagged behind all other regions in the number of national banks in operation. In portions of the Old South, national banks were mere rumors; 123 counties in Georgia had no formal banking facilities at all at the turn of the century.[17] State banks were unable to pick up the slack. As part of the National Banking Act, Congress imposed a 10 percent surcharge on all state bank-notes, which effectively prevented their use as circulating currency.[18] Private banks, never popular in the South, likewise were not able to loosen the tight credit in the postbellum South. Southerners made little use of the few banks that did exist. As a result, the money available for bank loans remained minuscule. In 1880, southerners and others doing business in the region deposited an average of $5.09 per person in all categories of banks in the South (national, state, and private). In contrast, the national average was five times that: $26.61 per person. Even in the underdeveloped West, banks registered per capita deposits averaging $19.98.[19] Limited deposits meant limited loans, and limited

15. Hahn, *Roots,* 171–183; Woodman, *King Cotton,* 246–254.

16. U.S. Comptroller of the Currency, *Annual Report for 1869–70* (Washington, D.C.: Government Printing Office, 1871), 23. Also William Laird and James Rinehart, "Deflation, Agriculture, and Southern Development," *Agricultural History* 42 (April 1968): 117.

17. Laird and Rinehart, "Deflation, Agriculture, and Southern Development," 117, 118.

18. Laird and Rinehart, "Deflation, Agriculture, and Southern Development," 115, 116.

19. John A. James, "Financial Underdevelopment in the Post-Bellum South," *Journal of Interdisciplinary History* 11 (Winter 1981): 443.

bank loans meant that southern farmers continued to look elsewhere for means of raising capital.

Second, the decline of factorage was accompanied, and probably hastened, by changes that the growth of rail lines brought into the southern interior. Formerly isolated regions were brought into direct contact with national and international markets; so too were yeomen farmers, whose connection to these markets was no longer necessarily mediated by the market power of local planters.[20] The same rails that took cotton from the interior to port brought supplies from the coast. The railhead and the merchant replaced the plantation and the planter as the center of economic activity in communities in the South.[21]

Together, a continued lack of capital and a more formalized market changed the way business was done in the agricultural South. These changes led, first, to makeshift and haphazard credit arrangements between local merchants and yeomen that took advantage of the merchant's central position in both the distribution of credit and supplies as well as the marketing of the cotton crop.[22] The system by which yeomen and tenants obtained seed and supplies in return for the promise of payment, secured by their crop, was formalized by a series of laws passed in southern states during and shortly after Reconstruction. As Woodman has shown, these laws steadily reinforced the rights of merchants and other creditors.[23] Merchants, then, were in a unique position to take advantage of the credit crisis, filling their own pockets while they filled a pressing need in the southern economy. They borrowed from northern banks and financial institutions and loaned to farmers in the field, making their share on the difference between the interest rates they paid and those they charged their customers.[24]

A third factor that worked to alter the nature of the southern economy was, of course, the change from slave to free labor. Eman-

20. Woodman, *King Cotton,* 279; Hahn, *Roots,* 173.

21. See, for example, Woodman, *King Cotton,* 273, 304–307; Clark, *Pills, Petticoats.*

22. Clark, *Pills, Petticoats* is the standard work; see also, Woodman, *King Cotton,* 295–314; Hahn, *Roots,* 173–176; Schwartz, *Radical Protest,* 34–39, 41–45.

23. Harold Woodman, "Post Civil War Agriculture and the Law," *Agricultural History* 53 (January 1979): 319–337. Also see Schwartz, *Radical Protest,* chap. 4; and Joseph Reid, "Sharecropping as an Understandable Market Response—The Post-Bellum South," *Journal of Economic History* 22 (March 1973): 106–131

24. See Hahn, *Roots,* p. 173, on prices. He estimates that mark-ups may have run as high as 40 percent. See also Woodman, "Post Civil War Agriculture and the Law," 327–329; Schwartz, *Radical Protest,* 36–38; Ransom and Sutch, 128–131; Ransom and Sutch, "The Lock-In Mechanism and the Overproduction of Cotton in the Post-Bellum South," *Agricultural History* 49, no. 3 (April 1975): 418.

cipation created a free labor market in the agricultural South that called upon land owners to make adjustments in the structure and organization of farm labor in the region.

Initially, planters tried to replicate the conditions of slavery as closely as possible, hiring former slaves and poor whites to work on the plantation for a flat wage, either in money, in a kind of scrip, or simply in return for the planter's promise of food and shelter.[25] Laborers worked ten to twelve hours each day, six days each week. They worked on Sunday, but "claimed Saturdays as their own."[26] On Saturday the laborers and their families gathered for society, friendship, and amusement. By implicit agreement the landlord not only declined to interfere with these activities but often surrendered the mess and the grounds to the laborers and their kin.[27]

Planters often took advantage of the ignorance and innocence of the freedmen by signing them to labor contracts that bound them in virtual slavery. These kinds of agreements were not satisfactory for the freedmen, who saw land ownership as the ultimate expression of their freedom.[28] Blacks became reluctant to sign labor contracts, and it became more and more difficult for white planters to ensure themselves a steady supply of wage labor from year to year.[29]

White and black laborers, moreover, used agricultural labor to satisfy immediate financial needs. They worked in order to build up a stock of cash, then quit, and returned to work only when their nest egg was exhausted. Reported one planter, "when hired labor is employed, the hands are irresponsible, lazy, and vicious . . . when paid, they leave, when broke, they return."[30]

Some plantation owners tried to forestall such transience by tying workers to long contracts, with payment deferred to the end of the

25. Annual contracts for 1874 and 1894 for the Lewis Plantation, in I. F. Lewis Plantation Records (Southern Historical Collection). See also, U.S. Congress. *Proceedings of the Select Committee of the U.S. Senate to Investigate the Causes of the Removal of the Negroes from the Southern States,* Senate Report 693, 46th Cong., 2nd sess., 2 vols. (1880) I: 214–218. Hereafter cited as *Exodus Committee.* For a survey of cropping agreements across the South see *George Committee,* vol. 1, passim.

26. *George Committee,* 2:173.

27. *George Committee* 1:105; 2:173–174.

28. *Exodus Committee* 2:243, "The first want of the colored laborer is to become a landowner."

29. The twin ills, inability to secure land and inability to provide for the education of their children motivated blacks to leave the South and seek their fortunes in the North. See Nell Painter's The *Exodusters: Black Migration to Kansas after Reconstruction* (New York: W. W. Norton, 1976) for an analysis of the movement to one state.

30. *George Committee* 1:105.

contract's term. In Georgia and Alabama, contracts were customarily executed for one year. Laborers lived on the plantation, earning eight to ten dollars each month, including board at a central mess. Except for emergencies, workers never saw a cent of their wages until the year's term was out.[31] In Texas, Oklahoma, and parts of Arkansas, where land was plentiful and labor was in short supply, employers were unable to force workers to sign yearlong contracts. The comparative economic power of laborers there resulted in short contracts, high degrees of labor mobility from one farm to another, and wages that rose 10 percent above those in the Deep South.[32] In the Old South, planters' efforts to secure a stable and tractable supply of labor became desperate. They turned to schemes to entice immigrant labor south, and when these failed, they purchased gangs of convicts from the state prisons.[33]

Regardless of whether or not the agricultural laborers of the cotton South exerted market power over their employers, the widespread concern of landlords over the quality and continuity of their day-labor supply led them to search for other means of agricultural organization through which they could extract the maximum amount of labor from workers with a minimum of cost, both in time and actual money. Under slavery, landlords made profits on the difference between the value of the product of a slave's labor and the cost of his or her upkeep. For landlords in a free market, the task was the same: extract surplus value from laborers.

As early as 1867 the editor of the *Southern Cultivator* wrote to his planter readers that ". . . the experience of the past two seasons has demonstrated that plantations . . . with free labor, cannot be made profitable." He recommended that "[t]he first change that must occur . . . is the subdivision of landed estates."[34] This subdivision occurred most dramatically between 1860 and 1880. By the latter year the size of the average southern farm fell to only 39 percent of its antebellum counterpart.[35]

A second change, concomitant with the division of the large planta-

31. *George Committee* 1:150–155; 2:173–174.

32. *George Committee* 1:79, 105. Also Reid, "Sharecropping as an Understandable Market Response," 112.

33. *Exodus Committee* 1:xxiii.

34. Quoted in Reid, "Sharecropping as an Understandable Market Response," 110.

35. U.S. Department of Commerce, Bureau of the Census, *Historical Statistics of the United States from Colonial Times to the Present,* 2 vols. (Washington, D.C.: Government Printing Office, 1976), 1:461. Hereafter cited as *Historical Statistics of the U.S.* See Reid, "Sharecropping as an Understandable Market Response," 110.

tions, was the growth of sharecropping and share rental in the cotton South.[36] In the 1870s and 1880s sharecropping came to replace gang labor on the largest plantations in the South.[37] As croppers, black and white families farmed a section of a large holding in return for a percentage of the crop, minus deductions for supplies. The terms of the customary crop agreement included a four-year commitment on the part of the tenant and a one-half split on the crop from the tenant's section. By 1880, nearly all share agreements stipulated that shares would be computed on the basis of cotton produced. This ensured the landlord of a marketable return and forced tenants to devote an ever larger percentage of their arable land to the cultivation of the King.

The shares were often negotiated up or down depending upon the amount of material support the tenant needed.[38] If the cropper needed to rent the landlord's mule, plow, or barn, the cropper's portion of the crop decreased, often to one-third of the year's crop. Tenants could increase their share by agreeing to make capital improvements on the land, such as building new fences or a new cabin. Expenses— seed, fertilizer, clothing, and food—were added to the cropper's bill by the landlord. It was not uncommon for the tenant's end-of-year bill, crop-rent plus expenses, to equal the value of the entire harvest. Croppers regularly received no net income from a season's crop after settlement of the year's debt.[39] Nevertheless, for the family farming on shares there was always the hope that, whatever the hardships of tenancy, the next year might bring a surplus large enough to buy land.

For the landlord, sharecropping achieved the goal of finding a method to induce laborers to remain on the land for extended periods, at low rates of pay. In addition, there were other advantages for the landlord. When hiring a laborer, planters hired an individual for a wage. In signing a crop agreement, the planter gained control over the labor of not one man, but a whole family, at the same time giving them an incentive to work long hours in the hope of making a profit over the rent and expenses they owed. While the exploitation of family labor is a feature of agrarian societies, what made the postbellum South different from its antebellum counterpart was the division of

36. *Eleventh Census, Farms and Homes*, 25.

37. For a discussion of the ways in which blacks were pressed into chain gangs and hired out as convict labor see *Exodus Committee* 1: passim; and Matthew Hammond, *The Cotton Industry* (New York: Macmillan, 1897), 180–187.

38. Cropping arrangements became standardized in the 1880s. See Kenneth Coleman, ed., "How to Run a Middle Georgia Cotton Plantation in 1885: A Document," *Agricultural History* 42, no. 1 (January 1968): 58–59.

39. *George Committee* 1:iii–xx.

the surplus. Merchants and landlords replaced the yeoman family as the beneficiaries of the long hours of toil.[40]

Some planters, though, after trying the cropping system for a few seasons, found that while croppers had great incentive to produce large crops in the short run, they had little or no incentive to maintain and preserve the land or the facilities on their share farms. After a few years, the quality of the soil on these farms deteriorated to the point where yields per acre began to decline.[41] Planters and landlords reported that heavy use of expensive commercial fertilizers was needed to restore the nutrients necessary for the production of cotton and corn.

Landlords also reported that tenants were often demanding and difficult to control. According to one landlord, John Dent, the most obstreperous tenants were whites. After "hiring white and black laborers on the same terms," Dent found that while blacks were generally "accommodating," the "wants of white men were insatiable, their discontent . . . and their efforts to take advantage . . . constant.[42] If Dent's complaint can be seen as a general one, it appears that the white tenant, more even than his black counterpart, was working for the main chance and demanded of his circumstance a degree of traditional autonomy and control. While there are suggestions that antebellum tenancy afforded the renter a great deal of control over family labor, landlords became increasingly preoccupied with "managing" their tenants.[43]

A chorus of progressive and business-minded landlords dismissed the complaints of their neighbors as the whining of ineffective managers. The deterioration of land, the misuse of farm implements, and general insubordination, wrote one landlord, "is almost entirely attributable to the carelessness or mismanagement of the owners." Remarked another, "the soil improves if [the croppers] are properly managed."[44] This management meant more direct supervision of the labor of cropping families and greater restrictions on crop mix.[45] Supervision was, as one observer reported "as close as the planter can make it . . . riding from farm to farm watching the state of the crop, deciding on the method of cultivation, requiring the tenant to keep up his property, and above all, enforcing regularity of work."[46] But land-

---

40. See comments in *George Committee* 1:105; 2:173, 174.

41. *George Committee* 1:321, 325–326; 2:171.

42. Hahn, *Roots,* 163.

43. Hahn, *Roots,* 189–203; also Gallman, "Self-Sufficiency," passim.

44. *George Committee* 2:173–174.

45. Hahn, *Roots,* 69; Woodman, "Post Civil War Agriculture," 321–327.

46. Brooks, quoted in Reid, "Sharecropping as an Understandable Market Response," 114. See also David Montgomery, *Worker Control in America* (New York: Cambridge University Press, 1979), 4.

lords were not alone in controlling the labor and crop of southern farmers. Broader forces—economic upheaval following the war, the lack of banking institutions, and the concomitant destruction of traditional local markets and rise of merchant capitalism in the region—combined to restrict the economic and social independence of both tenants and yeomen farmers.

3

Signs on store windows and advertisements for merchandise in local papers read "Terms, Cash or Cotton."[47] First cotton and then cotton futures became kinds of supplemental currency in the South. The rebirth and transformation of the cotton economy served to support trade and commerce in the region, but it also tied yeomen and tenants into a kind of economy that reduced their independence and contributed to poverty and misery experienced by men like Samuel Beard and noted by observers of every political stamp.

General economic conditions after the war required large numbers of southern farmers to borrow money in order to buy seed and supplies between harvests. The decline of the factorage system and rise of the railroads brought a new set of actors onto the scene. Small merchandisers set up shop at crossroads, often with little capital but much hope. One, George Bennett of Rapides Parish, Louisiana, opened his store between Cheneyville and Bunkie with financing from two New Orleans companies and a New York financial house.[48] The merchants, like Bennett, were themselves men in the middle. They furnished goods to farmers and they owed backers for most of their stock. Unlike antebellum planters—who, when they sold or lent grain to area yeomen, were dealing away their surplus—furnishing merchants sold goods on which they owed money. This meant a newly rigid system of accounting for buyer and seller.[49]

Cash was obviously the most satisfactory way of doing business. Cash exchanged for grain could be credited immediately toward what the merchant owed his creditors. But two factors made cash transactions difficult. First, it was a rare farmer who generated a surplus after the harvest to last the remainder of the year. This lack of liquidity was the case, as Hahn has shown, in virtually every section of the South in the decade following the war. Second, commercial credit,

47. Quoted in Woodman, *King Cotton*, 336. See also Clark, *Pills, Petticoats*, passim.
48. Quoted in Woodman, *King Cotton*, 305.
49. Quoted in Woodman, *King Cotton*, 297.

as we have seen, was limited. Merchants themselves became credit institutions.

Typically, merchants advanced to growers the seed and equipment for planting the crop, and throughout the year they satisfied the growers' needs for everything from grain to fancy ribbon. In return, farmers promised to pay the account in full on a specified date, usually coinciding with the final harvest. Merchants, themselves debtors, refused to carry their customers on promises alone and demanded security. This security took the form of crop liens, agreements between a creditor and debtor that gave the creditor legal claim to the crops or their proceeds until the debt was settled. Because of its storability, its reliability as a cash crop, and the well-developed infrastructure for its sale, cotton became the basis for most crop liens. Merchants advanced goods in return for a claim on a crop whose makeup they began to determine. Like tenants, yeomen working on the credit extended by merchants lost some of their autonomy, their ability to make independent decisions about the production and sale of their crops.[50]

As liens were codified in the laws of the southern states, merchants' ability to protect their investment increased and the ability of farmers to protect their crop declined.[51] First, liens were made exclusive. That is, once a lien agreement was signed, a grower was prohibited from signing a second lien. This was, in fact, the basis of the case against Samuel Beard. The exclusivity of the lien put the grower at the mercy of the merchant, mercy not marked by its tenderness. Second, lien laws were extended to cover other forms of security, including mortgages.

Before 1880, yeomen had been protected by homestead provisions in most statutes. Under these provisions, land and implements up to a certain value were held exempt from foreclosure. As merchant capitalism spread, such limitations discouraged some merchants from lending. As in so many cases, informal arrangements to get around such impediments quickly became formalized. Merchants simply required yeomen to sign waivers of the homestead provision before signing mortgages. Whether under the burden of lien or mortgage, southern growers became increasingly unable to protect their economic security. The vortex of the cotton economy pulled yeomen down, some into landlessness and many to despair. The dependent relations be-

50. Hahn, *Roots,* 52, and Schwartz, *Radical Protest,* 63, argue convincingly that the structures of cotton marketing reduced independent production decisions.
51. On the process of tightening regulation see Woodman, *King Cotton,* 303-04; Schwartz, *Radical Protest,* 36-40. On legal changes see Woodman, "Post Civil War Agriculture and the Law."

tween farmers and owners of either land or capital were not static. Rather, indebtedness compounded as a result of the structuring of the cotton economy and as the result of cheating and chicanery on the part of some landlords and merchants.

Abuses of tenants and debtors by landlords and merchants were apparent to contemporary observers as well as to historians. Whitelaw Ried, in his tour of the war-scarred South, found that the inhabitants of the Georgia Sea Islands called the group of local stores "Robbers' Row."[52] It was an apt description.

It was in the merchant's interest to maximize the debt owed him by the farmer without driving him into bankruptcy. This was easily accomplished. First, merchants charged differential prices to cash and credit customers. The markup on supplies for the grower buying on time ranged from 40 to 70 percent, and at times higher.[53] Second, merchants charged interest on liens that ranged from "25% to grand larceny."[54] In testimony to Congress, one planter reported that rates went "from 20% up, I do not know of any less than 20%. Frequently," he stated,

> they [growers] will buy stuff in August, and may pay for it with picking of the first crop in September or October, and when you calculate the annual interest it is 200%.[55]

Other reports bore similar testimony to the exorbitant rates of interest charged to farmers, tenants and yeomen alike.[56] As merchants maintained all accounts, there was ample opportunity for inflating the current charges against clients either by manipulating rates of interest or prices. Moreover, as merchants came to be the marketing center for the cotton harvest, they gained control of grading, weighing, and

52. Quoted in Woodman, *King Cotton*, 304.
53. *George Committee* 1:368, 76, 415; Hammond, *The Cotton Industry*, 153; C. Vann Woodward, *Origins of the New South, 1877-1913* (Baton Rouge: Louisiana State University Press, 1951), 180-181; Roger Ransom and Richard Sutch, *One Kind of Freedom* (New York: Cambridge University Press, 1977), 120-123; Woodman, "Post Civil War Agriculture," 327-329; Hahn, *Roots*, 173-174; Schwartz, *Radical Protest*, 36.
54. Quoted in Schwartz, *Radical Protest*, 37.
55. *Agriculture Report*, 776.
56. See Schwartz's table of interest rates in *Radical Protest* on p. 37 and his discussion of payments on pp. 36-37. See also, Theodore Saloutos, *Farmer Movements in the South, 1865-1933* (Berkeley: University of California Publications in History, vol. 64, 1960), 23.

assigning dollar values to growers' crops. In many cases, the merchant or landlord

> who has the measuring and weighing of the crop, and the handling and calculating of these orders, makes it out, somehow, so that they not only have nothing, but are in debt.[57]

A witness told Senator Henry Blair that the feeling among tenants especially was that "they found themselves at the close of every year as far behind, as deeply in debt as at the beginning of the year."[58] But the immiserization of southern farmers did not depend upon these intentional and sometimes illicit efforts of merchants to increase their profits.

Farmers, whether yeomen, tenants, or landlords, became involved in a new credit market based on the production and sale of cotton. If they needed credit, and most did, they were forced to grow cotton. As James McLendon, of Montgomery County, Alabama, reported, "custom has established the rule that almost all trades made on credit were made on cotton as a basis."[59] This was a rational economic decision on the part of merchants that forced farmers into deepening dependency. As individual farmers grew more cotton they grew less in

57. O. H. Wall testimony, *Exodus Committee* 1:29.
58. Cromwell testimony, *Exodus Committee* 1:5.
59. *George Committee* 1:318. Cotton production in the face of its declining profitability has spurred a lively debate among economic historians. The position I have taken here, that cotton production continued because of its liquidity on commodity markets, its storability, and its nonperishable nature is supported by contemporary observers like Matthew Hammond in his article, "The Southern Farmer and the Cotton Question," *Political Science Quarterly* (September 1897) and by several modern students of the postbellum economy including Ransom and Sutch, "Debt-Peonage in the Cotton South." The opposing view, that cotton production remained a profitable enterprise, or at least held out the promise of profitability for the small farmer as well as the landlord is represented by William W. Brown and Morgan Reynolds in their "Debt Peonage Reexamined," *Journal of Economic History* 33 (December 1973) and by Stephen DeCanio, "Cotton 'Overproduction' in Late Nineteenth Century Southern Agriculture," *Journal of Economic History* 33 (September 1973). DeCanio and Brown and Reynolds argue that prices for cotton fluctuated in ways similar to those for corn and wheat, allowing them to assert that farmers would have been as well off farming cotton as either of the other two crops. This argument assumes that farmers had a choice in determining their crop mix. They did not in many cases. Moreover, the declining prices of cotton did not often transfer into low profits for the merchant. It was simple for him to transfer low returns directly to the farmer, in the form of higher interest rates. Thus, prices are not the best indicator of the division of revenue, only of its level.

the way of food crops.[60] They became dependent upon merchants to supply them with the grain and meat that they had once produced themselves. This, in turn, deepened the indebtedness of farmers as they borrowed on future cotton crops to meet current needs. To complete the cycle, as the account at the local merchant's grew, so did the merchant's insistence that the farmer produce more cotton. This demand, of course, led to a further reduction in the production of foodstuffs. The cycle became more vicious in the 1880s when cotton prices began to decline, responding to increased supply on world markets. It took more and more cotton to raise sufficient revenue to purchase necessary supplies. Roger Ransom and Richard Sutch have aptly described this cycle as a "lock-in" mechanism, locking growers into the production of ever more cotton independent of rational economic decision making.[61]

Debt peonage had other meanings, meanings particularly poignant to southern farmers. Debt was, as we have seen, a pervasive feature of southern farming.[62] And debt created conditions whereby farmers lost control over their labor. For some, debt peonage led to an outright forfeiture of clear title to land.

Rates of tenancy rose throughout the period. Aggregate rates of tenancy rose by 10 percent in each census year between 1860 and 1890.[63] In Carroll County, Georgia, tenancy increased from 40 percent in 1880 to 52 percent in 1890.[64] In 1890, Mississippi led the nation with a tenancy rate of 62.3 percent. Kentucky, whose 34.7 percent rate was the lowest in the South, still exceeded the tenancy rate of any nonsouthern state.[65]

Mortgage rates, the percentage of titles held as security for debt, rose faster than the rate of tenancy. In Carroll County, Hahn calculates that the number of mortgages increased 5,000 percent in the ten years between 1875 and 1885. W. Scott Morgan, an Alliance leader and author, was himself a victim of what came to be called "Anaconda" mortgages. Like a lien holder, the farmer with a mortgage on his or her land

60. Hahn, Roots, 141–142.

61. See Ransom and Sutch "The Lock-In Mechanism;" Schwartz, Radical Protest, chaps. 2 and 3; Hahn, Roots, chap. 3; Wiener, "Class Structure and Economic Development;" People's Party Paper, November 26, 1891.

62. Schwartz, Radical Protest, chap. 5.

63. Schwartz, Radical Protest, 75.

64. Hahn, Roots, 167.

65. Eleventh Census, Farms and Homes, 24, table 94, 243–284.

> . . . became practically a slave of the mortgagee; he is deprived of all means of obtaining credit elsewhere; he cannot object to the quantity or quality of the goods offered him, nor to the prices charged.[66]

Actual foreclosure seems to have been rare, as low land values made it more profitable for merchants to continue to carry debt over from one year to the next, insuring themselves a steady, if small, stream of income.[67] In 1890, the average southern farm was worth only 34 percent of the same farm in New England, 36 percent of that in the North Central U.S., and just 19 percent of the value of the typical farm in the western states. While some of this difference, particularly that between the farm values in the South and the West, is captured by the greater average size of western farms, the difference in value between the small farms of the Northeast and those of the South is striking. For yeomen, often in name only, this meant toiling on the brink of bankruptcy and increasing dependency on the holder of the mortgage.

In the postbellum South, then, new forms of agricultural labor, increasing rates of tenancy, and the controlling mechanisms of liens and mortgages combined to reduce the independence and self-sufficiency of southern farmers by reducing their ability to control their own crops and labor. To these changes, farmers responded in various ways.

First, they redoubled their efforts. "In an occupation known for hard work," wrote Lawrence Goodwyn, "they worked harder."[68] For those who stayed and tried to dig themselves out of debt, Senator Blair may have provided an epitaph: "his hope is crushed and his faith departed."[69]

Second, when hard work produced only debt, they migrated, sometimes skipping out on their creditors, to seek a fresh start on the western frontier. As Lawrence Goodwyn found, skipping became so popular in sections of the Deep South that signs reading "G.T.T." were enough to convey to the reader that another tenant had "gone to Texas."[70] Those who fled, seeking their independence in the piney woods of east Texas and the central Texas prairie, found fertile soil,

---

66. Morgan, *History of the Wheel*, 57.

67. *Historical Statistics of the United States*, 1:463, 465. Schwartz, *Radical Protest*, 40.

68. Goodwyn, *The Populist Moment*, vii, viii.

69. Minority opinion, written by Blair, on behalf of his Republican colleagues, *Exodus Committee* 2:234. The majority and minority reports split on party lines.

70. Goodwyn, *Democratic Promise*, 31.

sufficient rainfall, and conditions suitable for the cultivation of the crop they knew best, cotton. Through the 1880s and 1890s, while the deep South labored under declining per-acre productivity and declining cotton prices, Texas planters survived. Scott Morgan reported that nearly 77 percent of the farmers in his home state, Arkansas, were either in debt or farmed as tenants.[71] The Alliance organ, the *National Economist,* reported 70 percent indebtedness among the farmers of northern Louisiana.[72] In contrast, Morgan reported that indebtedness in Texas rarely rose above one-third of working farmers.[73] One witness to the Senate Cotton Committee reported that among his farmer neighbors in Texas, "not 1 percent is insolvent."[74]

There was a limit to this miniboom in Texas farming. As migration continued, successive waves settled farther and farther west, eventually passing beyond the region in which rainfall could support cotton cultivation. For west Texas settlers, their new freedom was bittersweet. They regained control of their labor and in many cases their new land, yet they found themselves in a semiarid high prairie. But there they stayed, "flattening their Georgia plows against the limestone strata lurking inches beneath the topsoil of the Edwards plateau."[75] The new Texans eked out an existence in struggle against the soil, the weather, and predatory cattlemen whose herds knew neither fence nor forage. The migration to Texas was the last straw, the last attempt by farmers to deal with their poverty in terms and with tools they understood from generations of tradition.

When, through harder work and migration, southern farmers failed to drag prosperity from the earth, they turned to political action within their party, the Democratic party. In this effort, too, farmers found their way blocked by changes that had limited agrarian influence on policy making within the party.

4

After the Civil War farmers faced an agricultural economy changed in ways that confounded their understanding of the world. Postbellum political changes left them feeling similarly confounded. In the two decades between Appomattox and the organization of the National Farmers' Alliance, southern farmers found themselves caught, polit-

71. Morgan, *History of the Wheel,* 670.
72. *National Economist,* June 15, 1889.
73. Morgan, *History of the Wheel,* 670.
74. *George Committee* 1:350.
75. Goodwyn, *Democratic Promise,* 30.

ically, in a pair of scissors, one blade forged of tradition, the other of change, leaving them, by 1890, cut off from both the past and the future of the major political parties. They were ignored in the councils of the Democratic party and their interests lost legitimacy in late nineteenth-century political debate.

Party politics immediately following the Civil War, as Goodwyn and others point out, served as a proxy for the expression of racial and sectional loyalties.[76] Party membership, which we treat so lightly today, was invested with enormous emotional and historical significance far surpassing the surface commitments to one or the other of the two main parties. History, particularly the history of the Civil War and Reconstruction, determined party membership and demanded party loyalty. In Goodwyn's view, people ceased thinking about politics as a set of ideas after the war, and instead remembered only the role the two parties had played in the conflict.[77] Over time, the historic and symbolic differences between Democrat and Republican overtook substantive differences in platforms and policies. During the 1870s, as Walter Dean Burnham argues, substantive differences between the parties decreased, yet members were more tightly reined in by party culture and the force of tradition than ever before.[78]

The two processes, substantive convergence and symbolic divergence, reinforced each other throughout the 1880s and 1890s. As the parties grew closer together ideologically, means of differentiation based on other factors increased. Strategically, it was important for both parties to play up their historical and traditional differences in order to limit defections and retain majorities in areas of strength. Admittedly the strategy was defensive, but it was designed to keep movement between parties to a minimum while both the Republican and Democratic leaderships groped their way toward redefinitions of party goals. With the exceptions of the Populist revolt in the South and the ethnic ties of many urban workers in the North to Democracy, the historical division between Democrat and Republican, South and North, showed remarkable persistence throughout the postbellum years and into the twentieth century. The failure of the Democracy to hold on to white Populists and of the GOP to hold on to blacks points

76. Goodwyn, *The Populist Moment,* chap. 1; Eric Foner, *Politics and Ideology in the Age of the Civil War* (New York: Oxford University Press, 1980), chaps. 1–4; and C. Vann Woodward, *Origins of the New South,* chaps. 6, 8.

77. Goodwyn, *The Populist Moment,* 3.

78. See, for example, E. W. Winkler, *Platforms of Political Parties in Texas,* University of Texas Bulletin, no. 53 (Austin: University of Texas, 1916), passim; and Walter Dean Burnham, *Presidential Ballots, 1836–1892* (New York: Arno Press, 1976), 130–131.

out the growing distance between the needs of agrarians and the platforms of the parties, a distance that even symbolic and cultural ties
could not bridge.

In the North as well as in the South, for blacks as well as for whites,
the Democratic party emerged from the Civil War as the party of the
lost cause and of white supremacy. Southern Democrats had led the
fight, first to preserve slavery within the Union and, when the North
refused to accede, to build a new nation from the ruins of the
American Republic. The Democracy had been the one party in the
Confederacy; the White South was tied to the party of its fathers by
memories of honor, courage, and even pride of purpose. Because of
this enormous cultural weight, the terms *Southern, white,* and
Democrat became, for the most part, politically redundant.[79] Pressure
to maintain party allegiance was great, failure to adhere to the party
was sometimes dangerous. Populists and Alliancemen, like so many
others, felt "the murderous hate" that threatened any white
southerner who forsook the party of his fathers.[80] A member of the
People's party reported that he "had been shot at many times," and
that there was little that legally could be done: "Grand juries will not
indict our assailants . . . Courts give us no protections."[81]

The other national party, the GOP, was of course the party that
"saved the Union." In the South, it was also the party that defeated
the Confederacy and then occupied confederate land with its troops.
Finally, the GOP was the party that freed the slaves and made them
citizens. For southern whites, their positive identification with the
Democracy was indivisible from their intense hatred of the Republican
party and its history during the war and Reconstruction. For blacks,
newly freed from the sorrows and tragedies of bondage, the associa-
tions quite naturally ran in the opposite direction. Republicans were
not the devils, but the liberators. Once they found that Union soldiers
did not eat black babies (a story that was told often by slaveholders
during the last desperate days of the war), blacks identified the Union
army, the North, and their own individual freedom with Mr. Lincoln
and his party. Coupled with this natural affinity between blacks and
Republicans, conscious efforts on the part of Reconstruction politi-

79. See Carl Degler, *The Other South: Southern Dissenters in the Nineteenth Century* (New York: Harper and Row, 1974) for the most complete account of dissent
against the tradition of deference in the South.
80. Quoted in Henry Demarest Lloyd, "The Populists at St. Louis," *Review of
Reviews* 16 (September 1896): 265. For a general discussion of the fate of southern
dissenters see Degler, *The Other South,* chaps. 9, 10.
81. Quoted in Degler, *The Other South,* 317.

cians to recruit blacks into the party in order to break the Democrats' electoral hold on the South resulted in virtually unanimous black membership in the GOP.[82]

The association did not last long, for a decade of being counted out, bribed, and "bulldozed" convinced blacks that "neither of these parties gives a tinker's snap" for their protection, much less for their advancement, offering only the barest concessions to their citizenship.[83] Only in areas like Virginia, where disputes over taxation and government spending or other overarching issues split white votes, did blacks make political gains, and these were largely transitory.[84] In the late 1880s the white Republicans in the South attempted to buy into the myths of section and race, and by so doing, to recruit more southern whites into the ranks of the party and deflect criticisms from the Democrats that Republicanism stood for black rule. The "Lily-whites" set out to prove, among other things, that Republicans could be as racist as Democrats if they tried hard enough. The best that blacks could expect from either major party in the South was a grudging and debilitating paternalism that carved out a "black sphere" of economic and social life that was to be formalized in the Jim Crow laws of the late 1890s.[85] The rise of the "Lily-whites" in the South and the progressive decay of support for blacks in the national GOP left blacks literally without a party.

Thus tradition and history tied southerners to one party or the other, depending upon their identities and histories. For whites, Democracy represented both an image of a better past and their hopes for the future. For blacks, the GOP tied them to the army of their liberation, their freedom itself. Such ties were not easily broken, even in the face of changes that made the parties disloyal to their members. For blacks, disillusionment and betrayal came earlier than it did for whites, but by 1890, both black and white farmers and small producers in the South realized that while they had been true to history and had kept the faith, the parties of their respective fathers had not. Politics and parties had changed.

Agrarians of both races and in both sections recognized that the parties were becoming less responsive to their needs during the 1880s. Contractionary monetary policy lowered prices for their agricultural produce and raised the real cost of their debts. At the state level,

82. Woodward, *Origins,* 218; Foner, *Politics and Ideology,* chap. 2.
83. Quoted in Woodward, *Origins,* 219.
84. See Degler, *The Other South,* chap. 9; Woodward, *Origins,* 99–100.
85. Woodward, *Origins,* 256; also C. Vann Woodward, *The Strange Career of Jim Crow,* 3d revised ed. (New York: Oxford University Press, 1971), passim.

Democratic legislatures refused entreaties to regulate railroad rates and passed restrictive laws governing the rights of tenants and agricultural labor. At the same time, they granted tax exemptions to mining, manufacturing, and transportation firms. To farmers, it appeared that the Democracy, in an effort to regain national influence, had gone a bit crazy and forgotten its roots, which had been nurtured by southern farmers under the hot southern sun, even in the hardest times. What farmers saw as a colossal mistake was actually the gradual and, as it turned out, permanent reorientation of American politics.

As the nation industrialized and urbanized after the war, so did the two major parties. Their focus, in both rhetoric and program, shifted from the agrarian heart of the nation to its industrial center. While the old parties still held southern farmers, they became less and less disposed to help them.

The Republicans' post-Reconstruction politics revolved around investment rather than abolition; the cause of free soil, free labor, and free men was lost in the rush to create a nation of industry.[86] Even southern Democrats, representing the least industrialized and most agrarian region in the nation, were lured by the siren song of industry and its seductive melodies which promised not only high profits and regional development but, through industrial employment, a solution to the "negro problem."

Democrats were hardly ashamed or secretive about their changing attitude. Grover Cleveland proudly proclaimed himself a "man of business," and called his administration "their [businessmen's] representatives" in government.[87] In January 1892, shortly after the People's party registered its greatest electoral victories in the rural states and districts of America, Cleveland addressed an enthusiastic crowd of businessmen and their wives in New York's Madison Square Garden. There he spoke in his booming voice of what he considered the essence of his party. "True Democracy," he thundered, has "a membership composed of businessmen!"[88] The business of the two major American political parties became business in the 1880s and 1890s. The Alliance was aware of this change and was angered by

86. The rise of the Republican party is ably told by Eric Foner in his book *Free Soil, Free Labor, Free Men* (Chicago: University of Chicago Press, 1973).

87. Speech to the Businessmen's Democratic Club of New York, October 27, 1891. In A. E. Bergh, ed., *Grover Cleveland: Addresses, State Papers, and Letters* (New York: Sun Dial Publishers, 1908), 250.

88. Speech to the Businessmen's Democratic Club of New York, January 8, 1892. In Bergh, *Grover Cleveland*, 313.

it. Macune covered Cleveland's speeches in the *National Economist* and never failed to quote "Grover" at length whenever he waxed euphoric about business. In one issue, Macune quoted the president as saying that in businessmen and merchants rested "the factor in civilized life which measures the progress of a people, [and] which constitutes the chief care of every enlightened government."[89] If business was the "chief care of government" then what was left for the farmers? Macune asked his readers. Clearly, they felt abandoned by their party and cut off from traditional political remedies to their economic problems.

5

In politics, as in economics, traditional modes of discourse and interaction were replaced by forms that were at once new and prejudicial to what many farmers saw as their interests. This experience was in the root sense "educative," whether for individuals like Beard or for those, like Macune, who had been a part of the migration of ruined farmers from the old South to the Texas prairie, or for others who simply watched as their neighbors grew poorer, lost control of their land and labor, and ran out of places to turn for help.

The Alliance grew as an organized attempt to understand and combat the immediate and often local issues of stock laws, foreclosures, and high prices. As it matured, as it generated a cadre of intellectuals and a discourse of its own, the Alliance moved to a general critique of the changes in the political economy that resulted in farmers being disenfranchised and deskilled politically and in the pauperization of tenants and yeomen. The changed conditions facing producers demanded explanations, clarifications, and remedies. These demands focused the structure and content of the Alliance educational program at every juncture. As Polk told an audience in Indianapolis,

> The gray-haired sire, whose sinews and muscles have been toughened and hardened through a life of toil and labor in the production of wealth has been forced to address himself to the sole important problem of securing a just and equitable distribution of that wealth. Intelligent, honest, and earnest research and investigation as to the causes that have brought the American Farmer to the verge of bankruptcy and ruin have been forced upon him . . .[90]

89. *National Economist,* January 4, 1890.
90. *People's Party Paper,* December 3, 1891.

Education was particularly important to the Alliance movement in three ways. First, the lack of educational opportunities made southerners especially vulnerable to the kinds of changes that shook traditional southern society. Minimal opportunities for schooling and correspondingly high rates of illiteracy made southern farmers, for example, susceptible to the kind of fraud that appear in the reports made about country storekeepers and merchants. Second, education was the means through which Polk and others saw "research and investigation" taking place within the Alliance. Finally, the Alliance leadership assigned great value to the enrichment of rural culture socially, politically, and economically, and they saw, there too, education as the means to that end.

The educational program organized by the Alliance attempted to provide basic skills and to apply those skills to the environment in which farmers found themselves. Alliance educators taught skills in the context of the political and economic environment. Their curriculum drew upon the language of liens and mortgages, the mathematics of store accounts, and the history of working people. The effort was intended to create a critical and involved citizenry and, by so doing, to create a new political culture based on broad substantive participation that would serve the interests of rural producers.

2   Educating for Organization

The Structuring of Experience

> *Those who have combined by organized effort, secured special privileges through legislation, state and national, dread us because they know that our organization is a school, and through its teachings the road to liberty will soon be available to the oppressed. Knowledge is power and when the masses become educated their power will be irresistible.*
> —Evan Jones, *Southern Mercury,* December 17, 1891

1

Rising incidence of tenancy, growing dependence on merchant capital, and a general breakdown of traditional political and economic relations demanded explanation, and explanation demanded, as Leonidas Polk called it, "honest and earnest research and investigation." As Charles Macune stated the general problem, when "civilization advances, society becomes more complex and the questions arising for solutions become more complicated, requiring a higher standard of intelligence to solve them."[1] Existing educational institutions, though, could provide neither the simple quantity nor the quality and type of opportunity required by the circumstances as defined by the leaders of the movement.

The basic lack of schooling facilities in the region and the inattention of the few existing schools to political and economic education left "knowledge of political economy monopolized by comparatively few" men of affairs.[2] It was the educational goal of the movement to "educate the great mass of the people in the principles of economical government," and, by so educating "the mass," contribute to the Alliance's political goal of creating and sustaining a more democratic, producer-oriented political culture.[3]

Polk argued, and the Alliance maintained, that farmers learned best from their straitened circumstances, that experience in the productive

1. *National Economist,* November 2, 1889.
2. *National Economist,* November 2, 1889.
3. Col. R. J. Sledge in Dunning, *Farmers' Alliance History,* 330.

world was the best teacher. But that experience needed focus, it needed universal and collective expression. One of the first things farmers learned was that they needed to know more.

2

Some came on horseback, some on foot. Families loaded on wagons trundled slowly along the road in the early morning hours. Some five hundred strong, men, women, and children, black and white, headed toward the church at the crossroads town of Shady Grove, Georgia. What drew them was not Sunday service; they would make that trek from their homes and farms the next day. They traveled to town on what promised to be a hot and muggy June Saturday in order to take part in the Shady Grove Farmers' Alliance Rally.[4]

By 11:00, the church was packed and the temperature inside the church climbed. Following a benediction and a hymn, "the ball was opened with a rattling speech by Charlie Sewell." Sewell was the county Alliance secretary and did not disappoint his listeners. "We all knew Charlie was the best county secretary in the state, but his speech astonished his friends and confounded his enemies."

One of those enemies spoke next. Colonel C. D. Phillips, planter, landlord, and Democratic solon, "spoke for over an hour in behalf of the Democracy":

> He made an eloquent appeal to the old soldiers to stick to the old party because of its good work during reconstruction times and waved the bloody shirt in the regulation way; but strange to say, the old soldiers didn't enthuse worth a cent—they evidently were thinking of the fact that the Democratic party was the sole cause of the war, which resulted in maimed soldiers, reconstruction, etc.

By 1:00 P.M. the temperature inside had risen to daunting levels and contributed to a sharpening of rhetoric and tempers. Phillips' voice rose in a series of questions aimed at building support and momentum in the crowd.

> But the answers he got from all over the audience did not suit him, in fact, he came near losing his temper when the wool hat

4. For the account of the Shady Grove rally, see *People's Party Paper,* June 14, 1891.

boys would knock his arguments into a cocked hat with their quick replies to the questions he insisted on being answered.[5]

Phillips withdrew from the pulpit having failed, it seemed, to bring the assembled farmers back into the fold.

Despite the heat and the air that must surely have become dank, Georgia State Representative John Sibley rose from his seat to deliver "one of the best speeches ever delivered in the state." He "completely answered every argument advanced by Phillips and clinched every assertion with incontrovertable proof." His speech, according to one observer, "carried conviction with it." At the end of the speech, as Sibley, too, urged his audience to speak, "over a dozen farmers, who had heretofore hesitated joining . . . openly announced that they were full fledged [members.]" On this high note, the rally moved outside, into the full June sun to enjoy a meal.

"Too much could not be said" about the dinner. "The ladies of the community certainly showed their devotion . . . by the elegant feast they spread." Sweet potatoes, collards, cold pork, corn bread and baked sweet breads, cakes and pies were the staples of these Alliance rallies.[6] After eating, men tended to their animals with water, oats, and hay. They found shade under trees, shared their tobacco, talked about the morning's speeches, and news of themselves and their families. Women tended the meal, also talking of themselves, their families, and the events of the day. Meanwhile, children played in the church cemetery, dodging between the grave markers and weaving in and out between the wheels of their parents' wagons.

In Shady Grove, "after the whites had eaten, the colored men, of whom there was a goodly number present, were invited up." They had listened to Sewell, Phillips, and Sibley, from the back of the church, and now they ate. The socializing between black and white was limited, but the separate effect of the morning's speeches on the black audience was still profound. One black farmer said "we have had our

5. *People's Party Paper,* June 14, 1891.
6. This was not the only role for women in the Alliance. They were from the start integral parts of the movement and of its campaign of education. Most Alliance thinking in the role of women focused on empowering women within their traditional roles as mothers and managers of the household. In these roles, they were to exhort their men to greater efforts on behalf of reform, teach their children the fraternity and solidarity among rural people, and always seek to improve their understanding of the conditions that faced them. For more, see Betty Gay, "The Influence of Women in the Farmers' Alliance," in Dunning, *Farmers' Alliance History,* 308-313.

eyes opened today and you can count on me . . . what is good for the white laborer must be good for the colored laborer.''

After lunch, Secretary Sewell called the rally to order and introduced speeches by J. L. Dobbs, J. D. Cunningham, and several others. Phillips, who had been invited to stay and rebut any Alliance arguments, ''evidently thought the argument unanswerable for he did not remain.'' In high spirits, ''the association then adjourned to meet on the 2nd Saturday in July at Smyrna, for another Grand Rally.''[7]

3

Known by different names throughout the South—*rallies* in Georgia, *gatherings* in Virginia, *camps* in Texas—the periodic assemblies brought together the faithful, the curious, the skeptical, and sometimes the opposed for a day of respite from toil, a day of socializing, playing, eating, and political educating. The rallies were constructed and organized to be educative in all their constituent parts.

At the most basic level, these rallies brought farmers and their families together with others. That was not a small triumph. In the rural South only churches had succeeded in gathering together, on a regular basis, the dispersed population of most southern farm communities.[8] As mass meetings, the rallies generated a sense of group identity that circumscribed the identities of individual men and women. In the informal interaction between people at the rallies, in the preparation of the food, in the setting out of the luncheon, in the games, storytelling, and songs, formerly isolated farm families shared their individual experiences. As farmers found commonality, those stories, those experiences, took on more than individual meaning. As they were shared by others, experiences such as low cotton prices, high commodity prices, and ''anaconda mortgages'' bridged the geographical and sometimes ideological distance between individuals and fashioned a common bond between them.

The meetings were, in other words, important in broadening individual connections with the outside world. They were also moments for celebration of common bonds. In the fall of 1889, for example, the Alliance attempted to break the monopoly on jute bagging, in which their cotton was shipped. As the jute companies raised their prices, Alliance-sponsored companies began producing cotton wrappings for the bales. The early trust busting focused farmers' attention and gave them a common cause. Alliance efforts did not destroy the cartel of

7. *People's Party Paper,* June 14, 1891.
8. For a general commentary on rural life in the South, see Wilbur Cash, *The Mind of the South* (New York: Vintage Books, 1969), chaps. 1, 3.

jute producers, but it did force it to lower its prices. Discovering such power brought farmers closer together and redounded to the social side of the movement. On one particularly jubilant occasion, a young Allianceman and his fiancée suited themselves in cotton bagging for their wedding. The event took place in the midst of an Alliance encampment in Plymouth, North Carolina, and was widely heralded by the movement's leaders.[9]

In addition to linking farmers with each other, the rallies and meetings served to link the Alliance and its individual members more closely with their communities, as the schedules of events make clear. Usually the program began with a benediction, offered by the minister of a local church, often in his own church, as was the case in Shady Grove. With the help of cooperative and sympathetic churchmen, growers bridged still another chasm in the postbellum South, that between piety and social action. Religion, in structure and form as well as in substantive ideology, became a part of the farmers' movement.

Often the meetings were pageants for the community as a whole. In Erath County, Texas, a rally was introduced by two bands and a chorus of local school children. The children later entertained the amassed farmers with plays and skits. Singing, whether accompanied by musicians or *a cappella,* was a large part of the encampment structure and as the movement grew, songbooks appeared with selections written or adapted specifically for the movement. The Vincents' *Alliance and Labor Songster* ranged from patriotic hymns to popular Alliance ballads, written to old familiar tunes.[10] Singing was among the most complete educational tools of the Alliance rally, combining sociability and implicit unifying meaning with explicit lyrical themes and messages.

J. J. Martin's "Song for the Toiler" often opened the singing, perhaps to give the assembly a sense of its broader goals:

> We have now in Council met
> In Freedom's ranks to serve;
> Our hearts and hands in union strong.
> No fear or threats can serve.
>
> For Justice is our cornerstone,
> And Truth our sword and shield
> Fraternity our battlecry
> The world our battlefield.

9. *National Economist,* October 5, 1889.
10. *Southern Mercury,* October 29, 1891. See Leopold Vincent's *Alliance and Labor Songster* for a host of songs popular at labor rallies in the period.

In "Once More We Meet to Clasp," farmers sang to the tune of "My Country Tis of Thee" of the need for unity:

> One more we meet to clasp
> In friendships hallowed grasp
>   The hands of men!
> Oh may our cause sublime
> Throughout the length of time
> In this our native clime,
>   Forever stand.
>
> Patrons, stand by your cause,
> Obeying Honor's Laws;
>   Move hand in hand.
> No rich monop'lies great
> Nor foreign syndicate,
> Shall guide this Ship of State
>   In this fair land.
>
> Brave Sons and daughters fair,
> By truth and Virtue heir
>   To honor's name;
> Stand by your colors pure,
> And may your strength endure;
> Reward, though slow, is sure,
>   In this high game.

"Once More" implicated monopolies and foreign syndicates in the ills of the farmer. Other songs were far more specific in both their assessment of the causes of the growers' plight and their prescriptions for reform. A song titled "The Future America" adopted the same tune as "Once More."

> My Country tis of thee
> Land of lost Liberty,
>   Of thee I sing.
> Land where the Millionaires,
> Who govern our affairs
> Own for themselves and heirs,
>   Hail to thy King.

Land where the wealthy few
Can make the many do
   Their royal will,
And tax for selfish greed
The toilers till they bleed
And those not yet weak-kneed,
   Crush down and kill.

My country, tis of thee
Betrayed by bribery,
   Of thee we sing.
We might have saved thee long
Had we when proud and strong
Put down the cursed wrong
   That makes a King.[11]

The "cursed wrong" in the future America was of course the development of a moneyed class with political power disproportionate to its membership. In "The Future America" the central problem is told in the second verse, that of the identity of power and wealth and power used in service of wealth. The mechanism of "put[ting] down that cursed wrong," we will see, had everything to do with the Alliance campaign of education. The singing gave way to the speeches, orations in the southern style, and then to eating. Here, too, structure and process created educative moments for the farmers and their families.[12]

First, the lecture format mitigated somewhat the pervasive problem of adult illiteracy in the region. Illiteracy was a much more salient feature of life in the South than in any other region of the United States (table 2.1). The differences in literacy rates, first between blacks and whites across the nation, and second between southerners and nonsoutherners, is striking. Moreover, illiteracy had important effects on the ability of southern farmers, especially tenants, to defend themselves in an economic environment fast becoming dominated by written contracts. Evidence from the eleventh census (1890) indicates that men and women involved in agriculture were twice as likely to be il-

11. Vincent, *Alliance and Labor Songster*, 4.
12. See Edwin Dubois Shurter, *Oratory of the South* (New York: Neale Publishing Co., 1908), passim. Also, Waldo Braden, *The Oral Tradition in the South* (Baton Rouge: Louisiana State University Press, 1983).

literate as their counterparts in manufacturing. Only those involved in domestic service, an occupation overwhelmingly black, approached the rate of illiteracy found among farmers in the region.[13]

Unfortunately, occupational literacy figures were not disaggregated by race in the eleventh census; it is impossible to determine whether white farmers were, as a group, more likely to be illiterate than were white workers in manufacturing enterprises. But some inferences may be made by comparing table 2.1 to 2.2 and deriving a constructed illiteracy rate for white farmers, tenants, and farm laborers (see table 2.3).[14]

From these constructed rates of illiteracy it is clear that, except in Virginia, the rate of illiteracy for white farmers exceeded that for all manufacturing workers, all professionals, and all tradespeople. In short, white southern farmers were more likely to be illiterate than were their counterparts in industry and commerce. Moreover, illiteracy was a persistent feature of life in the rural South.

The 1900 census shows that of the 231 counties nationwide with adult white illiteracy rates over 25 percent, 226 were located in the South.[15] Charles Dabney, a leader of the educational crusade, later used these figures to launch his own campaign for education.[16]

Illiteracy put the southern tenant or southern debtor at a significant disadvantage, indeed it put anyone who signed his name with an x at the mercy of the merchant or landlord who signed with his name. Blacks, as is easily imagined from the deplorable rate of illiteracy for freedmen, were particularly susceptible to fraud. Even the Democrats in the Senate were forced to acknowledge the fact that tenants were cheated daily by their creditors.

Perhaps more significant was that illiteracy closed off important parts of the world and important forms of discourse. Alliance meetings and lectures sought to reopen those doors. Speakers wove

13. On illiteracy, see also Charles Dabney "Report on Illiteracy at the Tenth Census," in *Annual Report of the Department of the Interior: Report of the Commissioner of Education for 1890* (Washington, D.C.: Government Printing Office, 1891) 1: 791–820.

14. Only in Louisiana was the black farming population greater than 50 percent of the total farm population. Only in Kentucky, Tennessee, and Texas were fewer than 25 percent of the farmers black. If we eliminate these four states, we can assume a maximum of 50 percent black farmers and a minimum of 50 percent white farmers in the South as a whole. In general, a minimum for white farm illiteracy can be established for each state by using the formula: I (white farm illiteracy) = 2 (total farm illiteracy) − I (black farm illiteracy).

15. Dabney, "Report on Illiteracy at the Tenth Census," 794.

16. See chap. 6 of this volume.

Table 2.1. Regional illiteracy in the United States by race and sex, 1890 (percentage of total population over ten years of age)

Region	White males	White females	Black males	Black females
North Atlantic	6.2	2.3	21.7	22.5
North Central	5.1	3.6	32.8	35.4
West	6.2	5.7	41.5	61.0
South Atlantic	14.5	15.7	60.1	62.6
South Central	5.3	16.2	61.2	64.1

Source: *Eleventh Census of the United States: Abstract of the Eleventh Census, vol. 1.* Department of the Interior, Bureau of the Census (Washingtron, D.C.: Government Printing Office, 1894), 64–67.

Table 2.2. Illiteracy in the southern states by occupational category, 1890 (percentage of the total population)

State	Agriculture	Professional	Domestic	Trade	Manufacturing
Alabama	52.4	1.1	61.9	17.8	21.8
Arkansas	38.1	.5	40.6	9.1	10.0
Florida	39.4	1.0	46.6	13.3	14.7
Georgia	49.3	1.1	58.5	18.5	23.8
Kentucy	28.3	1.2	41.4	9.1	7.9
Louisiana	62.9	1.2	54.8	11.8	13.5
Mississippi	52.4	1.4	63.1	15.4	21.2
North Carolina	43.3	1.1	58.4	15.9	24.4
South Carolina	58.1	.9	61.6	17.7	25.3
Tennessee	33.6	1.1	49.1	3.1	15.0
Texas	25.6	.7	40.2	7.6	9.2
Virginia	40.1	1.3	52.4	17.1	20.7

Source: Computed from *Eleventh Census: Population, Part 2* 302–303, 432–433.

Table 2.3. Constructed illiteracy rates for white farm populations, 1890

State	Constructed Illiteracy Rate
Alabama	41.1
Arkansas	15.5
Florida	18.1
Georgia	37.9
Mississippi	44.1
North Carolina	25.9
South Carolina	55.5
Virginia	19.5

Source: Computed from *Eleventh Census: Population, Part 1.*

detailed and intricate arguments before the crowds, spiced with demagoguery, anecdotes, and wit. Most played shamelessly on the emotions and prejudices of their audience to gain support, as did Col. Phillips at the Shady Grove rally. When he reached out to the "old soldiers" he appealed to the growers to put aside their disagreements with the Democratic party for the sake of sectional loyalty. It was a powerful emotional argument.

That Phillips' attempt failed points to the second educative feature of the Alliance lecture. In the sense that lectures are passive arrangements whereby those with knowledge bestow it upon those who lack it, the rallies were not lectures at all. Rather, events like that in Shady Grove pitted one point of view against another, gave farmers opportunities to debate the speakers and each other, and provided numerous means for social and intellectual interchange. Ideas were presented by speakers, countered by others, discussed by those in attendance during the meal and games, and refined or altered by still more speakers in the afternoon. In Shady Grove, the audience whitewashed Phillips' bloody-shirt argument and in the same way empowered the points of view proposed by Sewell and Sibley. It was a format that encouraged participation, which in turn directed the outcome of the educative process.[17]

Sometimes, as at the annual Texas State Alliance meeting, the rally lasted for two or three days, with farmers camping at the meeting site, talking until the morning around small campfires, discussing the speeches and speakers of the previous day. The 1894 encampment in Texas, held between August 7 and August 11, brought ten thousand farmers and their families together. The fires that burned through the night recalled to one veteran "an army in bivouac."[18]

This is precisely how the movement's leaders wanted their encampments seen—as an army. It was the duty of the lecturer not only to bring farmers together but to send them away, after the final song and the closing sermon, united in a common purpose, the basis of which lay in empowering farmers to act politically in their own interest. The identification of common problems and a common purpose reinforced the lesson the Alliance lecturers were attempting to teach about the existence of two irreconcilable classes and class interests in society. The camp meetings, if they did nothing else, contributed, as rituals, to the raising of farmers' morale and to the process whereby their in-

17. *Louisiana Populist,* July 12, 1892.

18. For further descriptions of these giant encampments see: *National Economist,* April 20, 1889. See also *Southern Mercury,* August 9, 1894; September 24, 1891; September 10, 1891; October 8, 1891; *Louisiana Populist,* October 12, 1892, August 16, 1895.

dividual identities became linked in a collective sense, and linked to the Alliance's ideology and its reform program. The agents of this linkage, and the central actors in the "movement education" fashioned by the Alliance were the lecturers who appeared at rallies and meetings throughout the region.

4

"Owing to the false education of producers in regard to economical questions which touch their material interest," wrote J. H. Robertson of Virginia, "the lecturer holds the most important office in our order."[19] In many ways lecturers were the keystone of the Alliance's broad educational program. These men (they were all men in the beginning) linked farmers with each other and provided the personal connection between isolated local chapters, called subordinate or suballiances, and the growing organization of farmers across the South. Lecturers personified the ideology that favored direct economic and social mobilization; they were exhorters, cajolers, and sometimes bullies. Their roles and their numbers grew dramatically from the appointment of the first "Traveling Lecturer," S. O. Daws, by the Executive Committee of the Texas Alliance in 1883, to the work of some forty thousand lecturers in the field in 1892.[20]

Lecturers traveled assigned circuits, publicizing their arrivals in the hamlets and dusty crossroads through leaflets and advertisements in local papers. When conditions were good, they spoke indoors—in schoolhouses, churches, and town halls—before hundreds of assembled farmers. More often, they spoke from the backs of wagons in a fallow field to crowds of fifteen or twenty. Their work was taxing and sometimes dangerous.

Local opposition to the Alliance, particularly as the movement increased its involvement in politics, usually came from Democrats. "At a meeting at Union Bluff Schoolhouse, in Bell County [Texas], June 4 [1894]," reported the Bell County Alliance Secretary, "the Democrats of that bailiwick became so exasperated at the lambasting they were given by the Alliance speaker, Mr. Sam Baker, that they resorted to the usual method of reply . . . rotten eggs." The strong-armed Democrats struck Baker "in various and sundry places, much to the mortification and chagrin of every respectable man and women in the audience."[21] After his experience in Bell County, Sam Baker con-

---

19. *National Economist,* September 13, 1890, supplement.
20. Goodwyn, *The Populist Moment,* xxi, 26.
21. *Southern Mercury,* July 5, 1894.

tinued on to give ten lectures in eleven days in other nearby counties, taking only Sunday off for rest.

In their speeches, the lecturers rehearsed the litany of ills facing the farmer, high freight rates, low prices for their produce, the suffering and degradation caused by their reliance upon the crop lien. They then identified and elaborated upon the causes of this immiserization. Spoke one lecturer to a crowd of farmers in Natchitoches Parish, "there are two distinct and well-defined classes composing society, the producing and non-producing classes." "Between these two," he continued, "is an irrepressible conflict."[22] "They" were the "plutes," Jay Gould, John D. Rockefeller, Leland Stanford, the Vanderbilts, the Morgans, and an army of faceless bankers who, by monopolizing capital and transportation and by securing legislation in their own financial interest, kept the farmer down. These men had created a two-tiered society that made a mockery of the ideals of justice, equality, and liberty.

"There is something radically wrong at the heart of things," John Gardner told a Texas audience, "and the toilers' keen intuition locates the spot pretty closely." For Gardner, the problem was expressed best in metaphor:

> this kitchen servant has never been invited into the parlor of the nation, and until recently has submissively attended to his scrubbing, while the protected manufacturer and his political pilots have been playing cards in the drawing room and euchering him out of the fruit of his sweaty face."[23]

The division between these two classes, the producers and the non-producers, manifested itself in ways other than economic, as the lecturers pointed out. "The assertion," said one, "that all men stand equally before the law is erroneous." While the "poor but honorable son of toil is said to stand upon a platform of equality with the wealthiest in the land, outraged justice is dealt out in proportion to the assets of the complainant or defendant."[24] The national newspaper of the Alliance often presented examples that supported the lecturers' arguments about systematic injustice. The *Economist* reported one instance in which "one man was sentenced for two years for stealing

22. *Louisiana Populist,* April 1, 1894.
23. *Southern Mercury,* September 24, 1891; also T. J. Morris in *Southern Mercury,* September 24, 1894.
24. *Southern Mercury,* October 8, 1891.

$1500 from a bank and another man to fifteen years for stealing a worn out suit of clothing." The editor, Macune, added that "perhaps 14 years of the latter's sentence was for the crime of being poor."[25]

After illustrating the ills of the farmer and drawing their audience together by rehearsing common experiences, lecturers typically turned to another purpose of their visit, to organize farmers, tenants, and laborers into the Alliance. As lecturer J. B. Gay put it, "by public lectures you educate the people, but by organizing you not only lecture and educate them but put them to work also."[26] There was a sense in all the educating done by the lecturers that an education demanded this "putting to work," active use of the ideas and principles that were the curriculum of the Alliance. The first task for farmers was to join the organization.

Lecturers signed farmers to membership petitions, and out of their traveling bag gave each group they organized a charter, a secretary's record book, an account book for the treasurer, and a form book, consisting of tear-out membership applications, four copies of the secret rituals of the Alliance, six copies of the national constitution, samples of minutes for the secretary's reference, and copies of the *National Economist*.[27] A minimum of five individuals was necessary to sanction the chartering of a suballiance; often lecturers could organize five or six suballiances at a single event. In return for their charter, the members of each newly created suballiance paid the lecturer an organizing fee of fifty cents.

After that, lecturers paid visits to suballiances during their travels, often dropping in on one of the local biweekly meetings to provide information about activities in other chapters or news about the movement at large. In between these visits, the suballiances were united in a loose way by county and state Alliance presidents and through subscriptions to Alliance newspapers.

The organizing fees paid to the lecturers were the mainstay of their personal economies. Only the National Lecturer, Ben Terrell, was ever paid a salary by the organization. The remainder of the forty thousand lecturer/organizers subsisted on these organizing fees alone.

Clearly, lecturers did not become rich by their efforts to serve their neighbors, but some did gain national fame and prominence within the organization. In addition Daws, lecturers Harry Tracy, Ben Terrell, and H. S. P. "Stump" Ashby made names as firebrands and as

25. *National Economist,* December 14, 1889.
26. *Southern Mercury,* October 18, 1891.
27. *National Economist,* September 13, 1890, supplement.

the most eloquent apostles of the Alliance creed that was based on the democracy of Jackson and the moral virtue of Christ. These men shared several characteristics that are illustrative of the background that produced this generation of Alliance educators.

All were born before 1850 and had lived through the terrors of Civil War. Tracy, born in Georgia in 1840, was the oldest of the group and fought in the Confederate Army as an enlisted man. Terrell, two years younger than Tracy, also served his section in uniform. At seventeen, Terrell enlisted in General John Hood's regiment. He fought with Hood under Lee and was wounded at Sharpsburg. Ashby, only fourteen when the war began, did serve in its last days. Daws, alone, did not wear the uniform of the Confederacy. Of the four, all but Daws grew up in landowning families. Terrell's family owned a stock ranch in Colorado County, Texas, before the war. Ashby and Tracy came from farm families in Missouri and Georgia, respectively. Daws's family did not own land but farmed a leasehold in Kemper County, Mississippi, before the war. Landowners or not, the fortunes of all four families declined after the war.

All four young men left home in search of better land and greater opportunity. Terrell, under the blanket federal indictment against Confederate soldiers, sat out Reconstruction in Mexico, farming there until 1880. Daws moved west from Mississippi as part of the great westward migration, settling in Wise County, Texas, where he purchased a small farm. Ashby, too, made his way to Texas, but as a cattle drover. Upon his arrival he dabbled in several occupations, including teaching school, until he settled on a job as a traveling Methodist minister. Tracy took the roundabout route to Texas, living after the war in Arkansas where he became a prosperous farmer and a member of the Arkansas legislature in 1866. For reasons we do not know, he sold his holdings in Arkansas and moved to Texas in 1868.

The most striking feature of these life histories is the cyclical process of setting down roots, pulling them up, and starting over. All of these men ended up in Texas after being forced by the destruction of the war to leave their homes. Even Terrell, who was born in Texas, felt it necessary to relocate for nearly twenty years.

Only Ashby had documented school experience, spending several years in the common schools of his home county in Missouri. Daws attended weekly lessons in the Sunday school in Kemper; it was his only formal educational experience. Of Terrell and Tracy we know little regarding their education. It is probable, though, that neither of them enjoyed more than a common-school or Sunday-school education.

What can be made of these histories?[28] Goodwyn has argued that the process of dislocation and westward movement along the southern frontier provided a radicalizing experience for men like Ashby, Daws, Terrell, and Tracy.[29] While this constant searching for land and security may explain in part the rise of sentiment that contributed to the rise of the Alliance, it does not explain the particular form of Alliance organizing, particularly the central importance of education. What the four stars of the lecture circuit shared, besides a history of dislocation ending on the Texas prairie, was a history of self-education and independence. They had never been well served by the traditional leadership of the South nor by the radical Reconstruction governors. They lost the war, their property, and their families. In the process, they learned to take their own counsel. As they matured, both within and outside the Alliance, they developed a critique of society based on their experiences and a blueprint for reform based on their own self-education.

Self-education was common to most Alliance leaders, editors, state presidents, and national executive committee members. Of the twenty Alliance leaders for whom education data are available, only five received more than a common-school education. In this way, as in others, Alliance leaders were typical of many of their followers.[30] Their histories of self-education combined to advance education as a means of reform.

The processes of their own education informed the way in which the Alliance lecturers organized their educational efforts. Involvement, unity, and camaraderie—these typified the structure of the lecturers' efforts. They also, but with less success, were recurrent substantive themes in the content of the education offered at the rallies and meetings of the Alliance. Lecturers and Alliance organizers found that it was one thing to bring disparate groups together socially and quite another to forge a strong bond between groups held apart by powerful tradition and by divergent self-interests.

The acts of organizing a movement, rallies, songs, and lectures aimed, then, at building unity between different groups of what Alliance leaders called "producers." The structure of these organizing acts did unify in a physical sense and did universalize the experiences of isolated farm families. They taught farmers as much about them-

---

28. Personal histories from accounts in Morgan, *History of the Wheel and Alliance*, 290–350, and from Dunning, *Farmers' Alliance History*, passim.

29. Goodwyn, *Democratic Promise*, 51–77.

30. Morgan, *History of the Wheel and Alliance*, 290–350.

selves and their neighbors as they taught about the movement and its program. The experiences associated with organizing also united action with learning, a hallmark of Alliance educational practice.

5

Structuring experiences that were educative was not limited to lectures and camp meetings. More specific collective efforts, like the cotton-bagging plan, coupled the Alliance's educational and political aims. A case in point is the development of the Alliance Exchange, a cooperative merchandizing campaign that was also a means of political and economic education for Alliance members.

As a response to high commodity prices and low prices for cotton at harvest, the leaders of the Texas Alliance, with Macune, as usual, in the fore, organized a system of bulk purchasing and selling along the Rochdale plan. The Central Exchange, located in Dallas, negotiated sales of thousands of bales of cotton directly with mills in Fall River and other textile centers. For its part, the Exchange guaranteed that the cotton would be sorted, graded, and baled to the highest specifications.[31] Macune estimated that the Exchange secured prices for its cotton 20 percent higher than those offered by local merchants.[32]

At a local level, involvement in this phase of the Exchange idea was deep. County Alliances were to elect a business agent whose responsibility it was to inspect the cotton of each participating grower. After classifying the crop, the agent sent, in code, a report to the Dallas office. It was on the basis of these reports that the orders were filled and shipments consigned from various depots throughout the state. "On one occasion," reported Macune, "1500 bales were sold in one sale for shipment to England, France, and Germany, and the cotton was shipped from twenty-two different stations in Texas."[33]

Shipment was made only after the business agent received from the Exchange a bill of lading with a draft covering the contract. The draft was cashed and the individual farmers were paid in full the day of shipment. The Exchange charged growers twenty-five cents per bale, a significant savings over the thirty-five to forty cents charged by factors.[34]

31. Charles Macune, "The Farmers Alliance," typescript in the Eugene C. Barker Texas Archives Center, University of Texas, Austin, p. 22. Macune was quite proud of the early achievement of the Exchange.
32. Macune, "The Farmers Alliance," 34.
33. Macune, "The Farmers Alliance," 22.
34. Macune, "The Farmers Alliance," 23.

On the merchandising side, the Exchange was equally effective in providing savings to farmers. Again, the Exchange in Dallas served as the central clearing house for orders, this time prepaid orders for merchandise collected from farmers and passed on by local business agents. Wagons, plows, some commercial fertilizer, cloth, and other durables were bought by the Exchange and passed back down the line to fill local orders at prices below the inflated prices charged by merchants.

In its first two years, 1886 and 1887, the Exchange worked effectively, but in limited ways. The major shortcoming of the program was its reliance on cash. While the Exchange did sell cotton at higher prices than factors and did buy durables at lower prices than could be had from merchants, both high returns and low costs helped only those free from liens or other obligations. Growers under liens were not free to market their crop unless through the holder of the lien. Growers without ready cash could not place prepaid orders with the Exchange for goods they needed. Tenants and impoverished farmers responded to the problems in the Exchange by calling for a change, demanding that "the crop be made independent of the merchant."[35] For the Exchange to fulfill its promise, it would have to benefit all of the organization's members. To do that, the Exchange would need the participation of each one of those members.

The basic need was to provide a means for farmers and tenants to obtain supplies for the following year's crop on credit from the Exchange rather than from local merchants. In the fall of 1887 the directors of the Exchange, led by Macune, made public their answer. "By the conditions of this plan," wrote Macune, "the members of each subordinate Alliance should club together in buying supplies and giving security for the payment of same."[36] In order to do this, the business agent estimated the supplies needed by the farm families in the suballiance. The suballiance, as a whole, then issued a "joint note equal to the sum total." The notes were collected by the county agent and forwarded, with the orders for supplies, to the Exchange.

The notes, signed by each farmer in the program, promised as much as three times the value of the note in cotton. Notes were cosigned by prosperous farmers in the movement in order to further legitimate the transaction.

The Exchange then used the notes as collateral to borrow money with which to purchase the bulk supplies and ship them to the various

35. Quoted in Goodwyn, *Democratic Promise,* 124.
36. Macune, "The Farmers Alliance," 23.

stations in the state. For their costs—including credit costs with lending agencies, shipping, storage, and salaries for the Exchange agents
—the directors charged a 1 percent interest fee on the joint notes for
their term, six months between November and May 1888.

For farmers, the joint-note plan meant living from one crop to the
next on 1 percent credit instead of sixty, gaining lower prices through
bulk purchase, and still retaining the ability to get the best price for
the cotton in the field, probably the price negotiated by the Exchange.
Unity, as a concept, may have brought farmers to the rallies in Shady
Grove, but unity, as practiced in the Exchange, taught farmers the
power of united action and cooperation.

Throughout the spring and summer of 1887 Alliance lecturers criss-
crossed Texas raising support for the joint-note plan and discussing its
particulars with Alliance members and prospective members. The plan
provided a wonderful vehicle for the economic and political lessons
the Alliance attempted to teach. The forces of capital had achieved
their great strength by combination. The farmers could do the same.
The Alliance argued that the lien system was not a necessary part of
doing business in the region and attempted to circumvent it entirely
by the system of joint notes. Most of all, the Alliance hammered home
the point that farm families, by taking initiative, by familiarizing
themselves with the principles of political economy, by becoming active as a group in the interests of that group, could wield power and
could regain a measure of control and dignity.

But as the year ended it became clear that not all of the lessons of
the Exchange would be celebratory. By March of 1888, the capital
stock of the Exchange amounted to "about seventeen or eighteen
thousand dollars."[37] The sum was significant, coming as it had from
the pockets, mattresses, and coffee tins of farmers, tenants, and
laborers. Yet it was clearly insufficient backing for the kind of loan
Macune tried to sell to the banks of Texas in the Spring of 1888. The
joint-stock notes had poured in from all over the state. Orders for
wagons, tobacco, and flour piled up in the offices of the Exchange.
Macune met failure with the banks in Dallas, Houston, Galveston,
and finally, the financial center of the South, New Orleans. He managed to secure a small loan with one Dallas bank, and several supply
companies agreed to accept the notes directly as payment for supplies.

"The business, however, went steadily on," wrote Macune. "Purchases were made on a large scale to meet the demand for supplies,"
but instead of the favorable cash price Macune and the directors had
hoped for, the Exchange was forced to buy on credit and pay credit

37. Macune, "The Farmers Alliance," 24.

prices. Still, the business "went steadily on." One order was placed with the manufacturer for one thousand wagons to be shipped to various points . . . tobacco was purchased in car-load lots; five hundred barrels of molasses was purchased."[38] In May some of the short-term notes advanced by the Exchange to manufacturers came due, and the agency was unable to meet the obligations. At the end of May, in a report to the directors, Macune estimated the indebtedness of the Exchange at four hundred thousand dollars and the value of the joint notes on hand at one million dollars. The problem, though, was not one of ultimate solvency, but one of cash flow. The Exchange was out of cash.

To save the Exchange and salvage the attempt at breaking free from the crop lien and the merchant, the Alliance put its communication apparatus, its educational apparatus, into high gear. If lecturers were busy before the crisis, they became frantic now. Newspapers, particularly Evan Jones's *Southern Mercury,* ran weekly stories extolling the virtues of the Exchange and reminding farmers of the need to break free from the cycle of increasing poverty and powerlessness.

In late May, a rumor circulated that Macune had absconded with Exchange money and was headed to Mexico. Lecturers wrote to Dallas with the news that wherever they went, the rumor preceded them. To clear the air, the directors ordered a full investigation of the affairs of the Exchange. The report, authored by Jones and published in his paper and elsewhere, cleared Macune in unequivocal terms and warned farmers of the dangers ahead. "It is now time," wrote Jones, for each brother

> to realize the fact that faltering now means unconditional surrender; it means a perpetuation of the invidious discrimination which now deprive, and have in the past deprived, us of a just share of the proceeds of our labor."[39]

The Texas Alliance Executive Committee recommended that every suballiance in the state call an emergency meeting for the second Saturday in July in order to raise the capital stock of the Exchange, enabling the agency to pay off its immediate obligations and soothe the grumblings of its other creditors.[40]

38. Macune, "The Farmers Alliance," 24–25.
39. In Dunning, *Farmers' Alliance History,* 364; *Southern Mercury,* May 31, 1888.
40. Macune, "The Farmers Alliance," 25. Foreign investors were getting edgy and representatives of the Exchange and its creditors met and arranged the capital fund drive. See *Southern Mercury,* May 31, 1888.

There was no party spirit in the air on July 9, 1888, as farmers throughout Texas rode, drove their teams, or walked to the meeting of their suballiance, each ready to dig deeply to save the Exchange. Two dollars per farmer, that is what Jones and Macune had asked for. The *Austin Weekly Statesman* was "completely astonished by the mammoth proportions" in which the farmers responded to the call.[41] Farmers crowded into schoolhouses and churches and offered their two dollars to save both the Exchange and the idea of the Exchange. Evan Jones received over twenty telegrams in the days following the July meeting, all proclaiming that the Alliance had been saved.

The capital campaign raised pledges totaling over $200,000 by the end of July, a remarkable feat for an organization representing farmers of modest means. In the pages of the *Mercury,* Jones was justifiably proud of the membership. Yet he was also understanding of those who could not pay. "We voted the two dollar assessment for the exchange," wrote one suballiance president, "and as soon as we are able, will pay it, we are not able to do so at present."[42] Many were never able to make good their well-intentioned pledges. Macune estimated that $58,000 was raised by September 1.[43]

The Exchange weathered the summer and eventually made good on its obligations at the fall harvest. Although imitated in other states and carried on in Texas through 1890, the exchange idea never managed to deal effectively with its central problem, the lack of credit, even on a large scale, for supporting farmers from one growing season to the next. Yet the experience of the Texas Exchange and of all those involved in its successes and failures was educative in the most basic sense.

For the leaders of the Exchange, particularly for Macune and Jones, the failure of the Alliance to negotiate reasonable credit with the financial establishment proved radicalizing. Macune abandoned efforts to advance the farmers' interests within the network of existing organizations and institutions and searched for the means to fashion new mechanisms for the extension of credit and the development of cooperative buying and selling. He organized the Alliance purchase of a cotton compress and of a mill to produce bagging for cotton bales. Macune aimed at cutting out the manufacturers of jute bagging and the merchants who charged high fees for the preparation of cotton for transport.

41. Quoted in Goodwyn, *Democratic Promise,* 132.
42. *Southern Mercury,* May 31, 1888.
43. Macune, "The Farmers Alliance," 26.

More than Macune, Evan Jones was embittered by the failure of the Exchange to dramatically alter the way farmers lived and earned a living. Rumors circulated in the spring of 1888 that a combination of banks had decided to crush the farmers' movement by denying credit to Macune and the Exchange. Jones did nothing to denounce the rumors and issued statements that made clear his increasingly steadfast opinion that all banks, all merchants, all financiers were the enemies of farmers.[44] Until his death in 1900, Jones spoke for the most radical wing of the Alliance and later of the People's party. Never did he lose his sense that the remedy for farmers lay in struggle against the "money power." It was a sense of the world shaped by the lessons of the Exchange.

What that experience taught members of the Alliance is, of course, far less certain. That the Alliance unlimbered its educational apparatus to advance the joint-note idea suggests that the general issue of cooperative marketing and the specific program of the Exchange were discussed, debated, and argued in suballiance meetings and in rallies throughout Texas in the summer and fall of 1887. The fact that the drive to extend the Exchange, from a simple cooperative store on the Rochdale model to a credit-granting institution, came from the ranks of the yeomen and tenants suggests that a great many farmers learned the lessons well. They were able to examine the original plan and show the leadership how it failed to meet their needs, particularly the need to escape the weight of the crop lien.[45] Such demands seem to show a substantive assessment of the original system and of the early program of the Exchange.

Active participation in the Exchange taught lessons of a different order. For farmers who were able to market their crop and buy their supplies through the business agent and the Exchange, higher returns and lower costs showed in material ways the value of cooperation and consolidation. The ideas that the lecturers had been articulating and that the farmers had been debating were brought home.

For tenants and others whose first participation in the Exchange came with the creation of the joint-note plan, cooperation meant even more. They needed the pledges of more prosperous neighbors on the note to enhance the value of the collateral promised in each note, for it was the aggregate value of the crops pledged that offset the order for supplies. And these more prosperous growers cooperated, promising more than their share, because of the advantages to be gained in bulk

44. *Southern Mercury,* May 31, 1888.
45. Macune, "The Farmers Alliance," 22–23.

purchasing. Although some grumbled, it is testimony to the honor of even the poorest of these farmers that not one joint note was ever called, that all obligations were met on a net indebtedness of over $200,000.[46]

For all concerned, the lessons of the Exchange were complicated. On one hand, participants learned the power of cooperation, unity, and solidarity, shown so clearly in the pledges of July 9. On the other, they learned the power of the system they sought to alter, and they were forced to confront the possibility of failure. They also learned that unity was not automatic. Rumors about Macune, dissatisfaction among some signers of joint notes—these were signs of an organization whose cohesion depended on success.

In 1889, when the Executive Committee of the National Farmers' Alliance and Industrial Union met for the first time, it committed itself to a campaign of political and economic education designed to extend the lessons learned in Texas.[47] The committee urged other state Alliances to establish modest exchanges of their own, to authorize Alliance newspapers at the county level, and to increase the number of lecturers in the field. Their attempt, more determined after 1888 than before, was to combine a campaign of education with a campaign of action in order to unify producing classes and transmit the kinds of knowledge and experience that would empower them politically and economically. R. J. Sledge of Kyle, Texas, wrote that "during its brief existence the Alliance has done more to educate the great mass of people in the principles of government than all the schools and colleges have in the past century."[48] That teaching took place implicitly in the structuring of experiences and explicitly in the lectures and writing disseminated to the membership. In both forms, that teaching embodied the themes of unity, knowledge, and power—themes that shaped, and limited, Alliance members' ideas about their world.

46. Macune, "The Farmers Alliance," 26.
47. Dunning, *Farmers' Alliance History*, 130–158.
48. Dunning, *Farmers' Alliance History*, 330.

3 Educating for a Moral Polity

The Alliance Critique of Political Economy

Education is the only means within the grasp of the great mass of ballot holders in this land that can give them power to right existing wrongs. Read, study, and reflect!
—Editorial, *Southern Mercury,* October 15, 1891

It is a living, active, practical, and present embodiment of the cause of Jesus Christ.
—Charles Macune, "Purposes of the Alliance"[1]

1

It fell to the thousands of lecturers to carry, literally, the message of the Alliance to the isolated communities of the region. They played the central role as its master teachers, in disseminating Alliance ideas, and in setting up the small suballiances in which farmers across the South continued the process of self-education in economics and politics. As teachers, their role was twofold. First, lecturers had to break down barriers to active, critical political inquiry among farmers. These barriers were both technical, as in the matter of illiteracy, and cultural, as in the automatic support given by most white southerners to the leadership of the Democratic party. Second, lecturers transmitted a curriculum that legitimated active modes of political discourse, within which they then embedded Alliance proposals for specific reforms. These tasks came together in the critique of the Gilded Age political economy that lecturers led in their travels through the South in 1890 and 1891.

On April 3, 1891, Virginia state lecturer W. F. Jackson spoke to a crowded audience in the Amelia County Courthouse. His topic was the lecturing system, and his audience was the lecturers of the Virginia Alliance. "This system of lecturing on economic questions carried out in our broad land," he said, "will educate those who now feel the agricultural and other depression, but who do not fully understand its cause." The task of the lecturer was to "give them but a clew," as to

1. Charles Macune, "Purposes of the Alliance," in Dunning, *Farmers' Alliance History,* 260.

these causes, "and they will trace them in their feelings and to a man they will become zealous members in the Alliance lodges and earnestly apply the proper remedies."[2]

Alliance reform curriculum reflected the need to tie new knowledge about the political economy, the themes of unity, cooperation, and independence, to current "feelings" and traditional expectations. The "clew" that Jackson hoped his lecturers would give to audiences throughout Virginia was just this combination of the old and traditional with the new and revolutionary. It was an easy task when the two sets of ideas corresponded. The traditional idea of a moral economy with reciprocal relations, for example, went hand in hand with ideas of cooperation. There were traditional ideas, though, that contradicted the goals of reformers. The notion of a unified class of producers, for example, implied at least some connections with black farmers and croppers and with urban workers, yet traditional divisions between blacks and whites and between urban and rural workers made such unity problematic if not impossible. But easy or not, the development and dissemination of a reform ideology was the task of the lecturers and writers who populated the front lines in the Alliance campaign of education.

2

Some of the movement's leaders saw the educational campaign primarily as an offensive against the cultural fortifications of northern, urban, financial, and industrial capitalism. The wall between farmers and the set of ideas espoused by the Alliance, leaders like Harry Tracy argued, was built of an ideology whose elements mystified the true nature of farmers' circumstances and whose structure was held in place by its own educational process. Tracy and his fellow lecturers encountered a widespread uncritical acceptance of the rhetoric and ideas that supported the economic status quo. Tracy coined the term *miseducation* to describe what he found.

"Those who labor," Tracy wrote, "are educated (in the school of life) to be abject slaves and the rich are educated to be tyrannical, presumptuous, and vicious." Moreover, Tracy continued, "all the people have been educated to bow submissively at the feet of Mammon."[3] This understanding of the miseducation of the working men and women of the United States led Tracy to comment that "the condition of things is the result of education, good or bad."[4] The domination of

2. *National Economist,* May 16, 1891.
3. *National Economist,* June 29, 1889.
4. *National Economist,* April 20, 1889.

"moneyed interests" extended beyond financial transactions to ideology and the ways farmers thought about their proper roles. Economic domination was legitimated by a structure of ideas that made farmers individually responsible for their own poverty and powerlessness. Being educated to accept "abject slavery," those who labored were less able to recognize and reject the commercial domination by the merchants, middlemen, and bankers whom the Alliance blamed for declining farm prices and increasing rates of bankruptcy and tenancy. As Alliance member W. B. Hayden remarked, "the ignorance of the average farm boy is great . . . no wonder this country is becoming the home of the greatest money kings on earth."[5]

Part of this miseducation, part of the dominant ideology against which the Alliance struggled, taught farmers to separate politics from economics and then in the political realm to defer to the political opinions of professional politicians, social elites, and men of affairs. "So you think politics has nothing to do with your wages or your chance of getting employment, or your debts or your poverty," wrote one Alliance editor to his farmer audience,

> The banker tells you so, the politician tells you so, the monopolist tells you so, the people who live well and do nothing tell you so, isn't it funny that all these people are of the same mind?

The politicians and the bankers, he continued, have "trained you like a soldier so you can't think, but obey orders," What these elites want is not a citizen, but "a voting machine to help them live in luxury and power, and you've been doing it," he added incredulously. "Don't read up on the money problem," he finished, "you might learn something and not be so docile as a slave."[6]

Thinking about miseducation included thinking about the processes by which miseducation came to dominate. "By controlling the channels of information," wrote W. L. Garvin and S. O. Daws, "the capitalist holds your confidence with one hand, while with the other he picks your pockets."[7] Garvin and Daws referred to newspapers, but they and others mounted similar attacks on the publishing industry and on the public school.[8]

5. *Southern Mercury,* February 18, 1892.

6. *Louisiana Populist,* April 12, 1895; Woodward, "The Populist Heritage and the Intellectual," 61.

7. Garvin and Daws, *History of the National Farmers' Alliance,* ix.

8. Garvin and Daws, xi; see chap. 6 for a discussion of the Alliance and the public school. Polk's 1890 presidential address railed against the capitalist dominated press. See Polk, "Presidential Address: 1890," 141.

The ideology that taught political obedience and the mechanisms through which that teaching spread were anathema to the intellectual and political activism around which Alliance leaders built the agrarian movement. It is no wonder that for lecturers across the South, the first order of business was to scale the ideological walls that sustained and legitimated the system of production and social relations under which farmers and their families suffered. It was not an easy battle. Many of these obfuscating elements of the dominant ideology were deeply rooted in southern tradition. In countering these traditional ideas Alliance ideology met its toughest resistance, within and without the movement.

First, as an obstacle to reform, tradition made itself manifest in what Scott Morgan called "sentimental politics."[9] The Democratic party was, literally and symbolically, the party of the fathers, and southern farmers adhered to party lines even in the face of statements and legislation contrary to their own interests. According to one anonymous contributor to the *Southern Mercury,* "the great misfortune is our people worship party instead of principle. We have listened to that siren [the Democratic party] until we have been transformed into beasts of burden."[10] Regional honor and historical necessity demanded that white southerners vote the Democratic ticket. Insofar as casting Democratic tickets became automatic for the isolated rural farmer, votes for Democracy made southerners vulnerable to the machinations of the Democratic solons. According to the anonymous writer, "we have lost our spirit of self-independence and assertion . . . it places the people completely at the mercy of our dictators."[11] Milton Park, editor of the *Mercury,* was even more biting in his criticism of party loyalty: "Every vote we henceforth cast for either of the old parties is a vote to continue . . . villainous robbery."[12] "Villainous robbery" had not always typified yeomen's perception of relations with their elected representatives.

The destruction of the moral economy of the cotton South; the creation of divergent political, economic, and cultural agendas; and the reorientation of southern elites to new industries and new ideas created contradiction where once there had been broad consensus. Within this consensus, as Eugene Genovese put it, "the path of social

9. Morgan, *History of the Wheel and Farmers' Alliance,* 717–718.
10. *Southern Mercury,* August 6, 1891.
11. *Southern Mercury,* August 6, 1891.
12. Park in *Southern Mercury,* January 7, 1892; see also *National Economist,* February 13, 1892; and R. K. Sledge in Dunning, *Farmers' Alliance History,* 330.

duty emerged as the path of self-interest.''[13] Even when those two paths seemed to diverge, social duty was a difficult habit to break.

The persistence of sentimental politics was tied in with a more general form of symbiotic politics whose roots Genovese and others trace back to the political economy of the slave South. In the period after 1819, a stable elite in the South maintained electoral office, commercial sovereignty, and cultural dominance, ruling a well-defined lower class of whites and a legally enslaved black population. Their dominance, though, was ensured by their adherence to a complex set of reciprocal duties and responsibilities. Plantation owners, for example, were expected to share slaves with slaveless neighbors and kin, to provide loans in hard times and a ready market for goods during prosperous times. Yeomen deferred to the elites in matters of state and national politics, but only within the logic of and surrounded by the net of tightly woven social relations.[14]

As white farmers emerged from the destruction of the Civil War to find their livelihoods threatened, their first instinct was to turn for help to those who had led them into battle, made their laws, and judged their claims. The old planter elite, working to preserve its own position, encouraged the persistence of deferential politics and urged the farmers, black and white, to trust them as they had in the past. For multiple reasons, including the change in economic orientation of the old aristocracy from agriculture to industry, the interest of the farmer was not, in the 1890s, served by his allegiance with the social elite of the New South.[15]

The problem, wrote Charles Macune, was that "the masses of America have been seeking through others that which they should have done themselves." The masses, "have been looking to others, to

13. Genovese, "Yeomen Farmers in a Slaveholders' Democracy," 338.

14. Eugene Genovese, *Roll, Jordan, Roll; The World the Slaves Made* (New York: Random House, 1972), and Eugene Genovese, "Yeomen Farmers in a Slaveholders' Democracy," 331–342 attempt to discuss the way slavery determined the shape of white culture. James Oakes, *The Ruling Race* (New York: Alfred Knopf, 1982) brings slaveholders into sharp focus. Woodward, in *Origins of the New South,* chaps. 7 and 8 brings the politics of deference up to the populist era.

15. For a careful analysis of the contribution of planters to the development of the New South, see Dwight Billings, *Planters and the Making of a "New South"; Class, Politics, and Development in North Carolina 1865–1900.* (Chapel Hill: University of North Carolina Press, 1979); Jonathan Wiener, *Social Origins of the New South: Alabama, 1860–1885* (Baton Rouge: Louisiana State University Press, 1978), chaps. 2 and 3; Wiener, "Class Structure and Economic Development in the American South." For an analysis of antebellum relations between planter and yeoman see Genovese, "Yeomen Farmers in a Slaveholders' Democracy," 331–342.

parties and politicians," to serve their interests instead of taking the responsibility on their own shoulders.[16] Here the more active orientation of Alliance political discourse became evident. Here the curriculum transmitted by Alliance lecturers became an exhortation to active, reasoned participation in the duties of citizenship. For Park, Macune, and others, the answer was "to educate the masses in political economy till they can see wherein their interest lies," in the rejection of sentiment, blind party loyalty, and deference.[17]

A second and closely linked obstacle to the development of this new kind of independence was the "bloody shirt," traditional symbol of white southern solidarity. With encouragement from Democratic office holders and office seekers, it waved like a flag in the face of the conservative southern farmer, wrapping race, party, and section evermore tightly together. The wounds of the war and Reconstruction were slow to heal, leaving a ragged scar of sectional prejudice and hatred that moved southerners of all stations to believe that their interests were antagonistic to those of their northern brethren.[18]

For Alliance leaders the perpetuation of sectional antagonism was particularly vexing as it effectively prevented the development of any universal understanding among northern and southern agrarians of the changes occurring in the structure of social and economic relations in late nineteenth-century America. Whereas networks of industrialists and capitalists spanned regional and sectional boundaries, organizations of laborers, workers, and farmers remained shackled by old hatreds that were bound up in ethnic, religious, and sectional differences and that were often kept alive in the popular and political culture.[19]

The Alliance intended to destroy sectional prejudice and replace it with an alliance of producers, North and South, united by their similar class positions and brought together in search of explanations and

16. Macune in *National Economist*, April 9, 1889.

17. *Southern Mercury*, January 7, 1892.

18. Goodwyn, *Democratic Promise*, 220–239; C. Vann Woodward, "The Populist Heritage and the Intellectual," *American Scholar* 29 (1959–60): 60–62.

19. This is not to imply that there were no similar prejudices among northern workers, nor that there were no divisions in the North. In the latter case, Herbert Gutman and David Montgomery both demonstrate how divisions between ethnic groups and religious groups served similar functions in the North as race and section served in the South. Both show as well that employers did not work energetically in any venue to encourage worker solidarity. See Gutman's essays in *Work, Culture, and Society in Industrializing America* (New York: Vintage Books, 1977) and Montgomery's *Beyond Equality* (Urbana: University of Illinois Press, 1981), chap. 7.

THE BLUE AND THE GRAY.

"LET US CLASP HANDS ACROSS THE BLOODY CHASM."—Horace Greeley anticipated the inevitable. The Farmers' Alliance takes up his burden twenty years after he laid it down.

"The Blue and the Gray," cartoon from *Southern Mercury*, September 10, 1891

remedies for their perceived immiserization. County lecturer E. H. Belden wrote enthusiastically that "the North and South can no longer be divided by designing politicians." Rather, the "old animosities [lie] buried in the midst of a common oppression that rests alike on producers of both sections."[20] Belden's conclusion was probably too optimistic, as the prejudices between North and South were not as easily bridged as the handshake between Billy Yank and Johnny Reb in Alliance editorial cartoons might suggest.

A third and more subtle piece of the miseducation encountered by Alliance lecturers was the farmers' continued belief in classical eco-

20. *Southern Mercury,* December 17, 1891.

"Gathering of the Clans—On to Washington, Via St. Louis," cartoon from the *People's Party Paper,* February 25, 1892

nomic doctrine, which the Alliance argued obscured the power and penetration of monopoly in local markets and sent the farmers battling the wrong enemies.[21] As one contributor to the *National Economist* wrote, "the law of supply and demand becomes an absurdity when it is comprehended that capital controls both."[22] It was the control of the economy by capital through both economic and political means that the Alliance campaign sought to illustrate and end, creating in its place a national economy dominated by and for the interests of producers.

Finally, racism and racial antagonism determined a large part of the culture of the region, and so shaped the consciousness of southerners. For the Alliance, the race question proved the greatest ideological hurdle of all, and it proved ultimately insurmountable. Conflict between

21. Opponents of the Alliance argued that declining prices resulted from a simple overproduction of staples. Farmers argued that there was too little money chasing too many goods. The alternative offered by elite reformers, though, was to teach the farmers how to grow more. To the leaders of the Alliance, this was so much silliness.

22. *National Economist,* June 15, 1889; *Southern Mercury,* August 9, 1894.

blacks and whites was exacerbated in many states of the exconfederacy by the radical policies of Reconstruction. Few southerners were ready to accept blacks as citizens and free laborers, and fewer still to accept them as political and social equals.[23]

Like party and place, race was a banner easily employed to divide the producers against each other and to hide their essential commonality of interest in opposition to the interests of capital. Like party and place, race was used by those who opposed the Alliance as a wedge to create division and dissension within the movement. The Democratic press was unstinting in charging that the organization stood for racial equality, raising at every opportunity the specter of "negro domination."[24]

Tom Watson, the great Georgia Populist, grappled with the race issue longer and with more difficulty than many of his contemporaries. His analysis of the effect of racial shibboleths on the progress of the Alliance movement is instructive. "You might beseech a southern white tenant to listen to you upon questions of finance, taxation, and transportation," wrote Watson in the liberal journal *Arena,* "you might demonstrate with mathematical precision that herein lay his way out of poverty into comfort." Indeed, the tenant might be nearly convinced of the cause of his suffering. But, Watson remarks with a great deal of pain, "if the merchant who furnished his farm supplies (at tremendous usury) or the town politician (who never spoke to him excepting at election time) came along and cried 'Negro Rule!', the entire fabric of reason . . . would fall."[25]

The irony of Watson's remarks is that the Alliance never adopted a position close to "negro rule" nor even full participation for blacks in the councils of the organization itself. That "negro rule" was so far from the truth yet so strong in thwarting the efforts of the Alliance to organize white farmers highlights the power of the racism in obliterating almost all other questions and concerns in late nineteenth-century southern society.

23. See Foner, *Politics and Ideology in the Age of the Civil War,* chap. 4.

24. Bruce Palmer, *"Man Over Money"* (Chapel Hill: University of North Carolina Press, 1980), 152–168; Goodwyn, *Democratic Promise,* 337–338. Racism was an important impediment in the development of unionism in Gilded Age America. For a case study of one interracial organization and its problems, see Herbert Gutman, "Black Coal Miners and the American Labor Movement," in *Work, Culture, and Society* 119–209.

25. Tom Watson, "The Negro Question in the South," *Arena* 6 (October 1892): 541, parentheses in the original.

3

If traditional ideas about race, class, politics, and economics were the
boulders that formed the wall of miseducation standing between
farmers and social change, traditional ideas, albeit different ones,
were also the missiles launched against that wall by the army of Alliance lecturers. The curriculum they advanced to combat miseducation
was constructed of conservative ideas with radical implications that
linked Alliance teachings with the true democratic heritage of the
founders of the Republic, and in so doing drew upon another set of
culturally powerful political, moral, and religious traditions.[26] The
Alliance struggled to assert its traditions as the dominant ones and to
"falsify" the traditions maintained by the dominant culture. Like
those of their competitors, Alliance traditions encompassed ideas
about politics, race, and religion. What differentiated Alliance traditions, though, were powerful ideas about what they called class, about
class differences, and about the moral legitimacy of class action.

The leaders of the Alliance brought to the political debate powerful
elements of Jacksonian and Jeffersonian principles, claiming, first
and foremost, faith in government by the whole people. "We believe," wrote Ignatius Donnelly to the *Southern Mercury*, "that
government is simply aggregated humanity."[27] This vision of the State
contrasted markedly with the contemporary political scene, where
Alliancemen saw political power "monopolized by comparatively
few" individuals, who had turned the power of laws to serve their own
interests rather than the interests of the mass of citizens.[28]

Alliance ideas about democracy admitted the logistical necessity of

26. Sociologists and political scientists who have studied protest movements agree
that in fact the traditional and shared ideals of a culture are often the most radicalizing,
when it is perceived widely that these shared values are somehow being violated. In Anthony Oberschall's words, "it is not new ideas and novel techniques that have the most
far-reaching consequences, but . . . values and rights already enjoyed." See Oberschall,
Social Conflicts and Social Movements (Englewood Cliffs, N.J.: Prentice-Hall, 1973),
35. Ideas about "selective tradition" have been important in writings about literature
and culture. In particular, Raymond Williams has argued that any invocation of tradition or of conservation means in fact a selection of some elements of a vast and complex
past and a rejection of others whose legitimacy as "traditions" may be as strong. See
Williams' *Marxism and Literature* (New York: Cambridge University Press, 1977),
especially 108–121. Eric Hobsbawm has used Williams' work as the basis for collecting
historical examples of this kind of selectivity, focusing on "traditions" manufactured
out of a rather thin past. See Hobsbawm, ed., *The Invention of Tradition* (New York:
Oxford University Press, 1985).

27. Ignatius Donnelly, *Southern Mercury*, January 21, 1891.

28. Macune in *National Economist*, November 2, 1889. See also Polk, "Presidential
Address: 1890."

a representative government, and their emphasis was on representation. Lecturers returned again and again to the need for citizens to "recognize the officers of our government as . . . our servants."[29] Through the direct election of senators and widespread use of the referendum, the Alliance proposed to make the bonds of representation tighter while at the same time broadly diffusing political responsibility and political power.

Successful diffusion of responsibility and power among the citizens depended on the willingness of citizens to accept active political roles. Texas farmer Ella Castle made it clear that the Alliance sought to encourage acceptance of political responsibility. "Let the people become educated into a comprehension of their right and their duty to control and operate the government," she wrote.[30] The Alliance curriculum stressed this active citizenship, and inveighed against reliance upon political professionals. Like Castle, lecturers asked nothing less than that members assume responsibility for the political fortunes of the nation. Evan Jones reminded lecturers and representatives to the national meeting in 1889 that

> So long as our people neglect to inform themselves upon the great issues of the hour, and continue to follow blindly machine politicians to the neglect of their own interest, they will continue to lose their individuality, influence, and power in our political institutions, and be wholly at the mercy of the soulless corporations that are now wielding such an influence over our government.[31]

In the "full development of the individual citizen, and by the full exercise of individual sovereignty" lay "the safety of the Republic."[32] Accepting this personal responsibility for collective action meant, first of all, working to learn and teach about politics. "Anyone reading our declaration of principles," wrote Scott Morgan,

> will see that while we are seeking reforms that must in some instances come through the ballot box, yet by far the highest

29. Harry Tracy in *National Economist,* May 4, 1889.
30. Ella M. Castle in *Southern Mercury,* July 26, 1894.
31. Evan Jones, "Presidential Address: 1889," in Dunning, *Farmers' Alliance History,* 103–104. This is also one of the earliest references to the "soulless corporation."
32. Macune in *National Economist,* November 23, 1889; *Louisiana Populist,* March 29, 1897: "Direct Legislation is the string by which the people hold on to the government."

motive that concerns us is the education of the masses to that
point where they will finally see and know not only their own
wrongs and degradation, but see a full and final solution to the
labor problem.[33]

Political differences between educated active citizens were to be
resolved finally through the ballot. There individual sovereignty, exercised in the aggregate, would by definition choose a government
whose actions served the greatest good for the greatest number. Alliance rhetoric sustained great faith in this crude utilitarianism, bouyed,
perhaps, by an equal faith that their numbers were greater than any
other. Lecturers seemed untroubled by the potential for majoritarian
tyranny and even less troubled by the idea that an informed electorate
might reject their proposals for reform.

Anticipating success in the electoral struggle, the editor of the
socialist/populist paper *Argus* wrote, in 1890, that "quicker than
dynamite, more effective and more lasting than revolution, more far-
reaching than strikes, and more terrible to plutocrats than all is the
ballot."[34] Political education, that is education in both the goals of
political action and education in an active political discourse, was the
beginning of this revolution by ballot. By bringing the people "a
clew" Alliance lecturers believed they would rouse the masses of the
common people to throw out the rascals, and then conduct "this
republic as it was originally intended it should be conducted, in the interest of all the people."[35] But serving the "interests of all the people"
was not an easy nor even simple matter.

Interest was itself a complex term in the Alliance lexicon. On the
one hand, Alliance leaders and lecturers spoke of the "interest" they
defended as the universal interest of all Americans. They expressed
common interest very broadly as "fairness" or "independence," or
simply as common opposition to monopolists in economics or politics.
When they applied to economic or political processes, these normative
propositions about the political economy probably captured universal
interests. Fair elections; education in politics to the point at which
citizens could read, write, and understand contracts and ballots;
removal of structural inequities in economic power: these were goals
that reflected shared values that ran across traditional boundaries be-

33. Morgan, *History of the Wheel and Farmers' Alliance,* 751. See also Ella M. Castle writing in the *Southern Mercury,* July 26, 1894.
34. Quoted in Palmer, *"Man Over Money,"* 35.
35. *National Economist,* December 21, 1889.

tween urban and rural, capital and labor, and farm and factory. Alliance leaders found broad support on these broad issues. Broadening responsibility and power in determining the course of the political economy, although powerful in articulating a "process" for restoring true democracy, was not all that Alliance leaders had in mind when they talked about "the interest of all the people."

For on the other hand, the same Alliance lecturers who spoke so forcefully for the interests of all the people asserted that the interests of the producers were contradictory to those of the financiers and industrial capitalists. With this voice the Alliance argued on behalf of producers' interests over those of capital, rather than universal interest. The movement sought not just to restore democratic processes, but to make that process work to serve one set of class interests over another. Important pieces of the Alliance curriculum taught farmers and other producers to understand class and to calculate class interest.[36]

"There are two distinct and well-defined classes composing society: the producing and non-producing classes," wrote the editor of the *Louisiana Populist.* "Between these two is an irrepressible conflict."[37] As the lecturers saw it, the struggle was one between fairness and unfairness. Capital sought, through combination and political influence-buying, to restrict and control what Scott Morgan called "legitimate trade."[38] For Morgan and Charles Macune, the propensity for capital to centralize, to organize, and to restrain competition was not just episodic but endemic. To Macune,

Capitalism is but the modern development of despotism. Its sole aim is the increasing of its power and the absorbing of all values. It bases its rights on legal enactments entirely, regardless of the means used to secure such enactment.[39]

Alliance leaders blamed the agricultural depression of the 1890s on the success of capitalists in centralizing control of the political economy, and they pressed the membership to see that "centralized capital is a formidable menace to individual rights and popular government."[40]

36. Class identity was the goal, of course, addressed by the creation of a movement culture through the meetings, lectures, picnics, and encampments discussed in chap. 2.
37. *Louisiana Populist,* April 1, 1898.
38. Morgan, *History of the Wheel.* 16–17.
39. *National Economist,* June 8, 1889.
40. Polk, "Presidential Address: 1890," 141.

Morgan's critique of capitalism was damning at an even more fundamental level:

> Capitalism places property above life, thereby declaring war on
> humanity. This war must not cease until capitalism is van-
> quished and property becomes the servant, not the master of
> man.[41]

To return humanity to the system of laws governing American society,
and to return individual freedom, justice, and equity to the political
economy, noncapitalists needed to unite to restrain what was in equal
measure evil and inevitable about capitalism. This meant for Macune
that "our economic system knows too little of ethics; it has too great a
proportion of technical law for the quality of equity."[42] Alliance
leaders saw the agrarian movement as the vanguard in this "war" to
vanquish capitalism, defeat the interests of the "non-producers," and
create a system of laws that would raise to primacy the interests of the
producing classes.

Recognizing class interest entailed calculating economic self-
interest. The "interest" of the producing classes, in this sense, was to
ensure stable and high prices for farm produce, to ensure stable and
low prices for farm inputs and transportation, and to destroy the system of finance in the South that restricted farmers' economic independence or threatened the creation of favorable markets.

Class interest had a more subtle and pervasive meaning as well, a
meaning implicit in Morgan's critique of capitalism, This meaning
captured what Alliance leaders genuinely felt to be the moral/political
decay of American democracy at the hands of professional politicians
and slick financiers. Alliancemen saw themselves as the heirs to Jefferson as well as Jackson, and as the last repositories of the values, indeed of the very "humanity," that they believed to be the true foundations of American culture. So, when Alliance leaders spoke of a return
to "this republic as it was originally intended," they invoked a tradition of small-scale democracy whose control rested in the hands of the
yeomanry Jefferson trusted above all others. Only a dictatorship of
the producing classes could insure that American society would stay
on its proper course.

Some went even further, arguing that farmers possessed an endowment of moral vision in special measure. In the Alliance curriculum

41. Quoted in Palmer, *"Man Over Money,"* 203.
42. Macune in *National Economist,* June 8, 1889.

"United We Stand," cartoon from *Southern Mercury,* December 24, 1891

this right to stewardship in society derived from the special cultural position of agriculture itself, particularly compared with other forms of labor. Nelson Dunning, the Southern Alliance's scribe and house historian, rued the denigrated position of farmers in the Gilded Age. "We live," he explained, in a "parasitic age," and he recalled fondly a better time for farmers:

> Emerson says: "The glory of the farmer is that, in the division of labors, it is his part to create. All trade rests at last on his primitive activity. He stands close to Nature; he obtains from the earth the bread and the meat. The food which was not he causes to be."[43]

To the Alliance, farming, as an occupation, as a way of life, was worthy of protection above any particular demands for a greater percentage of the value of their crop. Theirs was a moralistic version of the Physiocratic doctrine that placed all productivity in the realm of agriculture. For both the eighteenth-century French economists and the leaders of the nineteenth-century American farmers' movement, tillers of the soil were the moral as well as material backbone of the political economy.

Evan Jones was moved to proclaim, in his 1889 presidential address to the National Alliance, that "[t]he hope of America depends upon the ownership of the land being vested in those who till the soil."[44] It followed from a sense of this dependence that the Alliance should support measures to raise the prices of agricultural goods without resorting to the reduction of acreage under cultivation, and at the same time assert the need to reduce the rate of farm tenancy in the South. The moral economy that the Southern Alliance hoped to create rested on this notion of the moral importance of small-scale agriculture, not as a museum of anachronistic values but as a foundation stone for the entire Republic.

In contrast to this ideal, what horrified farmers was "the wealth of the Vanderbilts, Rothchilds, and Goulds" on one hand and the "individual laborer who is not the master of his own actions," on the other. The "great wealth made by the representatives of this imperial despotism is made up of the aggregation of the sums wrung from the people," wrote Macune.[45] By explicating contrasts like this one the

43. Dunning, *Farmers' Alliance History*, 5.
44. Evan Jones, "Presidential Address: 1889," 102.
45. Morgan, *History of the Wheel and Farmers' Alliance*, 24.

Alliance curriculum combined a description of a "moral" economy with a critique of the "immorality" of currently dominant economic relations.[46] Market power exercised by the trusts cut away at the farmers' ability to convert their hard work into profits. Scott Morgan, speaking for the Alliance, called trusts "a conspiracy against legitimate trade . . . against the interests of the people and the welfare of the public."[47]

Thus in decrying Vanderbilt's $200,000 million personal fortune, the *Southern Mercury* captured the essential distinction between the moral and market economies:

> we do not want to discourage enterprise, neither private nor public. But everyone should receive the results of his own industry and enterprise. Please put the emphasis on his OWN . . .[48]

One month later, also in the *Mercury,* an article more fully explained how and why the makers of great fortunes, like Vanderbilt, were non-producers and leaders of the immoral economy. A capitalist, ran the article, makes his money on the difference between the wage paid his employees and the price gained from the sale of the products of their labor.

> One thousand workmen earning five dollars a day and getting two dollars a day, the unpaid three dollars remaining with you may, after your business gets running, make you a million in two or three years. But you will not have earned the million. Other men will have earned it and you will have taken it from them.

This expropriation was a first level of "immorality." As the enterprise grows, "you can go off and leave it." The capitalist can "hire men of executive ability to keep it running while you travel or indulge in yacht racing." Thus even while idle "you are still getting your hundreds of thousands a year."[49] These riches were the returns to idleness, and, when compared to the farmers' meager returns to toil, they lent a sense of outrage to the Alliance critique.

Alliance lecturers talked of this polarization not as the result of in-evitable realignment of capital among more and less profitable indus-

46. *National Economist,* April 5, 1890, and *Louisiana Populist,* February 15, 1896.
47. Morgan, *History of the Wheel and Farmers' Alliance,* 30.
48. *Southern Mercury,* January 16, 1902.
49. *Southern Mercury,* February 20, 1902.

tries, nor as a rise in the productivity of capital-intensive industries, but rather as a grotesque mutation of the classical economy spawned by corruption in politics and the emergence of oligopolies in the nation's most important industries. It was a situation in which the moral power of the agrarian citizenry needed to assert itself. The Alliance was eager to be the mechanism through which that took place. Empowered by a sense of stewardship, Alliance leaders felt little compunction in speaking for nonagrarians, for people whose material interests were not immediately identifiable as identical to those of small-hold farmers, because the Alliance program promised a morally superior political economy.[50]

For Polk, the moral superiority of farming flowed from "its higher character and function as the basis of all life, of all progress, and of all higher civilization."[51] The struggle for ideological supremacy, then, was more than an instrumental struggle waged in the name of one or another economic or political interest; it was a struggle to reestablish human values, guarded by the nation's agrarians, as the fundamental organizing principles of the political economy. Thus, while they attempted to educate citizens in the South to identify their interests and demand that those interests be met through the government, the leaders of the movement also fought to impose on the nation a set of values they saw as older, truer, and simply superior to those that bolstered the economy of the Gilded Age. For the Alliance the choice was between two different futures, one moral and upright, the other immoral and base. Theirs was a moral political economy, drawing, in Anthony Oberschall's words, from the "sacred documents" and selected traditions of the region and the nation. Perhaps the most significant of these traditions was the evangelical religious tradition that infused and empowered so much of the lecturers' rhetoric.[52]

4

Industrialization in America and the rapid demographic changes of the late nineteenth century gave rise to a peculiar crisis in Protestant circles.[53] A tension grew between evangelical churches and ministers

50. Perhaps more than any other single feature of the Alliance movement, this idea of stewardship, of moral supremacy amidst a whirl of competing moral visions, encouraged historians to see in the Populist agitation of the 1890s the antecedents of McCarthyism and more recently, of religious fundamentalism.
51. Polk, "Presidential Address: 1890," 140.
52. Anthony Oberschall, *Social Conflicts and Social Movements,* 35.
53. Robert Wiebe, *The Search for Order* (New York: Hill and Wang, 1970), 63-64. See also Kenneth Bailey, *Southern White Protestantism* (New York: Harper and Row,

on one side and millennial religious spokesmen on the other. Evangelicals, who dominated established religion in the South, saw their purpose as fostering individual conversion and salvation through faith.[54]
In contrast, millennial ministers propounded a more social form of
the gospel, urging Christians to reform civil society, to create "a
manifestation of . . . Divine life flowing into human history."[55]

Southern religious leaders extolled the virtues of passive acceptance
of social change, leaving southern churches with what Kenneth Bailey
calls "an almost single-minded emphasis on individual regenera-
tion."[56] Faced with the Alliance efforts at reform, the dominant sects
in the region, the Baptists and Methodists, took to "repudiating
reform as a denial of Christian Faithfulness."[57] Although they continued to count themselves members of the established churches,
many Alliance leaders broke with the southern Baptists and southern
Methodists, as they had with the Democrats. Both pillars of southern
society demanded of farmers a kind of deference that Alliance leaders
rejected in the pursuit of an educated and independent producing
class. Lecturer Billy Patterson wrote to the editor of the *Southern
Mercury* to ask "where in all the land is there a minister that will
preach to his people a discourse on usury?"[58] Joseph Downey wrote to
the *Mercury* the following week with a response that was supported by
the editor, Milton Park, and carried in the subsequent issue. "The
bosses of the state and the church," Downey explained, "are united
under the same power . . . the power of money." According to
Downey, "he [Patterson] cannot expect them to accept the subtreasury plan and preach against usury, as a man cannot serve God
and Mammon."[59] According to Frederick Bode, Populists and Alli-

---

1964); Harrell, *Varieties of Southern Evangelicalism.* Hunter Farish's *The Circuit Rider
Dismounts* (Richmond: Dietz Press, 1938) is still a classic study of southern Methodism
in the postbellum years. Robert Handy, ed., *The Social Gospel In America 1870-1920*
(New York: Oxford University Press, 1966) and Charles Hopkins, *The Rise of the
Social Gospel in American Protestantism 1865-1915* (New Haven: Yale University
Press, 1940) are notable in what they do not say about the Social Gospel in the South.
Temperance is the only manifestation of the social gospel they note in the region. Henry
May's otherwise fine study of the relationship of Protestantism to economic change,
Protestant Churches in Industrializing America (New York: Harper and Brothers, 1949),
lacks any substantive discussion of the South or southern religion.

54. Bailey, *Southern White Protestantism,* 18. See also Harrell, *Varieties of
Southern Evangelicalism,* 2, 3.

55. Thompson, quoted in Frederick Bode, *Protestantism and the New South,* 42.

56. Bailey, *Southern White Protestantism,* 28.

57. Hill, *The South and the North in American Religion,* 128.

58. Billy Patterson, *Southern Mercury,* December 17, 1891. The sentiment was
echoed by McGowan, *Southern Mercury,* August 20, 1891.

59. Downey in *Southern Mercury,* January 7, 1892.

ancemen in the upper South, in Virginia, North Carolina, and Tennessee accused the Methodist and Baptist hierarchy of taking refuge from their responsibility toward the poor behind a curtain of spiritual revival. Large contributions to the organized churches by the Duke family and other New South industrialists and financiers only encouraged the wrath of the farmers and their spokesmen.

Cyrus Thompson, incoming president of the North Carolina Alliance, claimed that "the Church stands today where it has always stood, on the side of human slavery."[60] In religion as in politics, the Alliance turned away from their traditional spokesmen and found new men, like Thompson, Isom Langley, and others, who were able to give voice to their circumstances using familiar ideas in new ways. For models, the Alliance turned to the social gospel that rang from northern pulpits. Indeed, scholarship on southern religion and on the rise of the social gospel identifies the Alliance movement as the one haven for civic millennialism in the region.[61]

Some of the most active Alliance leaders were men with backgrounds as preachers or ministers. For them the disparity between their faith, which emphasized individual conversion, and their experience among the poor of the South served to radicalize them and change their brand of Christianity. Langley, an Arkansas Baptist minister and Alliance lecturer was typical of this group. In his view it was "the duty of all [Christian] governments to eradicate the evils of extreme poverty and vice, restrain the strong and vicious, and strengthen the weak and helpless."[62] As leaders of the movement, in their positions on resolution committees, as lecturers, and as executives of state Alliances, these exponents of the social gospel mobilized farmers according to this vision of the State as an instrument of power to be used in support of the weak against the strong. This vision reinforced the Alliance's activist politics.

Although they broke from the theology of southern Methodism and southern Baptism, the leaders of the Alliance adopted much of the style and structure of evangelicalism for their own educational program. As Langley acknowledged, "the religious sentiments contained in the basic principles of the Alliance are giving it its wonderful power with the people."[63]

60. Bode, "Religion and Class Hegemony," also Cash, *The Mind of the South,* 140–146. Bode, *Protestantism and the New South,* 40, on Thompson.
61. Bode, *Protestantism and the New South,* chap. 2.
62. Langley, in Dunning, *Farmers' Alliance History,* 314.
63. Langley, in Dunning, *Farmers' Alliance History,* 314.

Alliance rhetoric resounded with Old Testament imagery. "Men of Israel," S. K. McGowan summoned, "gird on the whole armour and unsheath the shining sword of God's eternal truth and fell these traitors to the earth."[64] Their arguments claimed not just moral superiority but God's support.

As important as the reinterpretation of gospel in support of social reform, and certainly as important as the religious garb in which Alliance stump speakers clothed their arguments, was the appropriation by the Alliance of revival style gatherings. In these meetings, as in their religious counterparts, oratory mixed with song, food, and good company. The reliance on oral forms of educating met the needs of the largely illiterate and mostly isolated membership.

In addition to these general influences on the farmers' movement, Christian metaphor framed many of the specific issues addressed by the Alliance. References to the Bible, to Christ, and to Christian morality helped lecturers explain their positions to assembled audiences and forged a normative link between their audiences' traditional religious values and the arguments and proposals of the Alliance. Finally, religion lent a certainty and a sanction to the farmers' actions. "The Lord's side is the side of the oppressed," wrote Virginian T. J. Stone, and "the other side is the side of the oppressor."[65] Alliance political theology rested in this neat division of society into the oppressed and the oppressor, the Godly and the sinful.

In works like M. W. Howard's *If Christ Came to Congress,* writers sympathetic to the Alliance applied the biblical yardstick to contemporary politics and found it wanting in moral fortitude. *If Christ Came to Congress* was one in the genre of social gospel novels of the 1890s that, as a group, found fault with men of power and influence, blaming them for not using their power and influence to create or approximate Christ's kingdom on earth. Edward Everett Hale's *If Jesus Came to Boston* gave the genre a start and a pattern for its titles. Charles Sheldon's *In His Steps* won its author fame and commercial success, selling twenty-three million copies.[66] After Boston and before Congress, William Stead took Christ to Chicago.

Each of these novels put forth a central theme of stewardship. Christians, they argued, should dedicate personal resources to the task of social betterment. Alliance editors quoted often from Howard, and

64. *Southern Mercury,* August 20, 1891.
65. *National Economist,* April 25, 1891.
66. Charles H. Hopkins, *The Rise of the Social Gospel in American Protestantism,* 148.

this brand of social gospel came to legitimate ever-increasing Alliance political activity and eventually partisan political organization. "Vote as Christ would," urged Langley, "and see how soon all the wrongs would be corrected."[67] The moral standards advanced by the lecturers applied inside as well as outside the Alliance. The duties of membership, R. J. Sledge reminded them, "demand[ed] that the strong should help the weak; the educated, the uneducated; and the joyful, the sorrowing."[68]

The National Farmers' Alliance maintained an "official position" on religion that was much like its position on politics. The Order was, according to Macune, religious but not denominational, "it is not concerned with the discussion of doctrinal differences which too frequently disturb the harmony that ought to exist between Christian people." But, Macune continued,

> in the sense that religion underlies everything that is good, useful, and beautiful, that it is the mainspring in the force that directs the minds of men in comprehending what is right, and governs their actions in accordance with their perceptions of moral law, so too is the Alliance a religious organization.[69]

In this sense, religion in the Alliance was a kind of organized and focused morality, concerned with this world, moving toward a millennium without God, in the center of which was the agrarian class, carrying out Christ's designs.

Several specific elements of the capitalist economy came in for special scrutiny within the Alliance creed. Lecturers and editors used biblical metaphors and parallels in illuminating the sanctity of labor and the problem of poverty. Some conservative preachers dismissed this contradiction as the natural order of things, arguing that Christ himself stated that poverty was necessary. Isom Langley responded by writing that "it is God's plan that men and women who are able to work must live by their industry." The working men and women "are not the poor that 'we have with us always' who are spoken of by Christ . . . he meant that those who are disabled should be cared for by alms or charity, and not those who are able to work."[70] Alliance rhetoric contrasted the farmers, the honest sons of toil, with traders

---

67. Langley in Dunning, *Farmers' Alliance History,* 51. See *Louisiana Populist,* May 17, 1895, for sections of *If Christ Came to Congress.*

68. Dunning, *Farmers' Alliance History,* 328.

69. *National Economist,* March 30, 1889.

70. Langley in Dunning, *Farmers' Alliance History,* 31.

and financiers who did not labor for their earnings, but appropriated
their wealth from the labor of others. In the conflict that they defined
between the producing and the nonproducing classes, the farmers
clearly had morality and the force of the Bible behind them.[71]

The biblical injunctions against usury reinforced Alliance con-
demnation of moneylending, liens, and mortgages. The image of the
moneylender was decried throughout Alliance writing in religious and
sometimes ethnic terms. In one article on the crop lien system, Billy
Patterson quoted five biblical passages condemning usury.[72] The
editor of a local Alliance paper, the *Louisiana Populist,* wrote a
satirical letter "from the Devil" reporting on preparations to receive
Jay Gould. "The special fire I built for Jay Gould," wrote the
"devil," "was so hot it scorched the hair on my tail before I could get
away." The "devil" seemed to be warming to his task, enjoying his
role as tormentor of the greatest money king. "We are doing an excellent job of roasting on Jay," he reported, "but it will require a thousand years to bake his hide as hard as his heart."[73] At times, though,
this treatment of the moneylending theme went from the culturally
significant to the patently ridiculous. In one of his last editions of the
Southern Mercury, on February 6, 1902, Milton Park ran an article
entitled "Plutocrats Killed Christ," which purported to show that a
cabal of moneylenders conspired to condemn Christ.

But for these excesses, the treatment of Gould, of Rockefeller, Vanderbilt, and others of the moneyed classes of Gilded Age America,
and the invocations against usury, supported the farmers' insistence
that even individual economic activity not be separated from moral
considerations. Insofar as the Alliance rhetoric addressed capitalism
in general terms, it focused on its inherent lack of moral direction, its
inherent lack of "humanity."

5

An anonymous contributor to the Gainesville, Texas, *Signal* wrote in
1891 that "what the Reformation was towards the religious life three
centuries ago, the Farmers' Alliance is to the social life of the present
day."[74] This comment captures the important connection between
religious and political traditions that underlay Alliance ideology. Like
the Reformation of Luther, Zwingli, and Calvin, the Alliance sought

71. *Louisiana Populist,* April 1, 1898.
72. *Southern Mercury,* December 12, 1891.
73. *Louisiana Populist,* March 29, 1895.
74. Gainesville, Texas, *Signal,* quoted in *Southern Mercury,* September 3, 1891.

to democratize access to power and knowledge. Luther and his followers rejected the teachings of the priesthood in favor of their own understanding of the Bible. The members of the Alliance rejected, with the same kind of anguish and effort, the instructions of their political priesthood, the solons of the Democratic party. That the Reformation should be esteemed and the parallel noted is not coincidental but is, instead, an important example of how religious traditions gave meaning to the farmers' political and economic struggle. Religious traditions also gave that struggle voice and that voice power within the conservative culture of the agrarian South. Religious metaphors and religious ideas transmitted meaning and themselves shaped the Alliance critique of political economy and the Alliance curriculum in powerful ways. At the end of his history of the Alliance, even so worldly a critic as Scott Morgan turned to the spirit of the Old Testament. "Let every man," Morgan wrote, "study political economy, let him teach it to his children, expound it to his neighbors and proclaim it to the world." Then, "let the sword of justice fall, the bright blade gleams in the sunshine of liberty, equality, and justice . . . justice is mine, saith the Lord."[75]

75. Morgan, *History of the Wheel and Farmers' Alliance*, 283.

4 Educating for Political Action
Formal Pedagogy in the Farmers' Alliance

*No physician can prescribe for a disease until he knows its nature
. . . it is the object of these lessons to show the extent of the
disease . . . which is producing millionaires on the one hand and
tramps on the other.*
—"Economist Educational Exercises," No. 1 *National
Economist,* January 16, 1892

*Read! Read! The man who reads is the man who rules. We do not
ask you to adopt our principles before you understand them, and
not then, unless you think we are right.*
—*Louisiana Populist,* September 14, 1894

Out of crouching slaves they are making dauntless, intelligent citizens. . . .
—*National Economist,* August 9, 1890

1

The clearest tenet of the Alliance curriculum maintained that social
justice came from the work-hardened hands of a politically empowered and politically active agrarian class. But burdened by illiteracy, isolated from the centers of political discourse, and bound by
cultural traditions that militated against independent political action,
the average white southern farmer was ill equipped to shape the course
of the American polity. The configuration of Alliance educational efforts that included meetings and lectures encouraged farmers to take
greater responsibility for their own and the nation's fortunes, but
despite their ability to generate support and create class consciousness
these mass expressions of Alliance ideology could only begin to cultivate the individual intellectual skills that were prerequisites to the
kind of citizenship Alliance leaders demanded of the membership.

By 1889, the national leadership recognized that its educational efforts had produced a great amount of heat, but less light. Macune
worried that "while a person may be thoroughly cognizant of general
principles he often fails utterly to comprehend their specific application."[1] Even the most earnest members, while enthusiastic supporters
of the broad themes of equality, of justice, and of better distribution
of the returns to agriculture, were not necessarily able to understand

1. Macune's editorial in *National Economist,* March 7, 1891.

the implications of those themes.[2] What was missing from the configuration of educational opportunities fashioned by the Alliance was
a basic kind of education: individual training in intellectual skills, in
literacy, mathematics, and in the "sciences of social, financial, and
political economy."[3]

In 1888 the Executive Committee under Macune appointed a committee to explore the possibility of creating an Alliance newspaper.
The Committee on the National Organ included the major architects
of the Alliance educational campaign, Ben Terrell, Evan Jones, Harry
Tracy, and Macune himself. From the first, the committee used the
occasion of its charge to explore ways to deepen and broaden the Alliance campaign of education through the creation of an "educational
journal." Indeed, the committee recommended that the Supreme
Council appropriate funds to support a newspaper that would "be a
source of true education to the youth, of emulation to those in active
middle life, and of congratulation and comfort to the aged."[4] The
paper, the *National Economist,* did far more. Under Charles
Macune's editorship, the *Economist* became the lever by which the national leadership moved the educational campaign from mass meetings to individual skill-training. The *Economist* and other smaller
papers focused the movement's efforts to create local forums for
debate on national issues, to clarify Alliance positions in the face of
attack from outside and in, and most directly, to provide a substantive
text for the development of intellectual skills within the suballiances.
From the first, the nexus between the *Economist* and the suballiances
offered dramatic opportunities for political education.

Macune's editorial in the first issue of the *National Economist*
framed the premise of the entire enterprise. "Questions of public
policy are not too complicated for the average common mind," he
wrote, "the masses of the people should think more for themselves
and not, as is now too often the case, accept the declarations and conclusions of leading journals without understanding them."[5] Like lec-

2. Experiences like participation in the Exchange in the late 1880s added an important element to the educational configuration and enabled some Alliance members to
develop economic skills and a spirit of cooperative enterprise, but the Exchange reached
too few of the region's farm families. Moreover, the constant state of financial crisis in
which the Exchange was mired forced Macune to depend, for the most part, on using
individuals with previous experience and made it difficult to bring inexperienced
farmers into leadership roles in the project.

3. Harry Tracy, "Education," in *National Economist,* June 29, 1889.

4. Report of the Committee on the National Organ, in Dunning, *Farmers' Alliance
History,* 91.

5. *National Economist,* March 14, 1889.

turers, Macune and dozens of editors of small-town Alliance weeklies saw their role as equipping the "average common" farmer with the knowledge to examine "questions of public policy." Lecturers and editors shared many of the same goals within the educational campaign. Both sought to teach farmers a whole world view, one that emphasized the need for a conscious reconstruction of social reality in accordance with the aims and needs of rural producers. Both articulated a world view that identified class interest and class struggle as important determinants of social change, and urged farmers to think and act politically on behalf of their interests and ideology. But the editors saw their role a bit differently, attacking the problem of political education at a more fundamental level, with its concentration on skill building, and with more self-conscious attention to the process of educating, to pedagogy. Alliance pedagogy and Alliance curriculum differed, in practice, from expected modes of educating. They provided an alternative to the school and the party as sources of knowledge about and for politics.

2

Suballiances had always been the core organizational unit of the Alliance, bringing groups of five to twenty farmers and their families together in biweekly meetings to discuss Alliance business, exchange news, and socialize. By 1890, more than forty thousand active suballiances dotted the southern map. By 1891, many of them had embraced new roles as sponsors of the educational campaign. "These Alliance meetings are schools," wrote the editor of the Evergreen, Alabama, *Star*.[6] For Scott Morgan, the suballiance meeting was, "a school of education," where "the farmer discusses all of the issues that pertain to his welfare."[7] Acting in accordance with instructions from the National Executive Committee, each interested suballiance appointed a committee, sometimes an individual, to take charge over "the educational work."[8] This meant preparing talks on issues of the day, suggesting discussion topics, and leading these discussions. After

6. Robert McMath has uncovered the only membership lists extant for southern suballiances and has found that leaders of these groups tended to be wealthier than their followers, own land rather than rent, and be better educated than their compatriots. See McMath, "Agrarian Protest at the Forks of the Creek: Three Sub-Alliances in North Carolina," *North Carolina Historical Review* 51 (Winter 1974).

7. *Southern Mercury,* September 3, 1891; *National Economist,* March 14, 1889.

8. Report of the Atatosca County Alliance meeting of June 2 in *Southern Mercury,* July 5, 1894.

visiting several suballiance meetings in his home state of Texas, Macune reported to the membership that "hard financial and economic questions are being discussed in the suballiances now, with an ability and a calmness that would be truly astonishing to those who are accustomed to speak of the ignorant farmers."[9] These discussions of "hard financial questions" relied on farmers' discussions of their daily experiences, of what they heard from Alliance lecturers and other party spokesmen, and of what they read in newspapers like the *Economist*.

If the suballiance was the "school" of the educational campaign, then it is no overstatement to say that the network of newspapers supported by the Alliance in the South was its textbooks and lesson plans. We tend not to think of newspapers as means of education, yet the reform papers sponsored or approved by the Alliance set out to be textbook and teacher's manual for a generation of producers. Morgan argued that the "proper mission" of a newspaper was "to educate the people, to encourage progress."[10] Morgan dedicated his own journal, *Morgan's Buzz Saw,* to just this purpose. The model on which Morgan and other editors drew was Macune's *National Economist*.

The *Economist* reflected Macune's insistence upon educational activism as the cornerstone of the Alliance. His paper, he wrote, "is not, nor will it ever attempt to be a showy publication." Its object, "as the name indicates . . . will be to appeal to the reason and judgment of its readers and to educate in the principles of society, finance, and government."[11] The *Economist,* like other papers bearing the imprint of the movement, was financed by a combination of advertising revenue, subscriptions, and small appropriations from the Alliance treasury.[12] At the peak of its power and popularity, the *Economist* claimed a circulation of one hundred thousand subscribers across the nation, at a subscription rate of one dollar per year, and it probably reached several times that many readers as copies of the latest edition passed from hand to hand.

When farmers picked up their weekly *Economist* they found a paper of about ten pages in length. The front page bore the seal of the Alliance and was dominated by an editorial written by Macune, Ben Terrell, or Harry Tracy. The front page also ran comprehensive ac-

9. *National Economist,* November 14, 1891.

10. Morgan, *History of the Wheel and Farmers' Alliance,* 685. See also Thomas D. Clark, *The Southern Country Editor* (Indianapolis: Bobbs-Merrill, 1948). According to Clark, start-up expenses for publishing were low, particularly in comparison to today.

11. Dunning, *Farmers' Alliance History,* 74–77, 162.

12. *National Economist,* March 14, 1889.

counts of national political news, summarizing legislation, speeches, and presidential comings and goings. This political news paid particular attention to farm, currency, and tax legislation and to matters of industrial and trade regulation. Inside, farmers read excerpts from local reform papers about the progress of the movement across the nation.[13] Following the second page, Macune devoted the remainder of each issue to special features of interest to farm families and of importance to the educational campaign. The entire journal was framed by Macune's interest that its primary function be educational.

The extensive scope of his news gathering, for example, provided readers with a window on the world that they would not otherwise have had. In one issue, the *Economist* ran front-page articles on the capture of the Dalton Gang in the Badlands and on Lord Tennyson's death at home in England.[14] On page two farmers read of Pasteur's work on rabies, of the work of the Royal Society on germ theory, and of other discoveries in the world of science relevant to their lives as farmers and stock raisers.

It was particularly in its treatment of this kind of scientific news that the *Economist* linked the needs of its readers to ideas and events outside the normal sphere of farmers' daily discourse. As a good newspaper staff should, Macune and his writers kept farmers abreast of some of the latest and most important scientific research and political activity.[15] In politics and economics, what farmers read was again focused by relating outside events to immediate circumstance. The special sections in the middle of the paper consisted of rotating primers on politics, economics, and history. Macune called these sections "lessons" and crafted them quite consciously as means to advance members' skills in political analysis and political discourse.

The lessons on politics, entitled "The Republics of the World, a Brief Account of the Conditions Under Which They Exist," ran into eighteen parts and described the difference between direct democracy, representative democracy, and parliamentary democracy, using contemporary states around the globe as illustration.[16] After this groundwork was established, the lessons discussed the pattern of laws in several different countries, examining how certain legislation benefits certain classes while hurting others. Macune's series on economics, en-

13. *National Economist,* September 6, 1890. Here Macune began a "Telegraphic News Summary" in which he collected and commented upon the day's events at home and abroad.
14. *National Economist,* August 10, 1889.
15. *National Economist,* August 10, 1889.
16. *National Economist,* September 6, 1890.

titled "Political Economy" began in the fall of 1890. In twenty installments the Alliance's chief economic theorist labored to convey to
readers the sweep of the history of economic thought from the
Oeconomicus through Ricardo, Mill, and Smith. Complementing
these two series was a third, "United States History and Government," which was a concrete legislative history of the Union, with
emphasis on the effect of laws on the common man, and on the progressive influence of party professionals.

At the end of the weekly paper, after the news and the lessons in
politics and economics, farmers turned to household hints, farming
advice, and consumer warnings. Pieces on how best to tend hogs during winter, how best to mulch, and how often to weed cotton were
written and sent in by contributors ranging from U.S. Department of
Agriculture spokesmen to *Economist* subscribers who thought their
techniques could help others. The editors of the paper contributed
warnings about unsafe products, for example baking powders con-
taining high concentrations of ammonia and aluminum. Finally, the
Economist ran ads for the Alliance Publishing Company, which, during the late 1880s, kept up a steady stream of reform literature, including Morgan's book, *The History of the Agricultural Wheel and
the Farmers' Alliance,* and Dunning's *Farmers' Alliance History and
Agricultural Digest.*[17] Like the paper itself, these volumes included
information on a range of subjects, from political theory and the
ideology of the Alliance to practical farming tips and recipes.

By integrating theoretical and practical topics, the editors of the
Alliance journals sought to integrate new kinds of discourse, unfamiliar to farmers, into their daily experience. By its very comingling
of political news and agricultural tips, the *Economist* made political
education, like the latest information on mulching, a legitimate and
important part of what one needed in order to be a decent farmer. It
was a crucial connection. Alliance editors like Macune made an understanding of electoral politics a tool, and placed that tool in the hands
of southern farmers, to be used, much like any other tool, to more effectively pursue their chosen livelihood and to bring to fruition their
image of American democracy.

The *Economist* was the tip of a very broad pyramid of reform
organs that extended from the national paper to hundreds of tiny local
Alliance papers. Not all, not even the majority, of these Alliance
organs were owned by arms of the organization. The *Economist* was
the only paper subsidized by the national organization. State Alli-

17. See, for examples, *National Economist,* August 17, 1889, November 26, 1889.

ances, including those in Texas, Georgia, and North Carolina supported state papers. Local Alliance groups often did what they could to support editors who agreed with Alliance positions on issues. Haphazard though this pattern of support was, Alliance papers relied upon each other for much of their material. National and state papers drew stories, letters, and accounts of the activities of suballiances from the pages of county papers. These local organs, in turn, borrowed editorials, national news, and special sections—including the series on politics, economics, and history—from the *Economist,* in an early form of syndication. The goal of the National Alliance leadership was to "let every state have its own paper, under the control of the President and the Executive Committee."[18]

The national and state organs—along with the official paper of the Colored Farmers' Alliance, the *National Alliance,* and the journal of the Southern Farmers' Alliance, the *Southern Mercury*—were the mainstays of the agrarian reform press movement. They provided continuity where local papers could not, and linked local alliances and individual farmers with each other and with the leaders of the movement.[19]

Next to the *Economist,* the *Southern Mercury* was the most important paper in the pantheon of reform journals in the South. The paper was started in Dallas during 1881 by Harry Tracy and in 1886 was made the official organ of the Texas Alliance by the Clebourne Convention.[20] Tracy continued as the paper's publisher throughout the Alliance and Populist periods, but turned editorial duties over to Evan Jones and later to Milton Park, who continued to beat the drum for reform into the twentieth century. In 1892, estimates showed the *Mercury's* circulation at thirty thousand subscribers throughout the South. Park's sparkling editorials made the *Mercury* one of the most colorful and long-lived reform papers of the era.

Other papers aided the reform cause: Tom Watson's *People's Party Paper* ushered in the populist campaign in Georgia. L. L. Polk put out the *Progressive Farmer* to fifteen thousand subscribers in North

18. *National Economist,* April 6, 1889.

19. Humphrey in Dunning, *Farmers' Alliance History,* 290. There are no surviving copies of the *National Alliance,* nor of any of the estimated 200 black Alliance papers that had short runs between 1889 and 1892. For a summary of the reform press in Alabama see William Rogers, "Alabama's Reform Press," *Agricultural History* 34 (April 1960). C. G. Scruggs and S. W. Mosely, "The Role of Agricultural Journalism in the Rural South," *Agricultural History* 53 (January 1979) marks the change from politically oriented press during the Alliance period to technical advice in the earlier twentieth century.

20. Morgan, *History of the Wheel and Farmers' Alliance,* 102.

Carolina. These and other papers either received direct financial sub-
sidies from the state Alliances or operated independently with the
sanction and endorsement of state executive committees. All depended upon brisk sales and continuing advertising for their operating
revenue. Below the state level, literally hundreds of reform papers
opened and closed between 1889 and 1896. Some, the lucky ones, put
together fairly long runs. The Natchitoches, Louisiana, *Populist,* for
example, published for two years without a break in its weekly sched-
ule between the summer of 1894 and the winter of 1896. Most editors
and publishers, however, printed a few issues and folded, selling their
printing equipment to the next brave entrepreneur.

3

Editors persisted despite these problems because, in part, of what Alliance leaders saw as a monopoly on information and interpretation, indeed on knowledge itself, maintained by the Democratic dominated
press in the South. Certainly as far as the leaders of the Alliance were
concerned, "the newspapers lie because capital owns them or hires
them." Scott Morgan described the majority press as so many
"poisonous vapors" that "permeate the whole country with their
deadly influence, spread dissension, arouse the passions and smother
the nobler instincts and sentiments of manhood."[21] For their part,
major dailies, including Charles Dana's *New York Sun* and Henry
Grady's *Atlanta Constitution,* exploited most opportunities to paint
the Alliance as a socialistic, negrophile association of hicks ready to
drag the nation down in its schemes. Alliance editors saw their newspapers as essential weapons in combating the "miseducation" of the
Democratic press. They provided a competing perspective on events
and brought farmers face to face with competing world views.

In their rhetoric, Morgan and others argued that sources of information "must be owned by the people."[22] This solution, never fully
developed, matched in gross outline Alliance positions in favor of the
nationalization of railroads and telegraph lines. All these nationalization plans rested on the prior creation of a changed polity, in which
the state worked on behalf of the "common people," and in which the
state's activities were directed more completely by voters. This
changed polity, in turn, demanded a more politically independent and
active citizenry. For the Alliance educational campaign, this meant a

21. Morgan, *History of the Wheel and Farmers' Alliance,* 282–283.
22. *Southern Mercury,* January 21, 1892.

constant struggle against the information monopoly of the major newspapers.

Park's *Southern Mercury* and Macune's *National Economist* waged an ongoing battle against the representations of the Alliance in the New South and northern press. In 1891 Park printed excerpts from the *Sun,* the *Constitution,* and smaller journals like the Arkansas *Gazette,* that contradicted Alliance positions or the general ways of thinking encouraged and taught in the campaign of education. Next to these, he printed his own critique.

Sometimes, Park sought simply to combat opponents' perceptions of the movement. Quoting from the Alvarado, Texas, *Herald,* Park included the following clip:

> The sub-treasuryites have grown remarkably quiet. Have they shouted themselves too hoarse to talk or are they out on a still hunt?[23]

This and similar jibes in the Democratic press aimed at demoralizing the movement's membership. Park replied:

> They are all right! They are neither too hoarse to talk nor on a still hunt. The trouble is the partisans, like you, can't find any way to further misrepresent them.[24]

Park kept busy fielding and dispatching rumor and innuendo that reached Alliance members through papers like the *Herald.*

But Park's editorials worked at a deeper level, defending Alliance programs against substantive and symbolic attacks from the Democratic editors and writers. The editor of the *Fort Worth Gazette* opposed the Alliance subtreasury plan as a trick designed to throw even prosperous farmers into debt: "Thousands and thousands of thrifty and substantial farmers would be lured by the flattering promise of

---

23. The subtreasury was Macune's most direct and far-reaching plan for the reform of southern farm life. According to the proposal, the U.S. government would maintain branches of the federal treasury, subtreasuries, in each congressional district. In addition, the government would operate warehouses for grain and cotton. Farmers could warehouse their crops and borrow against their yield at a rate not to exceed 2 percent per year. By making the government the creditor of record in the region, Macune hoped to mitigate the problems of little circulating currency and loosen the hold of the crop lien. For more detailed explanations, see Macune, "The Farmers Alliance," 54–56; Goodwyn, *Democratic Promise,* 565–582.

24. *Southern Mercury,* January 14, 1892.

'cheap money' into the fatal policy of debt.''[25] Park's reply covered
two columns and ranged from invective ("The editor of the Gazette
. . . displays an aggravated case of debility of the mind . . . and a near
approach to mania . . .) to sober elaboration of the themes of the proposed subtreasury:

> Every person familiar with the present system of handling the
> farm products knows that at least thirty percent of their volume
> is uselessly frittered away in the hauling of it after it leaves the
> producers hands . . . [by warehousing crops locally] at least
> twenty-five percent of this waste will be saved.

Park explained that fees for warehousing and interest on money borrowed against these crops would never exceed five percent of the value
of the crop, saving all farmers twenty percent of the value of their produce over the existing system.

Park, then, created a kind of intellectual tension by countering
Democratic interpretations of Alliance programs with the Alliance
point of view. His rebuttals of arguments made or slurs printed in
local and even regional papers can be seen as direct efforts to defend
the Alliance and its programs from information that could affect
members and potential members and so erode support. They were also
efforts to contrast the way the Alliance saw issues of the day with the
way those same issues were interpreted by papers supporting and supported by the two major political parties. Park was not the only editor
to turn Democratic attacks to his advantage, as was evident in
Macune's ongoing sparring with Charles Dana in the pages of the
Economist.

When Dana and the *Sun* came out in favor of a protective tariff,
Macune used the occasion to show how the proposed tariff worked to
the advantage of manufacturers and financiers and to the disadvantage of the consumers of manufactured goods, including farmers.
More importantly, he showed that by looking at the tariff from the
businessman's point of view, the *Sun* ignored other lenses. The
Alliance, and its journals, he explained, worked to examine public
issues from the point of view of the farmer.[26] So, in addition to countering specific arguments in the establishment press, Macune and Park
used the example of these arguments to illustrate ways in which the

25. Quoted in *Southern Mercury,* August 6, 1891.
26. *National Economist,* September 3, 1892. For other examples of this type of explanation, see *National Economist,* August 27, 1892; *Southern Mercury,* August 12,
1891.

very paradigm within which "news" was produced differed between the Alliance and its rivals.

Highlighting this difference meant, in part, highlighting the difference between the political education offered by the Alliance and the technical education offered by others. Park quoted from the Tyler, Texas, *Democrat:*

> Some of the papers and politicians are crying out that a "campaign of education is needed in this country." True, but not exactly as intended by the demagogues and office seekers. A campaign of education out of politics and into the methods of economy and how to make a living at home is badly needed in this country, not only among farmers, but the people generally.

Park's response was to move the debate from technique (how to make a living at home) to the structure of the economy, which offered significantly different rewards to farmers and those involved in some industries:

> The farmers who till the soil in Smith County may need information how to make a living around home, but they don't need educating how to practice economy at home or how to make a living at home. Recent developments have demonstrated that there is a vast difference in cash receipts between those who till the soil and those who cultivate railroads . . .[27]

By turning to the structure of the economy, Park turned the focus of the debate, and of the Alliance educational campaign, to broad political questions about the distribution of economic rewards and away from narrower questions of farming techniques, productivity, and overproduction. By debating the point in the pages of the *Mercury,* Park took the time to show his readers what the Alliance meant by its campaign and how it differed from the kind of education, and the kinds of meanings, offered by the Democratic press.

4

The establishment press was often the butt of visual editorializing as well, in the form of editorial cartoons. The *Mercury,* in 1891 and 1892, ran cartoons with every issue. In its September 10, 1891, cartoon, the *Mercury* portrayed Charles Dana as a short fat figure

27. *Southern Mercury,* August 6, 1891.

"The Gold Bug," cartoon from *Southern Mercury,* September 10, 1891

pounding a bass drum while a multitude of politicians and statesmen clamored at the feet of a hideous "Single Gold Standard."

Like articles and editorials, the editorial cartoons were shared between reform papers. They added potency to the written arguments presented in the papers and, although certainly caricatures, presented salient parts of the Alliance message in easily understood and remembered fashion. It is possible, as well, that the cartoons offered a way for those with poor reading skills to penetrate the weekly journals.

Certain symbolic representations recurred in the art, conveying meanings that became universals and that needed no further explanation. Farmers were represented by broad-brimmed hats, beards, and homespun shirts. If it was their courage and steadfastness that was the theme of the cartoon, the farmers appeared as hardy, physically able men. If the degradation of the farmer was at issue, he appeared frail and weathered. Workers wore an omnipresent box-hat and often an apron; they were strong of limb and determined in features. Professional politicians sported suits and displayed enormous bellies, having eaten their fill, we are to infer, at the public trough. Their girth was barely spanned by great gold watchchains, or their pockets overflowed with greenbacks. Both were signs of ill-gotten gain. Bankers were often portrayed in the same mold as politicians, but sometimes also as "Shylocks," represented by the stereotyped Jew, with hooked nose, stooped shoulders, and deep-set eyes.[28]

Honest blacks shared with farmers and laborers robust physiques

RECIPROCITY AND RETALIATION.
United labor is able to protect its own, to avenge injustice and reciprocate favors.

"Reciprocity and Retaliation," cartoon from *Southern Mercury,* February 4, 1892

28. The anti-Semitic features of Populist writings are ably discussed by Barton Shaw in *The Wool Hat Boys* (Baton Rouge: Louisiana State University Press, 1984), 178–181. Earlier accounts from the 1950s overemphasize the characterizations by Populist writers of their enemies as Shylocks. See Oscar Handlin, "Reconsidering the Populists," *Agricultural History* 39, no. 2 (April 1965).

"Farmer Honesty's Experience with the Politicians," cartoon from *Southern Mercury*, September 17, 1891

and bore few of the degrading characteristics—huge lips, flat noses, long limbs—that marked the representations of black Democrats and Republicans.

It would be possible for even an illiterate "reader" to garner meaning from the cartoons. But in general, the cartoons, many crowded with print, served as supplements to and not replacements for the prose arguments. In one case, a weekly cartoon in the *Southern Mercury* was so complicated that not even the captions sufficed to explain its meaning. Park devoted several column inches to its explanation.

So, for the most part, the effectiveness of newspapers as modes of educational discourse depended upon the literacy of their audience and the ability of that audience to pay subscriptions. The Alliance audience tended, of course, to be rather poor and shared the illiteracy problem of the region. Yet newspapers became useful means of education in the hands of the Alliance leadership.

First, newspapers were relatively simple to produce and distribute. Editors did not need to possess specialized skills or expensive equipment. "A small stock of type, a printer's stone, four iron cases, an inking pan and roller, a couple of crude tables, a filthy towel, and a Washington or Franklin hand press were all the equipment necessary," according to Thomas Clark.[29] This meant that Alliance leaders could quickly translate the movement into print even in tiny localities.

Second, newspapers spread the cost of production beyond the readership. Through the sale of advertising space, merchants subsidized a portion of the printing and editorial expense—merchants who, in this case, may not even have sided with the goals of the movement. Advertising costs, when passed on to customers, again extended beyond the readership to buyers not connected with the Alliance or its program.

Third, as the only medium for mass communication, the newspapers allowed the leadership to communicate quickly and efficiently with large numbers of members in a way that was simply not possible otherwise. Park's editorials repudiating Democratic claims and slurs exemplify the "quick response" capability of nineteenth-century print journalism. As a means of mass communication, newspapers spread Alliance ideas farther and faster than could any other mechanism and extended the reach of the movement's leaders to literally millions of literate farmers and rural producers.

Finally, newspapers carried out a function much like that of the traveling lecturers. Both carried the message of the Alliance and its educational campaign to geographically and culturally isolated farmers. Like the lectures, the papers unified farmers through a sharing of common problems and the identification of common interests.

But still, the reach of the news was limited by poverty and illiteracy. To address both, and to deepen the campaign of education, Macune sought to refashion his *National Economist* into a political primer for use in suballiance meetings.

5

The idea of using the paper as a focus for suballiance discussions was an old one with Macune, dating to the discussions of the Committee on the National Organ and the inaugural issue of the *Economist*. His first attempts at instigating political discussion were the series on

29. Clark, *The Southern Country Editor,* 44.

"American Government" and "Political Economy." But the abstract content and dry style of the pieces daunted local Alliance leaders. Macune next tried to interest suballiances in a thirty-part series on the "History of Land," which summarized the condition of the "agricultural classes" from prehistory to the present. Although not popular in themselves, in this history of agrarian peoples Macune found his educational stride; he discovered a language and a system of metaphor that were to support all successive attempts to direct the political learning within the movement, the language and metaphor of history.[30]

"A knowledge of history," wrote Macune, "is to fit men to act intelligently on all political and social questions."[31] Through history, Macune found that he could turn popular moralizing about progress on its head; his was a morality play in reverse. In Macune's hands history became the story of the progressive degradation of the masses of men under the tyrannical rule of a powerful and morally bankrupt minority. He wrote history to be a set of object lessons to the membership of the Alliance, lessons that drew parallels between earlier times and their own. Greek history provided Macune with his first point of reference.

The history of Periclean Athens "is the most striking illustration of the dangers to which republics are exposed."[32] By Macune's account

> the conflict had narrowed down to a contest between the rich and the poor, the rich desiring ultimately to establish a strong central government and the masses contending for reform in the land and commercial system.

30. Macune had a sense of history that extended to his conception of the role of the reform press. "The historians who record the conditions of the present for the benefit and use of the future must tale their facts and draw their deductions from the current literature as found in the newspapers," he wrote. "The press is the storehouse to which those who write accurately, and honestly, trust for their information." More, he understood the power of traditional historical records and historical writing to swallow without traces oppositional movements: "When the history of the Alliance Movement comes to be written, if care is not taken, nothing save the falsehoods and misrepresentations of its enemies will be found in the Public Libraries." To him, the solution was the creation in each Congressional District of a storehouse for historical documents relating to the Alliance, including membership lists, collections of county newspapers, and records of Alliance meetings. We can only regret that the Alliance did not follow Macune here as it did in so many other areas. See *National Economist,* November 7, 1891.

31. *National Economist,* September 28, 1889.

32. *National Economist,* September 28, 1889.

The poor wanted "a system of distribution more in accord with the true principles of liberty and republican ideas."

Having drawn the history of Athens in these terms, Macune exploited its parallels with Gilded Age America for all they were worth: "It was with them, as it is with us, a struggle against the growth of monopoly."[33] He discovered parallels as well in the structure of Athenian politics. The political parties there "were divided by class lines . . . a conflict of the masses against concentrated capital."[34] Pericles' popularity among the people, according to Macune, allowed him to consolidate and centralize the government of Athens and to use the mechanisms of government to support imperial adventures, to overtax the producers, and to replace a democratic government with a near-permanent aristocracy. Macune interpreted these developments in the light of recent American history, particularly the strengthening of party hierarchies and American expansion overseas.[35]

"What then," Macune asked his readers, "is the lesson taught by this terrible experience of a noble people?" Clearly, he wanted his audience to learn that the people must "guard against the consequences of giving way to a thoughtless enthusiasm on any public question, especially of placing implicit confidence in any leader or public advisor." Instead, "the people must think for themselves and dictate to their leaders, not follow blindly." Macune concluded his lesson with a warning to his readers that "we have before us in the history of the Greek states a full illustration of what we are to expect if we continue in the same way and allow, as they did, designing demagogues to mislead and distract attention from vital questions."[36]

In practice, for Macune, history became a kind of laboratory in which he tried to demonstrate the elemental laws of social and political change as he and the Alliance leadership understood them. The

33. *National Economist,* September 14, 1889.

34. *National Economist,* August 8, 1889.

35. In his lesson in the *National Economist,* August 17, 1889, Macune glorified the order and egalitarian nature of Spartan society and condemned the rigid class structure of Athens. This is a telling divergence from the line taken in contemporary textbooks. See H. A. Guerber, *The Story of the Greeks* (New York: American Book Company, 1896), a high school text, for comparison. Macune referred to the Spartans as "austere, scorning wealth and the luxury it could buy." Both represented democracies, "one simple and of the crudest form, closely allied to the people; the other complicated with an aristocracy and commercial interests between the people and the state." The parallels are clear. Athens represented America as it was through Macune's eyes, Sparta what America could be.

36. *National Economist,* December 14, 1889.

prior validity of the laws themselves, of the moral virtue of manual labor, of the political power of the rich, and of the inevitable and ongoing conflict between the two classes for control of change—these Macune did not question.

As history, Macune's offerings fall short on many measures, but perhaps the most important is his selective use of examples from the historical record to prove the Alliance version of contemporary American affairs, without any attention to disconfirming or even simply confounding evidence. Certainly all history is the product of the selection of certain material and the omission of other. What is missing in Macune's histories, however, is a sense of complexity and context. Both are sacrificed when the purpose of history ceases to be the explanation of the past and becomes, instead, a window on the present. This proved to be the great strength and the great weakness of Macune's historical writing in the pages of the *National Economist*.

History proved a tactically useful medium through which to teach southern farmers the ideas of class conflict and class struggle. By drawing historical parallels to illuminate the condition of producers in the South, Macune hurdled the traditions of party loyalty and deference that limited farmers' ability to act in politically new ways. Democrat versus Republican, North versus South, black versus white: these oppositions had no meaning in Periclean Athens. Left were the ideas of the oppression of the poor by the rich and the centralization of power in the hands of a few. By displacing examples of power and powerlessness from their contemporary environment he was able to strip away potentially divisive issues and deal with political issues and political ideas in fairly pure form.[37]

"The History of the Land" gave Macune a part of what he wanted. The series gave farmers a base on which to gain some perspective on their own situation. The individual lessons challenged farmers to broaden their intellectual horizons and taught them that history could inform and propel their thinking. Yet Macune wanted more. The passive pedagogy of the lessons lacked the sense of involvement Macune sought. Moreover, the lessons' form and content did not address the problems of illiteracy and did not, in themselves, foster intellectual interaction between Alliance members. Dissatisfied, Macune developed still another "curriculum," the *Economist* Educational Exercises, a series designed to turn suballiances into schools. The Exercises captured the essense of the movement's educational aims. They taught analytic skills, including literacy and numeracy while at the same time

37. *National Economist*, June 24, 1889.

exposing members to democratic political theory, class analysis, and the social gospel through history. The Exercises ran in the *Economist* starting in January 1892 and continued through twenty installments. The Educational Exercises were the best developed of the Alliance's formal educational efforts and seem to have dominated the activities of suballiances throughout the South during the winter and spring of 1892.[38]

On January 16, 1892, suballiance presidents throughout the United States read in their *Economists* of a "series of instructive lessons for use in Alliances . . . to disseminate a correct understanding of the questions of the day."[39] Macune printed the first lesson, along with some general guidelines for the program, in the January 16 edition. He urged that presidents use the first lesson during the first week in February, giving them time to study and prepare.

"In the first four lessons we are about to study statistics to find out how much there is produced, who gets it, and whether there is enough to make all comfortable, or whether there is not," wrote Macune. "Read the lesson over carefully," he advised the Alliance presidents, "work out the problems carefully and study the lesson until there is no point in it which you do not understand." In addition to the material presented in the *Economist*, Macune urged members to "read up on the condition of the country a hundred years ago and add to the outlines interesting facts you come across." Macune asked local Alliance leaders to use schoolhouses for their educational meetings so that blackboards could be used for the arithmetic and grammar exercises in each lesson.

Finally, he had some advice on teaching. He urged the president to lead the first session but, after that, to assemble a list of volunteers to lead successive lessons. "All must work," he maintained, and the role of instructor could be used to build the confidence of a farmer not accustomed to speaking in public. Macune also urged the instructors to link the lessons with problems and issues of moment in their particular communities. Articles in local papers were of special value, and he urged instructors to pay special attention "whether [interesting articles] are three lines or a column in length."

Discussions would be lively, Macune promised, and the instructor needed to take care to keep out of deep water. "Avoid the discussion of party politics as you would avoid a poison," he warned. "Discuss

38. See reports on use: *National Economist*, February 13, 1892; April 23, 1892; *Southern Mercury*, February 18, 1892.
39. *National Economist*, January 16, 1892.

the condition of the country and the needs of the people, but let parties alone.'' In addition to discussion and blackboard exercises, Macune urged that the lessons be occasions for bringing together the whole reform community. ''Have plenty of music, get children to speak pieces, and have a short dialogue if convenient.'' In this way, Macune argued, education and social interaction would reinforce each other.

6

During the first week in February 1892, men, women and children of the Alliance moved through the chill of winter to attend their sub-alliance meetings. For some, it was a new experience to meet in the schoolhouse, for others the schoolhouse had been a familiar place for several years. When the membership had arrived and the business agenda dismissed, lecturers and presidents began the first Educational Exercise with a short lecture, outlined by Macune, or with remarks of their own. ''We have been repeatedly told by campaign orators that no country produces enough to keep all of its people in comfort,'' read Macune's outline. Farmers had been told ''that it is a matter of necessity that some people should suffer, even here.'' The crux of the problem lay in the credibility of these statements. Should farmers continue to take orators at their word, or ''would it not be well for us to study statistics, that we may decide for ourselves whether God has given enough for all, or whether there is only enough for a favored few?''

Following this preamble, instructors asked volunteers to move to the blackboard to work out some of these ''statistics.'' Farmers who ''hadn't handled chalk for ten or twenty years'' rose from their seats and walked to the blackboard. Boys and girls, in school or recently out of school helped the scholars at their ciphers. Together, farmers stooping at their task and young people standing squarely at the blackboard worked on problems as the instructor read them out: ''In 1790 the population of the U.S. was less than 4 million, in 1890 the population was about 63 million; how much has the population grown in 100 years?'' The lesson used $65 billion as an estimate for the total accumulated wealth of the nation in 1890, a figure which included GNP plus the total valuation of all land and capital equipment. ''What is the wealth per capita in the United States?'' the instructor asked.

With more background information, the scholar/farmers then computed the per capita debt and the net per capita wealth. Farmers quickly found that this figure for unencumbered per capita wealth vastly overshot their own wealth, making it clear that wealth was not evenly divided.

Other "statistics" derived by the members of the suballiance hammered home the same point. "The average amount saved during the last ten years was about $2,200,000,000 per year," the instructor announced. "How much was that for each individual yearly, how much for ten years?" The instructor hardly had to ask how much the farmers in the room had saved over the preceding ten years; the comparison was implicit, and painfully obvious to the assembled class.

As the blackboard exercises ended and farmers returned to their seats, the instructor called on other members of the lodge to read articles on the division of wealth and other related topics. Farmers stood and read, often haltingly and sometimes with the help of young partners, from county newspapers, magazines, or books. During the first of the lessons, instructors bore the responsibility of culling articles for use in these meetings. But as the lessons progressed the farmers could bring in their own articles circled on yellowing and torn newsprint. After an article was read, the instructor led a discussion on its importance to the object of the lesson and to the immediate concerns of the assembled membership.

Lesson 1, "The Richest Nation," ended with a selection of patriotic songs mixed with Alliance ballads and a group prayer. Farmers and

Table 4.1. *Economist* Educational Exercises

Lesson 1	The Richest Nation
Lesson 2	The Richest Man
Lesson 3	Our Millionaries
Lesson 4	Review: The Centralization of Wealth in the U.S.
Lesson 5	England: Its Privileged Class
Lesson 6	England: Its Workers
Lesson 7	Review: In Darkest England
Lesson 8	Scotland: Its Great Estates
Lesson 9	Glasgow: The Model City
Lesson 10	Ireland: Its Wrongs
Lesson 11	Germany: The Battleground of Europe
Lesson 12	Germany: Its Present Condition
Lesson 13	Historic France
Lesson 14	France Today
Lesson 15	Review: France and Germany Compared
Lesson 16	Historic Russia
Lesson 17	How Russia is Governed
Lesson 18	Russia: The Country of Peasants
Lesson 19	Review: The Power of Wealth
Lesson 20	Are Millionaires Beneficial to a Nation?

Source: *National Economist,* January 16, 1892, through June 25, 1892.

114   Educating for Political Action

their families left the schoolhouse and returned through the deepening darkness to their own homes and the warmth of their own firesides.[40]

Through the twenty lessons listed in table 4.1, the *Economist* Educational Exercises followed a similar structure which combined an introductory lecture, given by the instructor, with blackboard exercises in mathematics and, in later lessons, exercises in sentence construction. Oral reading and discussion followed in turn. Macune designed the lessons to introduce to the farmers general principles and unfamiliar concepts in ways that were relevant to their lives. The idea of per capita wealth, for example, is a powerful concept because of its implicit contrast with the farmers' actual holdings. The contrast between actual wealth and per capita wealth led to questions of how inequality occurs and why it persists, and to the moral question: should it be that so few own so much while the remainder suffer? The leaders of the Alliance were not dissuaded by these questions, indeed, these were the questions they wanted farmers to begin asking, not only of themselves but of their elected representatives as well.

The scope of the Exercises was quite broad. One week the scholars discussed Rockefeller's fortune and what it meant to be worth two hundred million dollars, and in the next lesson they computed the average farm size in England and the rate of pauperism throughout the British Isles. As they ranged around the globe and between time periods, some similar problems and topics recurred, giving the lessons both continuity and meaning within the educational campaign.

Unifying these disparate lessons is the warning that the centralization of wealth and power, a reciprocal process, always leads to the repression by the rich and powerful of the poor and powerless. The lessons on history and society led farmers to explore the historical process whereby privileged classes emerged and the processes whereby their privilege was preserved and extended, at the expense of the common people. The first point Macune wanted to convey was simply that "the concentration of wealth means concentration of power and accumulated wealth gives its possessor a decided advantage in the race of life and in the area of business."[41] He illustrated this notion with examples from the histories of England, America, and France, that showed how great fortunes were made, how political power aided the creation of wealth, and how the privileged construct laws and institutions that extend both their wealth and their power.

"In studying the early history of every nation," Macune wrote in

40. Quotes in this section from the first of the *Economist* Educational Exercises: *National Economist*, January 16, 1892.
41. *National Economist*, January 30, 1892.

one lecture outline, "the strongest man physically and mentally becomes the leader . . . but the leadership develops a strong tendency to become hereditary." Here, in this primitive form "is the origin of the privileged classes, the family of the chief gains powers and privileges which are not shared by other members of the tribe, although their bravery and ability may be equal to that of the chief." Through his mere familial relationship, "the son of the chief has greater opportunities to exercise his ability . . . to become skillful in the art of governing men."[42] This notion of the process of primitive accumulation establishes talent, strength, and ability as the basis for some original distribution of wealth and power. But successive generations inherit their position. By looking at the history of privilege across time and national boundaries, separate from personalities, it became clear that privilege is born of privilege, not effort or ability, and that men of wealth need not be "better men" than poor farmers.

"Today," wrote Macune in his introduction to the lesson "The Power of Wealth," "the same two classes exist as of old, not only in Europe but in this America." Rather than physical force, the privileged classes of America use "new methods of robbery . . . dividends, interests, and rents."[43] In England's House of Lords, in America's Senate and House of Representatives, privilege was defended and extended by the passage of laws favorable to the interests of the small social and economic elite. After two sessions on the legislative history of Britain, farmers discussed whether "Parliament ever enacted laws for the benefit of the people which were not first demanded by the people."[44] The following week, instructors asked if the farmers/scholars believed "that there are any laws in the United States which tend to increase the wealth of the rich at the expense of the poor."[45] This kind of analysis—reinforced by a series of exercises in which farmers derived estimates for the distribution of wealth in America, the rate of pauperism in England, and other telling indices of polarized economic conditions—led to normative as well as descriptive conclusions.

Centralization of power and wealth meant that the people were becoming both poorer and less able to exert power on their own behalf. "Is it best to continue a system of legislation which makes one man out of every hundred hold in his hands the wealth which should be distributed among 100 men?" Macune asked his students. For Macune, of course, the answer was no. The perpetuation of privilege and the

42. *National Economist,* May 28, 1892: lesson 16.
43. *National Economist,* June 18, 1892: lesson 17.
44. *National Economist,* February 27, 1892: lesson 6.
45. *National Economist,* March 5, 1892: lesson 7.

progressive polarization of wealth and power endangered the welfare of the mass of people so that a few could live in luxury. "By legislation, the English aristocracy have succeeded in enriching themselves and impoverishing the laboring portion of the nation; by legislation, American capitalists are seeking to do the same thing," argued Macune.[46]

The Alliance creed pointed the way toward what the leaders of the movement took to be a more just social order, in which legislation served the interests of farmers and some laborers rather than the interests of a few merchant capitalists and financiers. Centralization of power could be fought by the mobilization of the working people to regain control over government, to destroy the legal bulwark that protected and extended the power and wealth of the elite, and to reinject fairness into the race of life.

A certain utopianism infused Macune's histories as well as the general political philosophy of the Alliance. It was one thing to document and teach people to calculate the dimensions of the polarization of wealth and the persistence of inequality across the face of recorded history. It was quite another task to teach that inequalities—of wealth, of power, of cultural standing—could be swept away by one, or even repeated, gestures of the electoral hand. The fact of the persistence of inequality, well presented in Macune's scenes from the past, testifies to the historical complexity of the problem. Moreover, Macune's leveling rhetoric seems at odds with the essentially conservative social goals of the broader movement, goals that expressed simply a desire to equalize competition for wealth and power within a system of individual rewards for individual effort. It is important, then, to note Macune's qualification of his egalitarian message.

In lesson 2, in lesson 3, and again in lesson 19, Macune outlined the dimensions of John D. Rockefeller's fortune and illustrated the polarity in wealth distribution through a series of blackboard exercises. In asking how millionaires made their fortunes, in lesson 20, Macune and his students brought to the surface many of the assumptions the agrarian reformers held about the nature of work, labor, and economic rewards. "If a man made three dollars each hour, how long would it take him to earn a million dollars?" was one question designed not so much to test multiplication skills as to show that manual labor, even at the princely rate of three dollars per hour, could never earn a man a million dollars.

This kind of figuring made Rockefeller's estimated two hundred million-dollar estate and nineteen million-dollar per-year income stag-

46. *National Economist,* February 27, 1892: lesson 6.

gering and suspect. Another exercise derived a wealth distribution table, through which farmers discovered that between one and two thousand individuals owned more than 50 percent of the national wealth in 1890.[47] Is it right, Macune asked, that "one man have as much as ninety-nine other men?" "How much" of his fortune had Rockefeller "produced or earned by hard labor," and "what were the other ninety-nine men doing while he was getting his property?" Are "millionaires so much richer because they have worked so much harder than laborers or farmers?" "As society is constituted," Macune asked his classes throughout the South, "does the man who works the most get the most?"

These were questions that struck a chord with the farmers. They worked by the sweat of their brow and the strength of their hands, yet they barely managed to keep a roof over their heads and clothes on their backs. Was it possible that Rockefeller worked proportionally harder and with greater effect than the farmers to whom Macune addressed the exercise? Was it just or fair that men like Rockefeller, who only organized the labor of others, should earn so much more than they did and enjoy luxury while the farmers suffered in poverty?

The answer rested on the moral value assigned to labor, to manual labor, and on a neo-Calvinist notion that economic returns accurately represented the quality and quantity of one's effort. For farmers, work retained its moral value despite its declining monetary return. The dissonance between the intense moral and religious importance of labor and the apparent undervaluing of work in monetary terms created a sense of injustice about the nature of the American economy, reflected in the lesson on Rockefeller. In terms of physical production, actual labor remained the hub of economic activity. The reformers were correct to argue that workers and farmers held the American economy in their hands, but that was no longer the point.

The increasing dominance of wage labor and the rise of specialized marketing and distribution networks in the nineteenth century shattered the nexus between the activity of production and the realization of economic returns. But even though the economy was changing, and had for the most part eliminated the small independent producer except on the farm, the moral connection between labor and economic returns remained and was reinforced by the Exercises. The moral value of work remained a potent force in shaping the normative template of Alliance social reform.

These strands within the lessons bind together in a certain economic and political consistency. By tracing European history from its tribal

47. *National Economist*, January 30, 1892: lesson 3.

roots, Macune attempted to show that struggles between the masses of common people and privileged classes, whether chieftains, kings, aristocrats, or merchant-princes of parliaments, have animated most of the world's history. Moreover, through his histories of the French Revolution, the Chartist movement, and the struggle over reform in the English Parliament, he showed that reform had never come from the elite but instead had always emanated from impulses, often violent or threatening of violence, from the common people. "Have we any reason," he asked, "to expect those who have made great fortunes under existing conditions to give their help to change those conditions?"[48] In 1892, as in 1789 or 1350, the responsibility and the right and the power to reform society lay in the hands of the people, and it was their duty to effect such reform.

The Exercises, then, in Macune's hands became powerful tools for political education. They taught basic literacy and numeracy and created environments in which farmers and their families were encouraged to fashion logical and developed arguments on issues of the day. The lessons expounded a view of the American political scene that emphasized the conflict between classes. They created and disseminated a historical view of that conflict that showed "producers" to be morally superior to, if politically and economically weaker than, their merchant and capitalist enemies. Finally, the Exercises urged members of the Alliance to take direct political action to reorient the distribution of political power and economic rewards from the privileged class to the common man and woman.

7

It is no surprise that the *Economist* Educational Exercises embodied a set of values very different from those reflected in the school curriculum in the South at the same time. In its view of history, for example, we have seen that the traditional morality play, in which the history of civilization is one of unending progress, was reversed in the Exercises to describe not progress but progressive loss of economic and political liberties to privileged classes. The Alliance curriculum was based on the premise that American society was divided into two great classes, those who produced wealth with their labor, and those who extracted wealth from the labor of others. The lessons showed these classes in struggle over the control of government, law, and even culture, not just in the United States but in Europe and Asia as well.

48. *National Economist,* May 14, 1892: lesson 14.

In his survey of class struggle in Europe, Macune made every effort to identify the cause of working people as the farmers' own, to build upon their identity as workers and their opposition to organized capital. In the Alliance history, Irish peasants, Russian serfs, French *sanscullotes,* and American farmers shared in a struggle for liberty from the oppression of social and economic elites.

"Any system of government which tends to concentrate power of any kind in the hands of certain individuals tends to the formation of an aristocracy," Alliance students wrote as part of their July 4 sentence class.[49] The responsibility for preserving democracy lay in the hands of the men and women who gathered to participate in the Alliance lessons. Macune's text showed them the danger of relying on the state for relief of their grievances and preservation of their rights: "In studying English history do we find that Parliament ever enacted laws for the people which were not first demanded by the people?"[50] So, the lesson concluded, "our country will be what we, the people, make it; the day of hero worship is past; we are all heroes, or ought to be."[51] In practical terms, this meant increasing the political power and involvement of working people. It meant widening the electoral arena, where, by direct vote of the people, the course of the nation might be charted.

Direct election of representatives and increased use of the referendum would place the mechanisms of the state in the hands of the majority. State ownership of the means of transportation and communication, and direct government control over the distribution of circulating currency were aimed at widening the political control by voters over American economic and social life. The Alliance argument for the deepening of democratic action ran counter to trends in partisan politics which moved decision making up and, in the party hierarchy, away from popular control. A rationalist faith in the ability of working men to see their collective interest as such, and to vote accordingly, convinced Alliance leaders of the practical efficacy of their democratic ideas. A moralistic faith in the sanctity of their positions and their actions, in both politics and economics, convinced them of the righteousness of their aims. But a transformation of the social order, even one so rooted in righteous ways, depended first on the transformation of individuals, particularly on the legitimation of social activism in a population still tied by old bonds of deference. In

49. *National Economist,* June 25, 1892: lesson 20.
50. *National Economist,* February 27, 1892: lesson 6.
51. *National Economist,* June 25, 1892: lesson 20.

this transformation of the individual Alliance member, education played the central role, a tactical role this time, creating the "army" that Macune so desired.

Commenting on Sparta, Macune wrote that "a society that would be stable and harmonious . . . can not expect to accomplish this great good by merely establishing rules of action." It must, he went on, "carefully prepare and fit each individual for the responsibilities, duties, and requirements that will rest upon him as a member of society." The mechanism for this preparation "consists of education . . . men are but creatures of education and the history of Sparta proves that it is not impossible to instill a high regard for the common welfare . . . the low instincts of selfishness being crushed."[52] Macune's lessons, and their imitators, sought to design an education that would prepare farmers and others for duties and responsibilities in an America governed, in its particulars, by the vote of the people. The Alliance sought as well to create that America through collective action. While we may think of these as two separate processes, in the experience of the Alliance members they were integrated; education reinforced action and action demanded more education.

In structure, the formal educational program reinforced the message of the curriculum. The process of farmers' self-education placed a premium on cooperation and collective learning. Even the Educational Exercises, which were prepackaged, emphasized discussion and questions rather than rote learning. In many ways the pedagogy of Alliance skill training was as important as the content in creating the new citizenship demanded within the movement's ideology.

First, the curriculum drew from contemporary social conditions and current events for its substance. Macune and his colleagues fashioned a curriculum out of mortgages, terms of lease and sale, the economics of cotton marketing, and the *Congressional Record.* It was by understanding these features of contemporary life that suballiance participants gained some measure of intellectual power over their circumstance. At one level, the choice of a grounded curriculum indicates a strategic choice by the leadership to use education as a tool for social reform. The intellectual distance between an analysis of the economics of crop liens and support for regulation of interest rates was short, shorter than would have been the case if the Alliance leaders had, for example, begun their economics lessons with a discussion of how supply and demand function to regulate price. At another level, the choice to embed skill training in discussions of current prob-

52. *National Economist,* August 17, 1889.

lems demonstrates a great deal of sensitivity on the part of Alliance leaders to meeting the intellectual needs of their members with the raw materials that would best excite the members' need to learn.[53] What members wanted, after all, was a means to better control their fate in an environment that had become increasingly alien. But at a deeper level the Alliance's concern with the problems of everyday life suggests an epistemology that measured "useful knowledge" by its applicability to life as it was lived by farmers. Consequently, Alliance leaders often discounted theory without connection to events and criticized education based on theoretical issues alone.[54]

Second, Alliance pedagogy attended directly to adult learners and only indirectly to children. Macune's and Morgan's goal was for sub-alliances to become communities of adult learners organized by norms of cooperation and mutuality. It was one of the first systematic attempts in American history to provide supplemental education and literacy training to adults, and it is not coincidental that this effort was associated with an oppositional social movement. Pedagogic preference as well as political strategy made adult education the appropriate mode for building intellectual skills that could be used politically.

In this latter sense, adult education was a necessary component of the reform program. Traditional child-focused schooling has long been used as a means to defer social change into the next generation and school reform has often served as a compromise between those who want immediate social change and those who want no change at all. The Alliance leadership understood the danger of deferring their particular dream, and they could not wait. Knowledge of the sources of oppression and its persistence would do no good in the hands of children until they became old enough to take the kind of political action the Alliance deemed necessary. But knowledge in the hands of adults who possessed some social and political power and the ability to take swift action: this was indeed revolutionary.

Adult education served pedagogic goals as well as strategic needs. Leaders of the reform movement understood that education meant more than schooling. Increasing poverty and increasing economic and

53. This pedagogy has been rediscovered and repackaged in our own era in several settings. Its most detailed theoretical exposition comes from Paolo Freire in his book *Pedagogy of the Oppressed* (New York: Seabury Press, 1968). Freirian techniques have been central to the educational tactics of the literacy campaigns of the last twenty years. The best example is the Cuban, whose story is told by Jonathan Kozol in *Children of the Revolution* (New York: Dell, 1978).

54. This was an important part of the Alliance critique of the public school, a topic that is the subject of the next chapter.

political oppression were forces that educated southern farmers. The "school of experience" not only set an agenda for Alliance education, it prepared farmers to accept eagerly a curriculum that centered on understanding experience. The speeches at camp meetings, the arithmetic exercises on distribution of wealth: these had immediate and deep meaning to the farmers because of their collective history and shared experiences. The same curriculum, prepared and served to children, would have less meaning and correspondingly less impact on their future lives and actions. Some Alliance educators went further, arguing that all the schooling that came during youth merely prepared an individual for a more real adult learning. "The schoolhouse for the young," wrote one local editor, "is a mere gymnasium where the muscles of the mind are hardened." It was in "manhood" (sic) when finally the mind became "competent to grapple with the many problems of the day."[55]

Despite this overwhelming attention to adult learning, the political curriculum did participate in the training of youth. The spirit of mutuality and cooperation that reigned in the meetings of the suballiances extended across age boundaries. In creative ways, Macune urged the integration of children into the adult learning experience as teachers and tutors. Macune suggested, in the introduction to his Educational Exercises, that schoolchildren should help their elders with the math and spelling in the blackboard exercises. Children were more familiar, he argued, with the mechanical operations than were adults twenty years out of school.

Children participated in adult education in other ways, learning as well as teaching. Certainly some of the political discussions in the lodge stuck in the minds of the children present. What is more important, though, is what they learned about education itself. They were observers at the suballiance lodges. They sang, helped put on skits, and read aloud questions which were then debated by their elders. In this way, children and parents came to understand that education could indeed be a family affair that extended beyond the years and the curriculum of formal schooling.

Finally, while the Alliance tried to teach literacy and open the world of print to its members, leaders understood that not every farmer would learn to read, nor having learned, would spend the time struggling through his or her county Alliance paper. The curriculum of the suballiance meetings was carried out in such a way as to minimize the handicap of illiteracy. Oral presentations and debates punctuated readings and writing exercises. Macune, as editor of the Exercises,

55. *Farmers' Advocate,* July 1, 1891; and Woodward, *Origins,* 191.

refined the techniques of integrating oral and written work as the lessons progressed. In the final published session he added a section to the lesson plan outline called "Sentence Class."[56]

Sentence Class symbolized, in many ways, the complexity of Macune's formal curriculum. It stressed skill building within a language and a logic of reform. It encouraged cooperative discourse and debate. Finally, it reaffirmed the value of the very educational and social activities in which the farmers were engaged. In his introduction to "Sentence Class," Macune suggested that the instructor of the lesson pick "a class of seven children." The instructor read seven sentences aloud, one to each child. In the self-conscious script of the grammar school, children wrote their sentences on the board, and in turn, read them aloud. The adult members of the suballiance discussed the ideas captured in each sentence while the children listened.

The sentences suggested by Macune were, whether he intended them to be or not, a fitting finale to the *Economist* Educational Exercises. "Education," began the first one, "is the best inheritance which a nation can bestow upon its people; a nation which would retain its liberty must be worthy of liberty." It was the legacy of the Alliance campaign to bestow on those members witnessing its years of success a present and future hope that education could be used to create "heroes of the people" and to foster a reaffirmation that "in the people," as the second model sentence read, "there is a firmer foundation for justice than the strongest armor and the most powder and bullets."

These two sentences present a quandary. On the one hand, the Alliance supported education in all its forms. This included both its own educational campaign and the public school. In its constitution, its demands on legislators, and its actions, the movement consistently urged that a better and more effective system of public education be created and supported.[57] Through this work and their own, the Alliance attempted to bestow on generations to follow a legacy of education for active citizenship. On the other hand, though, Alliance leaders criticized public schools as falling into the same "plutocratic" hands as the other elements of civic government. They railed against monopolies in textbook publishing and of partisan control of educational governance. In facing this quandary, the Alliance faced in microcosm the issues and problems it addressed on a larger scale in politics and economics, with the same incumbent contradictions.

56. *National Economist,* June 25, 1892.

57. As early as the Clebourne meeting, the Texas Alliance demanded support for public education. See Dunning, *Farmers' Alliance History,* 76, and chap. 5 of this volume.

5   The Alliance and the Public School

We are unqualifiedly in favor of the education of the masses by a well-regulated system of free schools.
— Resolution passed by the Agricultural Wheel at its 1887 Convention.

Ignorance is today our curse and education must be our watchword . . . our country schools are the only hope for the farmer and the laborer.
— from a Resolution passed by the Shelby County, Tennessee, Alliance, April 1889.

1

"To arrange and display the needs of the South in their order as to importance, we believe the Alliance has well stated them: first we need education," wrote Congressman L. F. Livingston, President of the Georgia Farmers' Alliance in a contribution to Nelson Dunning's *Farmers' Alliance History*.[1] In 1889, the same piece, "The Needs of the South," was run, with an approving introduction, in the *Annual Report of the United States Commissioner of Education*.[2] For the Commissioner, N. H. R. Dawson, what Livingston was obviously talking about was schools. He was willing and eager to use Alliance sentiment in favor of education to spur efforts to improve the quality and quantity of public schooling in the South.

The Alliance leadership, too, seemed willing to be part of a movement to improve schooling. Livingston went on to argue that "we need, in the South, a thorough, practical, and economical system of common school education."[3] Macune, in the pages of the *National Economist* wrote that "what we ought to do is build up our public school system, build it up by providing a more liberal school fund." Milton Park echoed the sentiments of the national leadership. "Increase the number of schoolhouses," he urged, and by so doing, the Alliance would "increase the power of the people by educating them

1. L. F. Livingston, "The Needs of the South," in Dunning, *Farmers' Alliance History,* 284–287.
2. *U.S. Commissioner of Education Report,* 1889, xi–xvi.
3. Livingston, "The Needs of the South," 285.

"The Little Red School House," cartoon from *Southern Mercury,* November 26, 1891

to independent thought."[4] The People's party, when it emerged from the Alliance in 1892, supported public education. State and national Populist platforms carried planks demanding "an effective system of free public schools for six months in the year."[5] For these national spokesmen, public schooling fit into their program of education and reform in several ways.

First, public schooling in the South lagged far behind schooling in other regions, in enrollment per capita, expenditures per capita, and length of school term. This educational underdevelopment contributed to high rates of illiteracy, which made the kind of active citizenship the Alliance advocated difficult, to say the least. In an age before the adoption of the Australian ballot system (in which a ballot contains the names of all candidates) men merely collected a party ticket from a campaign worker, signed it, and stuffed it into a ballot box. Under this system illiteracy was no impediment to casting ballots, but it was a sure deterrent to an understanding of whose names were on the ticket.

4. *Southern Mercury,* August 9, 1894.
5. *Southern Mercury,* August 9, 1894.

From the point of view of the Alliance leadership, illiteracy was a form of de facto disenfranchisement. Worse, it put the votes of a large number of citizens at the mercy of last-minute party maneuvering. In addition, literacy tests became, in the late 1880s and early 1890s, a *de jure* means of denying voting rights to blacks and some poor whites in the South. "To take away a man's citizenship because he can not read and write," wrote one Louisiana man, "would be most unjust without first providing the means for such education."[6] What the Alliance attempted, through its support of public schooling, was to erase the problem of illiteracy and of manipulated voters, seeking a fair count and honest elections through universal literacy.

Second, public schools were and are institutions of the state. As with other elements of the polity, Alliance leaders demanded that the public school be directed "to promote the welfare of the people, the great struggling, toiling masses."[7] As in the larger political arena, the Alliance sought control over schools in part through the power of the ballot. To this end, every Alliance endorsement and every People's party ticket, even at the county level, targeted candidates for school boards and school superintendencies.

These direct electoral attempts to take control of the public schools were, however, halfhearted. The faith of the Alliance leadership in the ultimate importance of education could not compete for organizational resources with their immediate political aims in the direction of capturing legislative and executive control of government. Expenditures on these campaigns ran very low. Candidates for school posts languished in anonymity at the hands of reform editors. Park, a strong advocate of public schooling and a careful editor, misspelled the name of the People's party candidate for the Texas superintendency twice, before he finally gave the correct name. Even then, the retractions and corrections were the only bits of press E. P. Alsbury got from the *Mercury* in his losing campaign in 1894.[8]

Even more important than the organizational imperatives, though, in explaining this neglect of local school politics, was the understanding among national Alliance leaders that the public school was only one component of what comprised education in the rural South. In the public school children learned the rudiments of literacy and numeracy; their minds were "hardened" in these mental "gymnasiums." In

6. *National Economist,* September 7, 1889.
7. Donnelly pictured the best government as one that "pledges itself to promote the welfare of the people, the great struggling, toiling masses." *Southern Mercury,* January 28, 1889.
8. *Southern Mercury,* August 2, 1894.

the family, children and young adults learned the values and ideas that focused their parents' understanding of the world. There children began to use the skills they learned in school in the context of their lives. Finally, the third piece of this configuration was the "enrollment" of whole families in the great school that was the Farmers' Alliance. They became members and learned that there were names and reasons for the miseries they shared, and they learned how to take action in their own interest. When they thought about education for their farmer members, the leaders of the movement thought about this configuration as an integrated and interdependent unit.[9] The public school fit within the educational configuration as an important foundation through which future citizens could develop intellectual skills that would later be focused and directed within the educational program of the Alliance.

Thus the Alliance leadership supported public schooling on strategic, ideological, and pedagogical grounds, agreeing in general, if not in specifics, with the bullish school-building sentiment current in every region at the turn of the century. Over the period, public schooling was one topic upon which nearly every reform group could agree. Even in the South, where traditional opposition to public schooling continued into the 1890s, Alliance leaders could agree with industrialists and labor organizations that more schooling at state expense served the public interest. But this general consensus masked important particular conflicts over the nature and purpose of state supported schooling.

While national spokesmen and spokeswomen for the Alliance supported public education as an introduction to useful intellectual skills, they struggled politically and rhetorically against trends in educational governance that they believed would hinder the use of public schooling as a constructive element in their educational configuration. In fact, some feared that changes in schooling were fast making public schooling anathema to the reform cause.

These changes were of two kinds. First, the Alliance viewed with concern the growing power of private groups in the governance of education in the South. These groups, including the "school book trust" and various philanthropic organizations, were, through economic and bureaucratic means, wresting control of schools from the hands of elected or appointed school officials. Second, even worse was the fact that as they gained influence in the schools, these groups

9. Evan Jones in *Southern Mercury,* August 20, 1891; A. Severance in *National Economist,* September 7, 1889.

introduced a curriculum whose content contradicted the reform message of the Alliance educational program. Because of these changes, the use by the Alliance of public schooling as one leg of its educational triad became problematic. If the schools were teaching ideas antithetical to reform, then should the Alliance support public schools at all?

In some communities, the answer was no. According to the Choctaw, Alabama, *Advocate,* the county Alliance there established its own high school in 1891. In the same year, an Alliance cooperative school opened in Echo, Alabama, enrolling over one hundred students. The Echo Cooperative School employed two male teachers and held classes for seven months during 1891, nearly double the average length of school terms in the South.[10] Unfortunately, we do not know the fate of either of these two schools, and examples of this kind of direct intervention into schooling were few. The creation of alternative schools for the children of members was not an Alliance priority. In addition to the philosophical and ideological impediments to devoting organizational resources to the education of children, the Alliance, particularly local groups, could ill afford, financially, to create a system of Alliance schools. Rather than create a parallel system of schools, the Alliance launched a rhetorical attack on the educational "trusts" and mounted a campaign to debunk and discredit the standard curriculum.

National spokespeople incorporated schooling issues as part of their campaign to illustrate how combinations of the wealthy and powerful always result in the immiserization of the poor. In other words, the Alliance leadership fashioned its role in school politics in the same mold used for shaping its role in politics writ large: the leadership took upon itself the task of illuminating the underlying structures of power and authority which determined the course of so many outwardly democratic institutions. In this way the leadership carved for itself a niche as educators about education.

In 1890, the National Alliance accused a group of publishers including Harper Brothers, D. Appleton and Company, and A. S. Barnes and Company, of conspiring to consolidate contracts, control competition, and raise prices in the schoolbook market through the creation of a holding company, the American Book Company. This combination not only raised prices to schools and to parents, but also propounded, in the pages of its texts, the virtues of American indus-

10. *Choctaw Advocate,* September 2, 1891, quoted in William Rogers, *The One-Gallused Rebellion: Agrarianism in Alabama* (Baton Rouge: Louisiana State University Press, 1970), 140.

trial progress, particularly the virtues of the American industrial giants, the very enemies of the Alliance.[11] More, the Alliance found that the "trust" had insured its insidious effect on the public schools through an intricate and secret system of kickbacks to local and state superintendents. "The farmer will find this class of educators in hearty sympathy with this combine, and to attack one is to fight both," wrote Macune. Unfortunately, the Alliance did not rally to Macune's cry for action, perhaps not yet convinced that schools were a legitimate target for their political efforts.

National opposition to the increasing influence of philanthropic organizations on southern education was even more lukewarm. Occasionally Alliance papers denigrated the directors of the Peabody or Slater Fund through statements such as "that old Fraud R. B. Hayes is a member." More often, though, they criticized philanthropy itself: "Charity," Macune argued, "covers up no sins when the gift has been stolen from the poor."[12] Aside from these grumblings, the Alliance took no action against the philanthropic organizations which had begun to spread their money and influence throughout the South. One reason the leadership did not make more of the Peabody and Slater charity was that these organizations, officiated over by the ubiquitous Jabez Lamar Monroe Curry, ministered exclusively to black schools during the 1880s and until the late 1890s. While the Alliance leadership could and did disapprove of philanthropy and its effects, as long as the elite charities concerned themselves with black education they remained secondary targets, even within the realm of education.

2

The primary targets of Alliance opposition within public schools were curricular programs that the leaders felt eroded their own reform ideology. Their opposition in two particular areas, history and agricultural education, marked a struggle between the Alliance leadership and the educational leaders in the New South over what kind of knowledge was useful to the farmers of the region and what kind of knowledge was legitimate within dominant discourse.

It was not useful, in Macune's eyes, for the sons and daughters of southern farmers to study traditional narrative forms of history. He opposed history as it was written, arguing that the story of kings, queens, presidents, and wars obscured the historical pattern of oppression that dominated the real history of the laboring classes.

11. *National Economist,* July 19, 1890; *Southern Mercury,* October 1, 1894.
12. *National Economist,* July 19, 1890.

Macune intended to write just such a history, and his revision of traditional history turned even Greek history on its head. As an introduction to his series on Greece, Macune wrote that "the records are so encumbered by laudations of individual heroes that the condition of the people who composed the nations are overlooked and the evils entailed upon them are forgotten."[13] Historical knowledge of the common man and woman was important within the context of Alliance education for several reasons.

First, as Macune himself argued, it was through a sense of the great struggles that working people have always waged against privileged classes that southern farmers discovered a ready explanation for their own problems. The parallels between their own circumstances and those of agrarians in Greece, in France, and in Ireland, during earlier centuries, located the source of the farmers' poverty and eroding influence in increasing centralization of power by the wealthy.

Second, history offered a liberating perspective on current events. Action on behalf of social change was inhibited in the South by a set of myths and customs of national and regional origin that kept southern farmers tied to social and economic elites. White supremacy, party loyalty, and deference muffled cries of protest almost before they emerged.[14] Telling the story of oppression in historical terms stripped it of its contemporary cloaking. Race antagonism was not apparent in the struggles between Athens and Sparta, sectional hatred did not intervene in the English enclosure movement, and party loyalty did not have any determining influence on the early events of July 1789. Instead, what emerged from the Alliance "history" of the world was a series of illustrations of raw, unmitigated oppression and empassioned direct response that were intended as parallels to the farmers' current situation.

Third, this history of oppression presented a range of strategic options to the Alliance membership based on the actions taken by oppressed classes in past time. The range of responses and their consequences were played out in the pages of the *National Economist*. Russian serfs did almost nothing in response to the increasing restrictions placed on their movements and rights by the Zemstvo. As a result they were the most oppressed group in contemporary Europe, according to Macune's history. The French peasantry had achieved short-term freedoms through the most violent revolution to that point in history.

13. *Louisiana Populist,* March 26, 1897, *Tarboro Southerner,* June 4, 1891.
14. *National Economist,* March 30, 1889 and see chap. 2 of this volume.

The English peasants were only slowly achieved reform through peaceful and semidemocratic means. Through these historical experiments farmers were led to believe that the surest means of securing reform, although not the quickest, was first through education and then, once education had instilled in the masses a sense of their own interests differentiated from those of other classes, through political mobilization.

Finally, as a history of working people, Macune's pieces gave farmers and others a sense of their own agency. Not only kings and presidents but peasants and workers also made history. The "plain people" created the French Revolution; they forced parliamentary reform in England; and they defeated Athenian tyranny in the city-states of Greece. There was no reason, in the light of two thousand years of this history, that the farmers could not fashion their own future in similar ways.

Thus, it was Macune's intention, as the chief educator for the Alliance at a national level, that farmers learn from history the persistence of social divisions based on the unequal distribution of wealth and power and identify their suffering not only with the suffering of their contemporaries, but with the suffering of agrarians and workers in other nations and in other periods. This continuity, and the very weight of historical evidence, in turn, sharpened the issues at hand and pricked the membership of the Alliance to action in the cause of reform. The *National Economist* became the nation's first revisionist historical text, upending the traditional views and values put forth in school histories.

Those whiggish tracts, in contrast, portrayed American history as a semisecular "pilgrim's progress." The history of the nation was one of successive crises met with successive victories, resulting from the effort of American leaders and the smiling assistance of God.[15] In the best-selling texts of the late nineteenth century, as in the dominant culture, material prosperity and moral virtue coincided. In summarizing these texts, Ruth Elson shows that "the unique prosperity of America [was] an indication that it [was] uniquely virtuous and the chosen of God."[16] Politically, the texts portrayed American history as the progressive march of freedom, for the colonists, for immigrants,

15. See chap. 1 of this volume. Also see Ruth Elson, *Guardians of Tradition* (Lincoln: University of Nebraska Press, 1964) for the best analysis to date of nineteenth-century texts.

16. Elson, *Guardians,* 259.

for slaves, and for workers. Wrote G. P. Quackenbos in his *Illustrated School History of the United States,* "in no country is labor so highly respected as in the U.S.; and in none, therefore are the working classes so happy."[17]

The normative and descriptive content of these texts contradicted the drive of Macune's history. The very notion of progress in nineteenth-century texts, indexed by some ill-defined measure of aggregate prosperity, differed dramatically from the Alliance view that real progress must be accompanied by not only greater wealth but by better distribution of the products of labor. More, the dominant view that progress was continual implied that it might well be inevitable. If progress were the natural course of the nation's history, then struggle confounded that course. The normative implications were clear: working men and women, far from struggling against what they perceived as injustice, needed instead to march in step with the dominant drum beat of progress.

The appropriate role for the masses was passivity. This message was reinforced by the texts' "laudations of individual heroes," which, Macune warned, robbed common people of the history of their influence on events and served to make them distrust their power to influence affairs in the present or future. If heroes, presidents, generals, and industrialists made history, as they were shown to do in the nineteenth-century texts, then nonheroes did not. To the elite was bestowed the power to make history. To the masses was assigned the role of reacting to history, to following in the path broken by the great men and women of the age.

Still, the texts held out the possibility of heroship to individuals: "the humblest citizen may raise himself to the proudest position in the Republic."[18] But changes in individual status did nothing to alter the balance of historical power between heroes and the masses. New heroes emerged from the masses and worked their magic upon history, but, as heroes, they ceased to be part of the mass of common folk. No matter what the magnitude of this mobility, inside the covers of nineteenth-century schoolbooks the exclusive power to make history rested in the hands of the members of the elite. The Alliance history, in contrast, argued that it was the proper order of things for the common people to rule, not great men and women.

Their historical struggle to change American society was reflected quite clearly in their historiographical struggle. For Macune, one

17. G. P. Quackenbos, *Illustrated School History of the United States and Adjacent Parts of America* (New York: D. Appleton, 1872), 512.
18. Quackenbos, *Illustrated School History,* 512.

struggle advanced the other. If the common people were to change the course of the nation, then they first had to change the course of its written history, to find themselves in the past, not as a passive mass to be led about by their betters, but as a power in their own right, as actors in history. Only by discovering their power in the past would farmers and their allies be able to exercise power in the future. And by exercising power, by uniting in the Alliance, farmers came to understand history and the ways in which history reinforced the dominance of privileged groups. Macune resisted this curricular dominance of elite ideas throughout the period of his greatest educational influence. However clear his own opposition, though, he failed to convey to his readers the importance of critical evaluation of schooling.

A similar divergence between the national and local position on curriculum occurred around the inclusion of vocational agriculture in the South's high schools and colleges. Although supportive of the idea of agricultural education, Alliance leaders worried about the potentially limiting scope of vocational curricula particularly in the realm of politics and political education.

3

Professional educators and social elites believed that the classical curriculum wasted the time of children whose lot in life was to farm the fields of the South and West. Literacy and numeracy remained important within the school curriculum, dominating the common school. But in higher training, including both at the high school level and the land grant colleges, the skills and techniques of agriculture came to play a larger and larger role after 1880.[19]

By 1880, the land grant colleges that Congress had authorized in 1865 had become well established, even if their purpose remained ill-defined. Their charge to instruct students in the mechanical and agricultural sciences had been interpreted loosely. In most of the southern states, the A & M colleges were ruled by the faculty of the classical departments, with a farm attached to the campus on which students worked during a good part of the day.[20] In 1887, Congress appropriated funds for the establishment of agricultural experiment stations in the South; most were attached to these land grant institutions. At the stations, experiments were carried out with the goal of increasing

19. Beginning in 1886, the U.S. Commissioner of Education Reports contained segments on agricultural and industrial education. See also Bond, *Negro Education in Alabama,* chap. 16.

20. Dabney, *University Education in the South* 2:chap. 12.

per acre yield of various cash crops, including wheat, corn, and of course cotton.

The idea of agricultural education got a boost as well from the widely lauded industrial schools established for blacks. These schools, like Washington's Tuskegee and Armstrong's Hampton, became in the 1890s the paradigm for useful education for all members of the laboring classes. In industrial schools, blacks learned skills and habits commensurate with adult roles as hired labor or independent artisan. In other words, they were educated into, not out of, the lives assigned them through the rigid racial structuring of southern social life. Similarly, whites in agricultural programs within the public school learned modern methods of cultivation and fertilization. They learned how to make more from their lot (literally and figuratively). What Charles Dabney concluded about sentiment toward black education applied with similar force to whites by 1890. The question was not "whether he should be educated, but how he should be trained."[21] The rise of vocationalism, of training, in southern education encouraged conservatives as well as liberal southerners to support the spread of universal public education.

The leaders of the Alliance saw the introduction of agricultural education in both the schools and the colleges as a good thing.[22] At Clebourne, the Alliance approved a resolution demanding "for the masses a well-regulated system of industrial and agricultural education.[23] Similarly, the constitution of the Agricultural Wheel stated that one object of the order was to work toward the "improvement of its members in the theory and practice of agriculture, and the dissemination of knowledge relating to rural and farming affairs."[24] In its own educational campaign, the Alliance participated in the movement toward more thorough education in the science of agriculture. Most Alliance papers ran columns on farming and farming technique. The Dunning volume, *The Farmers' Alliance History and Agricultural Digest*, which was mailed free to every subscriber to the *Economist*, contained articles on "How to Plan a Barn," and "What is Under-Draining."[25] The *Digest* also included sections on fertilizers and soil

21. Dabney, *University Education in the South*, 52.

22. Theodore Saluotos, *Farmer Movements in the South*. University of California Publications in History no. 64 (Berkeley: University of California Press, 1960), 40–41, 86.

23. Dunning, *Farmers' Alliance History*, 76.

24. Dunning, *Farmers' Alliance History*, 209; also S. O. Lee in *National Economist*, March 14, 1891, and Morgan, *History of the Wheel*, 464.

25. Dunning, *Farmers' Alliance History*, 477–497, 526–550; *Farmers' Advocate*, 1891 issues; *National Economist*, beginning July 13, 1889, in its "Applied Science" series.

chemistry Suballiance meetings were arenas in which farming technique was discussed and new methods were disseminated.

In its support for better agricultural education the Alliance seems at, one level, to have been in sympathy with the school reformers and earlier agrarian groups, particularly the Grange.[26] But the Alliance position regarding agricultural education differed from that of either the New South reformers or the Patrons of Husbandry. Alliance opposition to certain aspects of the agricultural education movement illustrates, again, the struggle underway over what, exactly, was useful knowledge.

The major complaint of Alliance spokesmen regarding agricultural education as practiced in the schools of the South was that it was technical in nature, to the exclusion of all other epistemological forms. Macune responded to the popularity of agricultural education with typical insight, arguing that

> the purely technical effort of improving our methods of farming, by which we may possibly increase the amount of products we make in return for a given amount of labor and expense, although it be praiseworthy, is not a force or remedy [to the conditions faced by farmers].

"The influences that tend to depress agriculture and render the pursuit of that occupation unprofitable," he continued, "have rapidly gained the ascendancy over and neutralized the beneficient effects that should have followed the introduction of wise methods and new machines."[27] The old methods and the old logic—produce more to make more— had "proved ineffectual on every occasion," and the Alliance leadership found that political knowledge leading to political power held out hope where technical knowledge and technical prowess did not. The hope of the Alliance lay in changing the political economy in such a way that the laws and the courts worked in the farmers' favor, not in perfecting their techniques within a political economy structured against their interests.

L. L. Polk, speaking before an audience of the faithful in convention on a winter afternoon in Ocala, Florida, summarized the division he saw between technical and political means to achieve freedom from

26. On Grange education, see James Ferguson, "The Grange and Farmer Education in Mississippi," *Journal of Southern History* 8 (October 1942): 496–512. Also Saluotos, *Farmer Movements,* 30–45; Rogers, *The One-Gallused Rebellion,* 70–71; and Solon Buck, *The Granger Movement: A Study of Agricultural Organization, 1870–1880* (Cambridge: Harvard University Press, 1913), 290–293.

27. *National Economist,* December 14, 1889.

the grasp of poverty. "This investigation (into the causes of agricultural depression) has led to the general, if not universal conviction that it is due to discriminating and unjust national legislation. Were it due," he proclaimed, "to false or imperfect systems of farm economy, we would apply the remedy by improving systems of our own devising."[28] For Polk, technical training and technical knowledge, when substituted for political training and political knowledge, masked the true nature of the farmers' plight and militated against the organization and mobilization of any kind of protest. Agricultural and industrial education were simply parts of the "miseducation" of southern farmers. Improved technical efficiency, by itself, promised to make farmers more productive slaves to the lien system, the usury, and the declining prices that marked southern agriculture during the period. Political knowledge, not technical knowledge, offered hope.

Some of the conspiratorially minded leaders of the movement saw an even more pernicious meaning in the rise of technical agricultural education. A second complaint about the increasing focus on technical/vocational education was that it would actually deprive farmers and workers of access to political knowledge and so limit their legitimacy in future discussions of politics. By limiting the education of the masses, black and white, to technical training, elites would preserve political knowledge, and so political power, for themselves. The introduction of agricultural training in the purely technical aspects of farming was, for these members of the Alliance leadership, a first step toward the creation of a hierarchy of kinds of knowledge and toward the segregation of access to different kinds of learning on the basis of social class.

Thus Milton Park noted in the *Mercury* that it was the organized politicians and the professional educators who "advise the farmers to raise more corn, cotton, and grain." "We [the Alliance] say, study political economy and the social conditions more, work less for the plutocrats and bosses, and you will come out ahead."[29] The reform program of the Alliance depended on the movement's ability to appropriate the powerful language of politics for its own use. By limiting the curriculum for farmers' children more and more to technical, vocational areas, schools made it more difficult for the next genera-

28. Polk's presidential address reprinted in *National Economist,* December 13, 1890. For a similar discussion in a different setting, see Richard Johnson's "Really Useful Knowledge: Radical Education and Working Class Culture, 1790–1848," in J. Clarke, et al., eds., *Working Class Culture* (New York: St. Martin's Press, 1979).

29. *Southern Mercury,* October 15, 1891; also *Southern Mercury,* August 6, 1891; Morgan, *History of the Wheel and Alliance,* 205.

tion of farmers to grasp political ideas, to form political opinions on their own, and to take independent political action—in short, to support any ideology different from that of the dominant classes.

If the farmers became technicians, and intellectually came to accept that the solutions to their problems rested with improved technique, then the battle for reform would be lost. The Alliance based its reform impulse on a critique of the American political economy. This critique relied on the farmers' ability to distill from their own particular experiences perspectives on the state of the nation. It required that farmers measure the state of the nation against a normative template fashioned of economic moralism and equality of opportunity. In short, reform depended upon the ability of the farmers to criticize the system of American politics and economics. Park, for example, worried that, as technicians, farmers would be trained to take that system for granted and to puzzle over how to maximize their returns, social as well as economic, within it. It was a prospect that animated Alliance opposition to exclusively technical training in the schools, colleges, and experiment stations in the South.[30]

4

When the Alliance leadership looked at the economy, they worried about and worked against the concentration of wealth in the hands of a few industrialists and financiers, and the corresponding concentration of political power in the same hands. When they looked at what

30. The leaders of the Alliance could not have foreseen that during the twentieth century, technical expertise would come to dominate even politics. Nor could they foresee the way in which the centralization of political knowledge in the hands of social elites would limit the scope of political discourse. The power of hegemony has indeed restricted our sense of alternatives to the extant political economy. What the Alliance saw clearly as an expropriation of political knowledge by social elites would result in the elimination of informed dissent from American politics. In the sterile world of twentieth-century politics, in which the nature of the political economy is indeed taken for granted, problems like unemployment, high interest rates, and increasing inequality in the distribution of wealth appear not as endemic to the logic of corporate capitalism, but as what Apple has called "puzzles to be solved by technical expertise," within the ideological parameters of capitalism. Apple, *Knowledge and Power,* 119. Also Edward Thompson, "The Segregation of Dissent," in *Writings by Candlelight* (London: Merlin Press, 1978), 5-15. Farmers did not develop their own technology. Innovation trickled down from the universities and experiment stations. This was greeted with suspicion by Alliance leaders. Wrote one northern Populist, "our would be masters have a corner on the whole outfit of the inventions and they are now just as much employed to the destruction of human rights as formerly the peoples ignorance was used as a means." Quoted in Norman Pollack, *The Populist Response to Industrial America* (New York: Norton, 1962), 23.

was happening in education, a few, notably Macune and Park, saw that a similar process was at work: the "bosses" and the "plutocrats" intended to monopolize political language and political knowledge, setting themselves up as the experts in running the nation, and setting out for the farmers a limited and subordinate sphere for the development of their own agrarian expertise.[31] As they had gained control over the mechanisms of economic production, the privileged classes were well on the way to controlling the means of the production and legitimation of knowledge, through the segregation of technical and political learning along class lines.

The leaders of the Alliance saw that exclusive concentration on agricultural techniques would limit their claim to political knowledge and their claim that their particular political ideology was legitimate. As a result, their efforts to retain access to political knowledge and to battle for the legitimacy of their ideology centered upon ways to continue to train farmers in the language of politics and in the ideals of democratic citizenship, in spite of changes in publicly funded educational programs. For the same reason, the leaders opposed technical education without compensatory political education, both in and out of the public school.

For this remedial political training the leadership relied on its own educational configuration: the rallies, the suballiance meetings, and the news organs. The Alliance supported the public schools, the agricultural experiment stations, and the agricultural and mechanical colleges, insofar as these other pieces of educational apparatus contributed to a wellbalanced system of education, whose effect was "not only to teach our people to grow better crops," but also to "obtain control of products of the farm and prevent their passing into the hands of the great corporations."[32]

To some extent the Alliance leadership depended upon the movement's ability to maintain an ongoing critique of "miseducation" that was powerful enough to overwhelm the antithetical elements of schooling. In this expectation they were disappointed. The educational movement that sought to redefine the family does not seem to have done so. The campaign that was to create a permanent system of suballiance discussion groups produced only temporary successes. In other words, the distance between Alliance educational thought and its formal articulation restricted the effectiveness of the educational

31. Evan Jones in *National Economist,* March 14, 1889, and Macune, *National Economist,* August 24, 1889.

32. *National Economist,* August 24, 1889; November 2, 1889.

campaign. At another level, the success of Alliance educational opposition was limited by the narrow distinctions national leaders made between acceptable and unacceptable public school curricula.

Unfortunately for the fate of the educational impulse of the Alliance, these distinctions were too fine in most cases to influence local Alliance groups in their day to day interaction with particular schools. Debates over the nature of history taught in school and over the legitimacy of political knowledge did not penetrate to the local level, with an ultimately negative impact on the general oppositional education campaign. At the local level, only the bare outlines of the leadership's position on schooling were visible, and these outlines suggested one main position, namely that public schooling was good for the children of the South. To local Alliancemen the difference between several types of knowledge, between divergent means of control over that knowledge, and even between the focus of Alliance and state education simply did not obtain. What did, however, were sets of local political, economic and social conditions that varied substantially between communities. As a result, local support for or opposition to schools depended more upon circumstance than principle.

It is important to remember that although poorly supported and most often poorly conducted, the public school was an integral part of southern communities. In the South and in other rural areas, schools were much more than buildings in which children learned to read and write. The school was often a focus of public life, serving as an auditorium for community meetings and debates; as a courtroom in which the justice of the peace and the circuit judge presided; and as a hall in which community groups, including the Alliance, might find a temporary home. In the black half of town, the public school often doubled as a church, or the church as a school—at times it was hard to tell. But for both blacks and whites, in addition to its educative function, the public school served as no less than a community center in the postbellum South. As a community center, the school was symbolically and logistically important for local Alliance groups, and this importance favorably disposed local officials in their handling of public school matters.

The first meeting of the Arkansas Agricultural Wheel—one of the several organizations Macune brought together in Shreveport to create the National Alliance—took place in W. T. McBee's schoolhouse, eight miles southwest of Des Arc, Arkansas, in Prairie County, in February 1882. From that early moment in the history of the movement, local chapters of the Wheel and the Alliance met in school-

houses throughout the South.[33] The connection was auspicious, promising reform-minded farmers a firm link with the communities
in which they lived and worked. For, from the first, the Alliance
fought the stigma of a foreign element in the community body politic.
Members of the Wheel and the Alliance did not fit into traditional
political categories; their allegiance to the agrarian cause was something new. Naturally the movement came under suspicion. By tying
their organization to one of the pillars of the community (the school),
local leaders gained some measure of legitimacy. This linking with the
school meant more than simply using the building for Alliance events.
In most communities it also meant supporting the public school in
every way possible.

Ideological and rhetorical support for the schools came naturally to
local Alliance groups. From the national leadership they had learned
the value of education, which they translated into support for the
schools. Wrote the editor of the Tarboro, North Carolina, *Southerner,* "our public schools are the mainstay of our republic."[34] The
Farmers' Advocate of Tarboro echoed this sentiment, urging the
members of the Edgecombe County Alliance to "send the boys and
girls to school while they are young . . . educate your children by all
means." The schools could "make them not dumb-driven cattle, but
help them to be heroes in the strife."[35] In Tarboro at least, Alliance
leaders were not concerned with the niceties which caused the national
leadership to distinguish between schooling that served the cause of
reform and schooling that detracted from the movement. The situation in Edgecombe County, location of one of the more active local
Alliance groups in North Carolina, illustrates the interaction between
Alliances and schools at the county level.

5

In Edgecombe County, of which Tarboro was the seat, seventy-eight
separate public schools operated during 1890, thirty-eight for blacks
and forty for whites. Thanks, in part, to the efforts of the county

33. Rogers, *The One-Gallused Rebellion,* 122, 135. In 1892 the Virginia legislature
read a bill to permit the Alliances "to use the public schoolhouses for their meetings
provided their meetings do not interfere with the schools." The bill never came to a
vote, but the Alliances used the schools anyway. *House of Delegates Journal and
Documents,* January 20, 1892. Quoted in William Sheldon, *Populism in the Old
Dominion* (Princeton: Princeton University Press, 1935), 41.

34. *Tarboro Southerner,* September 3, 1891.

35. *Farmers' Advocate,* April 15, 1891.

Alliance, the schools held session between October and March, for close to twenty weeks, longer on average than any other county in the state of North Carolina.[36] Of the funds to pay for Edgecombe's schools, 60 percent, around five thousand dollars, derived from state and local property taxes. Another third came from local poll taxes, and the final third was raised by revenue from the sale of liquor licenses. In the balance between local revenues and state revenues, Edgecombe was typical of most other counties in the state.

Edgecombe also differed from other North Carolina counties, economically and educationally. The aggregate rate of tenancy for citizens of Edgecombe was 84.5 percent, the highest in the state. Moreover, as late as 1909 the rate of tenancy remained high, at 72.8 percent.[37] These figures suggest the ties that bound Edgecombe's farmers to the lien and mortgage system. The crushing tenancy rate probably played an important role in the growth of the Farmers' Alliance in the county. What differentiated Edgecombe educationally was the high percentage of its school funding derived from the liquor trade and the low tax revenues from its black citizens, as measured by poll and property tax revenues collected for school purposes.

Typically, counties earned less than one quarter of their school income from licensing liquor sales; one third of the counties earned no revenue through spirits at all. This was a feature of Edgecombe's financial base that was to come under careful scrutiny from the county Alliance in 1891. The heavy reliance on the wages of sin resulted in a battle over school finance in which the Alliance was to take a decisive role.

In 1891, the earliest date for which we have reliable figures, only 370 of the 1,870 black adult males in the county paid the $1.90 poll tax. In contrast, all but 5 of the 1,400 white males were listed as having paid. Despite this disparity in contribution, throughout the years between 1890 and 1895, disbursements for black schools remained within 5 percent of those for white schools. If, however, expenditures are calculated on a per-pupil basis rather than on a per-school basis, there was a significant disparity between the money spent on white and black education. In 1891, 1,297 white children enrolled in school in Edgecombe County. The same year, 2,495 black children enrolled. Thus, while the total expenditures for black schools were comparable to those for whites, the per-pupil rate for black children was half of

36. *Report of the North Carolina State Superintendent of Schools,* 1890 (Raleigh: 1890), table 4, pp. 74–75. Hereafter cited as *North Carolina School Report.*
37. *11th Census, Farms and Homes,* 29; Harlan, *Separate and Unequal,* 37.

that for whites. For each white pupil, the county treasurer disbursed $10.70; for each black pupil, $5.56.[38]

From these data, it appears that Edgecombe County's schools, both black and white, were in better shape than the average southern school system. Part of the credit must go to the Edgecombe County Alliance, which supported the schools of their community rhetorically, politically, and, despite extreme hardship, financially. What is more, during 1891, the county Alliance, through its two newspapers, the *Farmers' Advocate* and the *Tarboro Southerner,* waged a battle to increase the revenue available for public schools in the county.[39]

In Tarboro, the graded school was a central focus of community activity. School affairs received special attention in the *Southerner* and the *Advocate,* as they seem to have in the town. The children of the Tarboro Graded School put on a Christmas pageant in December. Farmers, their families, and the local shopkeepers and professionals crowded into the school to enjoy the spectacle.[40] Graduation day was also a special day for the entire community. Families arose early and dressed in the clothes they usually reserved for funerals and church. Fathers in ties, mothers in dresses and bonnets, and young brothers and sisters in cast-down finery all made their way to the outdoor ceremony. Under the Carolina sun the beaming parents of the new graduates sat along with the childless and the aged citizens of Tarboro, listening to speeches by the teachers, music and programs by the children, and the always important presentation of awards and diplomas. The whole town shared in the pride of the children and their parents, as they shared the event itself. Graduation symbolized both individual achievement and civic virtue, and it was clear, on this day over all others, that schooling embodied the town's hope for the future of its children, a hope that burned in Alliance families and non-alliance families alike.

The coverage given the graduation ceremony in 1891 was effusive. The *Southerner* and the *Advocate* both ran front-page stories on the events. They printed the speeches, described the program in detail, and listed the names of the graduates with great reverence. Even so, the editor of the *Advocate* apologized for being unable to cover graduation at the length it deserved. "On this line we could write at length," for "one of the greatest essentials of the age is education."[41]

38. Computed from *North Carolina School Report,* 1891, table 2, p. 5.
39. *Farmers' Advocate,* June 10, 1891, to December 12, 1891; *Tarboro Southerner,* January 8, 1891, to July 30, 1891.
40. *Tarboro Southerner,* January 8, 1891.
41. *Farmers' Advocate,* June 24, 1891.

The *Southerner* took great care to note the special achievements of every graduate, giving them places in the sun and special senses of accomplishment: "Sallie Lawrence deserves special mention for her punctuality and attendance; she has been neither absent nor tardy during the term."[42] One can hardly imagine a greater moment in the young life of Miss Sallie Lawrence than this simple statement in one of the local papers. One can hardly imagine, at that time, an event in Tarboro that meant as much to the citizens as that graduation.

This nexus between community and school was emotional and instrumental. Parents supported schools because schools held out to the children hope that their lives would be better than their own. But the school was more than a means to an end, it was an end in itself. Simply, in its various roles as a meetinghouse, a cultural center, and a repository of both the memories and the hopes of the adults of the community, the school was a part of community life, to be cherished and nurtured independent of the epistemological doubts that nagged the leaders of the National Farmers' Alliance. At the local level, abstract concerns paled before the significance of Sallie Lawrence's personal achievement, and before the symbolic importance of graduation day to all the members of the community.

Alliance editors and others in Tarboro worried that the school would be unable to maintain itself in years to come. "The township has a really first class graded school," argued the editor of the *Southerner,* but "taxation is the only way to keep it up."[43] Throughout the year, the Alliance pushed to pass a local levy, a property tax, designed to help support the school.

In 1891, the North Carolina legislature passed a law enabling local school districts to levy school taxes at a maximum rate of fourteen cents per one hundred dollars of assessed real property. At the beginning of the year, only four counties in the state had local levies. The local Alliance, uncomfortable in supporting schools through the sale of liquor, wanted to substitute tax money for licensing revenue and to expand the school's income base. The county leadership began its campaign at the year's first meeting of the county Alliance, held on January 7, 1891. There, the question of taxation was raised, and a long discussion ensued. Some of the members, particularly the landowners, were reluctant to support increased taxation during such hard economic times. Other members, the tenants and croppers, favored the move, since they would benefit from an expense they would not have

42. *Tarboro Southerner,* June 4, 1891; *Farmers' Advocate,* June 10, 1891.
43. *Tarboro Southerner,* February 5, 1891.

to bear. As the evening wore on, this division within the membership became more acrimonious and resolution became less and less possible. The group tabled the issue with the promise to take up taxation at its next weekly meeting.

The *Southerner's* first issue of the year came out on January 9, carrying an account of the meeting. Although the membership could not reach agreement, the editor of the *Southerner* was not reluctant to take a stand. "To maintain a graded school a special tax must be authorized by the legislature," he proclaimed in his editorial.[44] The next week, the county Alliance met and again raised the question of instituting a tax. Again the debate raged long into the winter night, again the rift between landowners and renters proved unbridgeable, and again the question was tabled.[45]

The editor of the *Southerner* stepped up his campaign in favor of taxation during the next weeks, carrying articles on schools reprinted from other Alliance papers, and quoting from national and regional educators on the need for more liberal school taxes. On January 29, 1891, the *Southerner* printed in its entirety a speech delivered to the North Carolina legislature by J. L. M. Curry, General Agent for the Peabody Fund. One of the most well known exponents of public schooling in the South, Curry was a spokesman for New South interests, and an advocate of industrial and agricultural training. He was also a fierce opponent of the Alliance and its educational and political activities. School politics, at the community level, made bedfellows of Curry, the antipopulist, and the leading Alliance editors. In their effort to improve the financial base of schooling, the local Alliance editors were willing to overlook many sins. At the local level, unlike the national level, the importance of maintaining particular schools overrode what the locals may have seen, if they saw them at all, as quibbling differences over philosophy. But the tentative alliance between the farmers and proschool advocates of the New South, even only in the pages of local papers, may have made Alliance men and women less critical of the specific New South educational program of the educational crusaders of the late 1890s. When the National Alliance fell in 1896, the only organizations working for public schooling were the educational crusaders of Curry's ilk. It was an easy thing for local groups, many still organized as Alliances, to turn to these men for help in carrying out what they still saw to be the ideals of the Alliance.

44. *Tarboro Southerner,* January 8, 1891.
45. *Tarboro Southerner,* January 15, 1891.

The *Southerner* kept up pressure in favor of taxation throughout February. "It is essential," wrote the editor, "that the people should come together in mass meetings and let the legislature know their views." "The National and State Farmers' Alliance," he went on, "have urged more and better education and thereby to bring it about, the *Southerner* therefore calls on his Honor, Mayor Clark, to call a meeting soon to discuss the matter of taxation."[46] This appeal, both to the mayor and the farmers, tied support of the Alliance to support for taxation. Cleverly, the editor mentioned the national and state organizations in an effort to sway Alliancemen to support taxation out of loyalty if not out of self-interest. The appeal seems to have worked in a limited way. The local Alliance still could not resolve to support or oppose taxation, but it did support the call for a mass meeting to discuss the matter.

The *Southerner* next turned its editorial guns on the avowed opponents of increased taxation, the large holders of commercial property and several of the wealthy merchants in town. O. C. Farrar, owner of the Hotel Farrar on Main Street, was the organizer of a petition drive on behalf of the opposition to the state legislature, urging that the representatives block Tarboro's proposed levy by lowering the ceiling on the school tax rate.[47] Meanwhile, Mayor Clark called on the town to meet on February 13 to decide whether or not to hold a special tax election in July. In two issues, February 5 and February 12, the *Southerner* tried several approaches to the opposition.

First, the editor worked on the merchants. "A settler," he argued, "looking around for a place of habitation, would give a wide berth to a town without such schools as he could afford to send his children to." What prosperity the town enjoyed would quickly disappear according to the editor: "If Tarboro permits the graded school to go down for want of proper support, then blow your boom to the wind," he admonished his opponents.

Next, the *Southerner* rang with denunciations of those who opposed the tax because they did not want to support the educational expenses of poor children. The editor called them unpatriotic and attempted, at length, to reason that what appeared to be charity was really self-serving in the long run. "Some object to the school from the most selfish of motives, that is they do not want to pay taxes for the benefit of the children of other men," he wrote. If their view prevailed, "poor men, without property," would be unable to send their children to

46. *Tarboro Southerner*, February 5, 1891.
47. *Tarboro Southerner*, February 26, 1891.

school. In this event, "this country would soon be remanded to the most benighted age of darkest ignorance and barbarism." Would, he asked, "such a country be worth living in; would it be safe to live in?"

Finally, in preparation for the town meeting, the *Southerner* reprinted highlights from Curry's speech that emphasized the benefit to industry, commerce, and agriculture accruing from an educated workforce. The day before the meeting, the editor of the *Southerner* reminded his readers to attend and to "reflect carefully, deliberately, attend the meeting, hear the speeches, put your shoulder to the wheel and keep the school afoot, as long as there's a pea in the dish."[48]

The meeting ran for several hours, and when it was over Tarboro had decided to submit the question to a vote. In July, after six months of campaigning by both sides, the citizens of Tarboro went to the polls and voted to tax themselves for the support of their schools. The editor of the *Southerner* was jubilant. "It is one of the straws which shows that the people of the South are becoming aroused to the importance of education."[49] The Edgecombe case illustrates several general points concerning the dimensions of Alliance support for local schooling.

First, the general pedagogical and epistemological concerns expressed by the national leadership simply did not obtain in Edgecombe, and likely did not exist in many localities. There, local Alliances were concerned with local issues and constrained by local circumstances.

Second, the most important of these local issues proved to be the centrality of the school to the cultural life of southern communities. As a result, it was difficult for members of the Alliance to separate the pedagogical process of schooling from the other roles the school served in the community. Their support for schooling was deep-rooted and extended beneath pedagogical concerns.

Third, decisions by individual Alliance families whether to support improvements or changes in schooling often relied on matters of household economy. The split between landowners and tenants in the Tarboro taxation debate illustrates how economic necessity and financial hardship limited the extent of local Alliance support for school-

48. *Tarboro Southerner,* February 5, 1891. The editor and some of the readers of the *Tarboro Southerner* appealed to the elites on the old immigration argument. More workers would migrate to Edgecombe County if they thought they could find good schools for their children. The editor wrote a story of a master mechanic who refused to take over the Edgecombe Iron Foundry because the schools were in bad shape. He used the tale to appeal to the more industrial-minded of his readers.

49. *Tarboro Southerner,* July 30, 1891.

ing. At the national level, ideology counted for more than money; at the local level, the balance was reversed. For many, while they believed in the importance of education and of public schooling, poverty and the weight of the crop lien prevented them from making long-term financial commitments to the public school.

Fourth, notably missing from the Tarboro debate over taxation was any discussion about black schools. In fact, the tax passed by the town supported schools for both races, but in proportion to the tax paid by each. That is, white schools derived revenue from taxes paid by white citizens, and black schools from taxes derived from blacks. The Edgecombe Alliance opposed a bill in the state legislature that would have equalized the apportionment of funds from all sources on a per capita basis, calling it the "Great Mendicant Bill."[50] In Edgecombe, white support for black schooling, within the ranks of the farmers' movement, was limited for the most part to a rhetorical solidarity. The *Advocate* reported favorably on the first black teachers' institute to be held in Edgecombe, pointing out how beneficial it was for the whole community that blacks were going to have a higher caliber of teachers, but more than this they did not offer. Nor were members of the Alliance concerned, at the local or the national level, that, as the commissioner of education put it, "education for the colored race is becoming more and more industrial."[51]

Only in Texas did the Alliance make any real impact on black education, there creating dual systems of control in counties in which Alliance superintendents gained power. The dual system allowed blacks to control black education for the first time since reconstruction.[52] At the opposite pole, in Alabama, Alliance leaders went along with proposed constitutional changes that robbed blacks of state as well as local school revenues and transferred them to white schools.[53] What blacks did to improve education for themselves and their children, they did alone.

In general, the Alliance members in Edgecombe County and elsewhere were unconcerned with the careful distinctions made by their national spokesmen and spokeswomen: between schooling and education, between knowledge supportive of reform and knowledge antagonistic to reform, and between political and technical learning. The notion of schools as one leg of an educational triad seems not to have penetrated to the local level. As a result, the decline of national leader-

50. *Tarboro Southerner,* January 29, 1891.
51. *U.S. Commissioner of Education Report,* 1892, 1559–1560.
52. *Southern Mercury,* August 9, 1894; Rice, *The Negro in Texas,* 210.
53. Bond, *Negro Education in Alabama,* 160–167.

ship left local reformers without a coherent educational policy, one able to discriminate between education that was useful and education that was not. Local leaders were concerned, on the whole, with easing the burden of undereducation for their children and their friends' children. Their choice to support local schools lacked the detachment that typified the careful distinctions drawn by the national leadership. The neat categories of political and technical education were far from neat to local Alliance members.

6

The national campaign of education in the Alliance began to deteriorate late in 1892, with the exit of Macune. He resigned as editor of the *Economist* and severed his ties with the national Executive Committee in opposition to its support of the People's party, believing that the only hope for the movement was to take control of the Democratic party in the South. Despite interim efforts at revival, the educational movement declined precipitously after 1894, when the *National Economist* shut its books and quieted its presses. With the *Economist* gone, there was no national voice for the campaign and no unifying structure for its curriculum. Some suballiances tried to carry on the struggle with direction from the leaders of the new People's party. Tracy and Ashby, in particular, continued to urge reform through education. But with the decisive repudiation of populism in the 1896 election, even this direction disappeared.

One of the greatest organizational strengths of the Alliance educational campaign—its independence from traditional child-focused schooling—proved to be one of its greatest weaknesses, for the focus on adult education left members unprepared to examine schooling critically. The failure of the Alliance to effect a change in the public schools arose from the campaign's optimistic reliance upon the continued existence of an independent program of adult education, which intended to counteract even the most reactionary curricular innovations in the state-supported institutions. But this notion never penetrated to the local level, where schools were not dealt with in the abstract but in the concrete, and where school support was a part of community life. Bolstered by the national leadership's broad support for public schooling and by their traditional links with particular schools, former members of the Alliance were easily recruited into the educational crusade that followed closely on the heels of the 1896 election. The Crusade for Education in the South, sponsored by Rockefeller and other northern industrialists, galvanized local school officials, university educators, and influential citizens in support of progressive-style educational reform. The effect of the Crusade was to bring southern education under the control of a newly minted cadre of educational professionals, men like Edwin Alderman, Charles Dabney, and Charles Duncan McIver. By centralizing the governance of southern schools into the hands of a strong private network, the crusaders accomplished in education what Macune and his associates feared most for the polity as a whole. It was ironic, to say the least, that the support the Alliance worked so hard to build for education could, in the end, contribute to the success of a Crusade so completely antithetical to the movement's aims. But this kind of ironic twist was typical of the legacy left by the Alliance in politics and in economic affairs as well as in education.

6 The Limits of Tradition

The Legacies of the Southern Alliance

The Negro is here, and he is a laborer and a voter; for this the People's Party is in no way responsible.
— Milton Park, *Southern Mercury*, July 5, 1894

[When the unions] find out for the hundredth time that strikes, even when successful, do not reach the root of the disease, we will argue with them for the substitution of a better and more effective method.
— Milton Park, *Southern Mercury*, August, 2, 1892

Avoid the discussion of party politics as you would avoid a poison and discuss the condition of the country and the needs of the people, but leave parties alone.
— Charles Macune's instructions to suballiance presidents discussing the first Educational Exercise in *National Economist*, January 16, 1892

1

Behind the irony of the Alliance legacies in education and in politics lay the continuing tension between conservatism and radicalism in the movement's ideology. To contemporaries united by their antipathy toward the agrarian revolt, the educational campaign of the Alliance was nothing short of radical "fanaticism," and "a piece of political intrigue and agitation."[1] Yet the leadership consistently pointed to the conservative nature of the movement's ideals. Alliance ideas and ideals were essentially conservative in that they used as reference points traditional constructions of key concepts like state, polity, society, and economy. What was radical, threatening even, to the dominant classes was the Alliance leaders' argument that these concepts should be applied to farmers' day-to-day lives. It was the application of the ideas of democratic participation, of universal education, and of economic equality, as much as the ideas themselves, that sustained the radical element in the Alliance movement.

Drawing upon traditional ideas for their radical application defines the Alliance as a truly organic oppositional movement, growing up from within the culture it opposed. In its connection to the South of which it was a part, the movement derived strength. But the same con-

1. *National Economist*, September 14, 1889.

nections that made Alliance ideas powerful within the dominant culture made intellectual and political separation from that culture difficult for leaders of the movement as well as its members.

A part of the real power of the Alliance curriculum, at all levels, derived from its attempt to draw together historically divided groups around several often-articulated fundamental principles and shared values. Clearly foremost among these were the ideas that all laborers or producers had similar interests and that these interests were opposed to the interests of the "moneyed classes." From the first, whether by intent or neglect, a certain murkiness appeared at the boundaries of these class definitions. Variable membership criteria, imperfectly applied, testified to the permeability of class boundaries even within the Alliance.

Originally, the Texas Alliance had only included men and women who farmed for a living. In 1882 the Committee on Membership inserted an amendment into the constitution "to limit membership to white persons only."[2] As a condition of merger between the Alliance and the Agricultural Wheel in Louisiana and Arkansas, more stringent membership rules were applied. The Wheel had offered membership to any "farmer, farm laborer, country mechanic, country school teacher, country doctor."[3] The new constitution included these and excluded "lawyers with a license to practice," owners of "stock in any national, state, or other banking association, merchants, merchants' clerks, or anyone who owns interest in a dry-goods, hardware, furniture, drug store or any other mercantile business." The exception to the exclusions was telling, as the Order accepted for membership merchants who were "selected to take charge of a cooperative store."[4] "Class" membership seemed to rely not on an individual's relation to labor but on that individual's relation to the ideas and programs of the organization. Fuzzy boundaries allowed the Alliance to draw membership and support from a wide spectrum of the agrarian population, from tenant farmer to large landowner. Similarly, broad goals, like justice, economic equality, and popular control of government allowed multiple agendas to coexist under the umbrella of the National Alliance. The reticence of the Alliance leadership to define its goals

2. Dunning, *Farmers' Alliance History,* 35. This prohibition was made in order, as one observer put it, "to preserve without even the pretext of disapproval" the inclusion of white women among the membership.

3. "Constitution of the Agricultural Wheel: 1882," in Dunning, *Farmers' Alliance History,* 171.

4. *National Economist,* November 11, 1889; also Dunning, *Farmers' Alliance History,* 209.

narrowly served the political and educational strategies of the broad movement well but brought confusion, conflict, and a certain irony when breadth gave way to specific analyses or demands. So when pressed to be specific, either by events or by pressure from its critics, the Alliance often found itself in a head-on conflict with the dominant culture inside the organization as well as outside.

2

In the matter of race, this conflict was clear. For some Alliance members, like Texas Alliance Treasurer Fannie Moss, blacks and whites were equal under God, who "made no distinction in men; they were created equal."[5] But for most agrarians, like most southerners, the issue was not that simple. Blacks were free citizens, by fiat. They were also free labor. In both positions blacks became the objects of intense struggle. In politics, both parties, and later the Populists, tried to enlist black support, and when blacks still showed signs of independent thinking, the parties resorted to force. At first this meant "bulldozing" blacks into the proper line at the ballot box; later it meant keeping them away altogether. As free labor, blacks probably worked less than they had as slaves. Among white landowners and planters, this decline in labor power came to be known as the "negro question." Successful resolution of the "negro problem" depended on the creation of managerial and legal instruments that approximated the slave system under the new "free" market conditions. Share cropping, gang labor, and crop liens all reduced the bargaining power of black farm workers, curtailed the mobility of labor, and attempted to eliminate individual decision making in the exercise of labor power among blacks.

In a society not bound by racism, the mass of black farmers and farm laborers might have been an important source of support for economic reform and of membership and leadership in organizations like the Alliance. But the leaders and members of the Alliance were bound by their culture and their history. As a result, the lecturers and leaders of the movement "taught" blacks contradictory lessons through the movement and its educational program.

Alliance support of black farmers, despite rhetorical flourishes to the contrary, was shallow and paternalistic, and never challenged the racial structuring of southern economic and social life. When the Alliance formally banned blacks from membership it did so on all-too-often heard grounds. One delegate put the decision into context:

5. Moss's letter in *Southern Mercury,* September 24, 1892.

> From its inception women were admitted as members of the
> Alliance . . . in order to preserve this, without even a pretext of
> disapproval, the Alliance at this meeting inserted an amendment
> in its constitution restricting its membership to white persons
> only.[6]

This is poignant testimony to the power of the dominant culture. The
Alliance could break new ground by encouraging women to become
full and active members in a political organization but not look
beyond the social sanctions against allowing black men and white
women to attend the same meetings. After closing the door to black
membership, the white leadership authorized the creation of the Colored Farmers' Alliance (CFA) in order to gain black support while
keeping blacks themselves at arms distance.

The Colored Farmers' Alliance was never close to an equal partner
in the agrarian struggle. Members of the black Alliance never met in
convention with their white brethren, and the organization itself was
headed by a white man, R. M. Humphrey. At the gatherings that were
so much a part of the movement education of white Alliancemen and
women, blacks participated tangentially if at all.

W. P. Martin gave an account of a typical rally, the 1894, meeting
of the Pine Tree, Texas, Alliance, "At Pine Tree," he reported,
"there was quite a number of colored people, and I noted with
pleasure that after the whites were through eating the colored people
were invited to the tables."[7] In the movement, as at lunch, blacks were
expected to content themselves with leftovers, to listen to the speeches,
and to fall into line after their white counterparts.

As the agrarian campaign picked up momentum in the region, the
Alliance and the People's party found even this limited "partnership"
with blacks to be a political liability. Democrats and "Lily-white"
Republicans charged the Populists with being traitors to the white
race. In an exasperated response to one such attack, Milton Park, a
conservative on racial matters, wrote, "the Negro is here, and he is a
laborer and a voter; for this the People's Party is in no way responsible."[8] Such sentiment promised few visits to the table for black
Alliance members.

Tom Watson offered a similar pragmatic view, this time to blacks
themselves. In return for support, "our platform gives him a better

6. Quoted in Dunning, *Farmers' Alliance History,* 35.
7. *Southern Mercury,* August 2, 1894. See also the account of the Shady Grove,
Georgia, rally in chap. 1 and in the *People's Party Paper,* June 14, 1891.
8. *Southern Mercury,* July 5, 1894.

guaranty for political independence; for a fair return for his work; a better chance to buy a home and keep it; and a better chance to educate his children."⁹ This was hardly a pledge for social equality or even a guarantee of support for blacks' constitutional rights; Watson merely offered to do better than the other two parties.

While the white Alliance never granted equal rights and privileges to the members of the Colored Farmers' Alliance, the latter was a vital organization in its own right. Members of the CFA took the task of education seriously, perhaps more seriously than their white counterparts would have liked. In the process of educating themselves on matters of the day, the CFA membership found that its interests lay along a different path than that of the white organization. They pursued that path, and by so doing proved again that education serves only imperfectly narrow partisan purposes. Just as dramatically the independent action of the CFA proved the ability of education to liberate the mind and empower the spirit.

The order began in Houston County, Texas, on December 11, 1886 and by 1890 had recruited nearly one million members throughout the South. According to the superintendent of the CFA most members were croppers or wage laborers. The interests of the black membership, as laborers, often conflicted with the interests of the white Alliance, many of whose members owned land and hired black labor.¹⁰ The result, in one illustrative incident, was a clash over Alliance policy that drove the two groups far apart and demonstrated, to the glee of Alliance opponents, how self-serving was the white order's commitment to the interests of black growers.

In 1891, groups of farmers and planters in the Cotton Belt tried to ally behind a firm wage standard for cotton pickers. For the pickers, nearly all of whom were black, the wage controls would have resulted in lower wages and elimination of the little bargaining power they had.

9. Watson, "The Negro Question," 548–549. For more on blacks in the Alliance see Gerald Gaither, *Blacks in the Populist Revolt* (Montgomery: University of Alabama Press, 1977) and the work of Jack Abramowitz: "Agricultural Reformers and the Negro," *Negro History Bulletin* 11 (March 1948): 138–139; "The Negro in the Agrarian Revolt," *Agricultural History* 24 (January 1950): 89–95; "The Negro in the Populist Movement," *Journal of Negro History* 37 (July 1953): 257–289. William Rogers' piece, "The Negro Alliance in Alabama," *Journal of Negro History* 55 (January, 1960): 38–44, gives a detailed account of the CFA in that state. Goodwyn's account of the "Populist Approach to Black America," is much too optimistic and ignores the white supremacist doctrine that underlay all such approaches and which so swiftly turned so many Alliance leaders away from blacks after 1896. See his *Democratic Promise*, chap. 10.

10. Gaither, *Blacks in the Populist Revolt*, 12; *National Economist*, December 14, 1889.

For white landowners, and even for white tenants who hired black laborers during the picking season, wage control presented one way to keep costs down and to increase, even marginally, their annual return. Black pickers appealed to the Colored Farmers' Alliance, which, in early fall 1891, called upon all agricultural laborers to go out on strike on September 20, 1891, and to let the cotton rot in the fields until farmers paid one dollar plus board for every one hundred pounds of cotton picked.[11]

L. L. Polk, a North Carolina planter as well as Alliance president, accused the black Alliance of trying to sabotage the cause of producer unity by pursuing its "special interest" instead of the general program of the National Farmers' Alliance. When the CFA refused to give in to demands that it cancel the strike, an angry Polk told farmers to abandon their crop rather than pay more than fifty cents per hundred pounds to the black pickers, less than half of what the pickers demanded.[12]

The "General Strike" which was intended to cripple cotton harvesting all along the Cotton Belt, did not materialize. There were only scattered work stoppages, mostly in Texas, where the CFA had always been strong, and in isolated counties in South Carolina and Arkansas, according to Gaither.[13] Even in these areas, the strike was abortive, as white militia intervened to make sure blacks returned to work, and a lack of strike funds made work stoppage economically impossible for most pickers and their families.

Although the strike was an immediate failure, it had lasting impact on the relationship between the black and white Alliances. While the *National Economist* tried to downplay the incident, stating that the black brethren were ill advised, the national press somewhat gleefully demonstrated that the incident reflected the paradox of Alliance efforts to include blacks in the agrarian movement but keep them as instruments of white leadership serving white interests. "This is not what the Alliance expected," stated the *New York Herald,* "when it kindly consented to receive colored men as members." The problem with educating and organizing blacks "to take part in the grand strike against capital" proved to be that "the colored man struck for himself . . . who says he never learns anything."[14] And indeed, this was the

---

11. Rice, *The Negro in Texas,* 176; Gaither, *Blacks in the Populist Revolt,* 14–17.

12. For a good account of the strike, see Abramowitz, "The Negro in the Agrarian Revolt," 90–91.

13. Gaither, *Blacks in the Populist Revolt,* 15–16; *Tarboro Southerner,* February 5, 1891.

14. Quoted in Gaither, *Blacks in the Populist Revolt,* 16.

point: educated in the Alliance to act to secure a fair return, blacks did just that. Education was a force not easily circumscribed, not even by the educators.

The strike and Polk's reaction as leader of the National Farmers' Alliance illustrates the limits of black-white cooperation within the movement. When blacks supported the white program, as indicated by Watson, they could expect to receive concessions toward their rights in return, but little more. On the other hand, the white Alliance was obviously unwilling to address the unique economic needs of blacks. While the Alliance did take strong rhetorical stands against lynching, did oppose convict labor leases, and did provide the smallest promises of support for black education, these approaches to black America were balanced by Alliancemen's instrumental understanding of the utility of black electoral power, power the Alliance needed. At the national level, at least, the Populist program was not qualitatively different from that of either of the two major parties. None offered blacks any power, but all argued that blacks would prosper from the ascension to power of their particular brand of white leadership. Intentional benefits to black America were clearly derivative in all three cases.

As the Alliance's admittedly halting efforts to draw blacks into the agrarian movement drew increasing fire from Democrats, the national and state organizations attempted to repudiate their connections with black America, through white primaries, through support of white supremacy candidates, and through an ever-increasing distance between the official black and white orders. Still, it is important to recognize that individual Alliance leaders, such as Scott Morgan, Stump Ashby, and even Macune, steadfastly supported existing black rights, limited though they were. Throughout the 1890s when the official line was hardening toward blacks, Ashby continued to lecture at gatherings of the Colored Farmers' Alliance and its state affiliates. Moreover, despite the tension between black involvement and white supremacy in the highest councils of the Order, real advances in black-white cooperation may have occurred at the local level, as Lawrence Goodwyn has shown in his illuminating study of Alliance politics in Grimes County, Texas.[15]

In Grimes, what began as an expedient alliance between black and white agrarians for control of local politics turned into a cooperative and supportive relationship that continued well past the fall of the national movements. Control of Grimes by a biracial Populist coalition

15. See Goodwyn, "Populist Dreams and Negro Rights," for an eloquent account of this kind of cooperation and this particular kind of courage.

brought fair treatment for black citizens at the hands of the law and real gains in black education. In Grimes, black teachers were paid more than their white counterparts into the twentieth century, and black schools were controlled by members of the black community, in direct contrast to the situation in most counties throughout the South where whites limited the amount of resources available to black schools and kept control over black education as a means of controlling black advancement and self-activity.

It took violent repression by white supremacists to split blacks and whites in Grimes and to sour the cooperative spirit that ruled in the county between black and white Populists for nearly fifteen years. Unfortunately we have no idea how often in communities throughout the South the heroisms that make Grimes memorable were replayed. While national leaders did not understand or would not admit that blacks and whites had different economic and social priorities in the postbellum South, their rhetoric of mutual interest and of mutual support may have given blacks and whites at the local level an excuse to look for areas of mutual interest. Moreover, the experience of Grimes surely did more to educate citizens there to the potential for interracial coexistence than could any tract or lecture.

3

In the Alliance's attempt to ally with still another group of producers, urban labor, there was no local interaction through which to produce a set of common goals or a program of cooperation. As a result, a monumental misunderstanding of the needs of urban workers left Alliance approaches to the Knights of Labor and other labor organizations quite impotent despite the agrarians' stated goal of uniting all members of the producing classes.

This is not to say that the national leadership did not attempt to secure the support of labor or to bring labor under the umbrella of the Alliance. The Knights of Labor sent representatives to every National Alliance convention, and throughout his career as president of the organization, Macune wanted nothing more than to unite the two organizations in the name of producer unity. But the ideology of the Alliance—particularly in sanctifying yeoman farming—and the vestiges of sectional misunderstanding left agrarian leaders unable to comprehend reform strategies and types of struggle different from their own. A kind of rural parochialism prevented an effective link from being made between the farmers and the workers.

From the first days of the Southern Alliance, the relation between labor and the agrarians was marked on both sides by a wary affinity. Organized labor and organized agrarians agreed to dance, but neither was sure who was leading. Terrence Powderly of the Knights of Labor wrote after the St. Louis convention of the Farmers' Alliance in 1889 that "we met the Farmers and we are theirs, or they are ours."[16]

At the St. Louis convention, the delegation from the Knights of Labor—Powderly, A. W. Wright, and Ralph Beaumont—formally endorsed a set of seven demands made by the Alliance. Included in these seven were the abolition of national banks, prohibition of futures sales of mechanical and agricultural goods, the free and unlimited coinage of silver, elimination of alien land ownership, and the operation of the means of transportation and communication "in the interest of the people."[17]

The language of these demands is important, as is the collection of issues around which the Alliance and the Knights could agree. Most significant are the ways in which the resolutions differ from the Alliance demands of both 1888 and 1890. In both years, Alliance conventions demanded not just that the means of transportation be operated in the interest of the people, but that the transportation and communication be owned and operated by the government. Whereas the Alliance relied on the democratic idea of the state as the aggregation of the people, the Knights were less willing to see government as a source of reform. No mention was made in 1889 of two important Alliance planks, the subtreasury plan and the direct election of senators. Instead, the document signed by representatives of the Alliance and the Knights contained the weak statement that "legal tender notes [should be] issued as needed . . . as the business of the nation expands."[18] No mention whatsoever was made of deepening the democratic involvement in the election of federal officials. In several ways, the nature of the rapprochement between the two organizations reflected Powderly's own agenda.

First, Powderly and the Knights of Labor had lost much of their industrial support to the new American Federation of Labor by 1888.[19]

16. Terrence V. Powderly quoted in Stuart Bruce Kaufman, *Samuel Gompers and the Origins of the American Federation of Labor, 1848–1896* (Westport, Conn.: Greenwood Press, 1973), 185.

17. Quoted in Dunning, *Farmers' Alliance History,* 123.

18. Dunning, *Farmers' Alliance History,* 122.

19. Philip S. Foner, *History of the Labor Movement in the United States* (New York: International Publishers, 1955), vol. 2, 166–168. On the particulars of the southern wing of the Knights of Labor, see Melton Alonza McLaurin, *The Knights of Labor in the South* (Westport, Conn.: Greenwood Press, 1978). McLaurin's perspective is limited by a lack of research on the history of the Alliance.

Their response was to redouble efforts to recruit members in rural areas, particularly in the South. Standing in the path of Powderly's rural strategy was the fast-growing Alliance. Accommodation without merger was the strategy Powderly employed to use the momentum of the Alliance to help save his moribund organization.

Second, the Alliance seems genuinely to have appealed to Powderly. The moralism and social gospel of the Alliance leaders echoed what Daniel Rodgers has called Powderly's "deep and encompassing sensitivity to the dignity of labor."[20] His discourse, like that of the Alliance leaders, glorified the virtues of the "sons of toil" and used Biblical allusions to show that workers' moral superiority should lead to material superiority as well.

Finally, although currency reform of the soft money variety did not spark much debate in labor organizations until the crisis of 1893, Powderly and his codelegate to the St. Louis convention, Ralph Beaumont, had strong ties to the Greenback movement of the 1870s. So, when Powderly appointed himself and Beaumont to the visiting committee, he signaled a predisposition to buy into the Alliance plan for monetary reform through expansion of the currency. As individuals, Powderly and Beaumont believed that labor as well as agricultural interests would benefit from the creation of a flexible circulating medium and an increase in the money supply. They came to St. Louis, in other words, with personal prejudices that may not have reflected the position of some of the rank and file in an organization in which Powderly was increasingly isolated.[21]

But the accommodation between the Knights of the Alliance was atypical and idiosyncratic, and it suggested far greater synergy between agriculture and labor than actually existed. More typical responses came from the ascending labor organizations, the AFL and the Socialist Labor Party (SLP). Daniel DeLeon of the SLP and

20. Daniel T. Rodgers, *The Work Ethic in Industrializing America, 1850–1920* (Chicago: University of Chicago Press, 1978), 175. For more on Powderly and his leadership of the Knights along the lines of social gospel, see Herbert Gutman, "Protestantism and the American Labor Movement: The Christian Spirit in the Gilded Age," in *Work, Culture, and Society in Industrializing America* (New York: Vintage Books, 1977).

21. The internal struggles of the Knights of Labor, and Powderly's increasing isolation in the leadership is documented by Foner in *The History of the Labor Movement in the United States,* vol. 2, 161–167. Powderly's own status as a greenbacker is the focus of his *Thirty Years of Labor* (Philadelphia: 1890), 203–209. McLaurin, in *The Knights of Labor in the South,* 80, provides a brief biography of Beaumont, including his years in the greenback movement. From McLaurin's and Foner's analysis, it is clear that Powderly appointed the visiting committee on the basis of its support for the farmers' monetary program.

Samuel Gompers of the AFL shared a critical view of the farmers' movement. To DeLeon, the movement's ideological allegiance to small-scale agriculture and small-scale independent production was anachronistic.

The movement's purpose, DeLeon remarked scornfully, was "to perpetuate a class that modern progress has doomed."[22] In an article in the *North American Review,* Gompers went further, saying that the Alliance represented and extended the interests of "employing farmers without any regard for the employed farmers of the country districts or the mechanics and laborers of the industrial centers."[23] Both labor leaders resisted pressure to ally with the agrarians and gave no official encouragement to efforts by Alliance leaders and other nonallied radicals, like Henry Demarest Lloyd, to bring the movements together in the creation of a workingmen's political party.[24]

Here again, the organic connection of the agrarian movement to the culture of the rural South prevented effective accommodation in Alliance thinking to the different needs and priorities of the urban working class, despite constant and sincere attempts to create unity among producers of all sorts. In general, such unity seemed natural, logical, and desirable. When it got to specific programs, however, such unity seemed elusive at best.

The National Alliance convention in Ocala, Florida, during the first week of December 1890 produced the most complete and pointed set of reform proposals to come from the farmers' movement.[25] The Ocala Demands were framed by the general position of the Alliance that "the world's stock of wealth and opportunity belongs to all mankind, to be won or lost on the basis of merit and demerit."[26] The basic demand was that farmers and other producers regain a more equal chance at the economic prizes of nineteenth-century capitalism. The means that farmers intended to use to accomplish this goal were far more specific and far more divisive, within the movement and without.[27]

22. In Kaufman, *Samuel Gompers*, 209.

23. Samuel Gompers, "Organized Labor in the Campaign," *North American Review* 155 (August 1892): 94.

24. See Foner, *The History of the Labor Movement in the United States,* 303–309. It is interesting to note that in the 1892 election, Gompers voted for the Populist candidate Weaver as the "lesser evil." See Kaufman, *Samuel Gompers,* 150.

25. The complete text of the Ocala Demands is included here as Appendix B.

26. Tom Watson, quoted in Palmer, *"Man Over Money,"* 31.

27. For a detailed analysis of the political intrigues of the Ocala meeting, see Goodwyn, *Democratic Promise,* 225–232. North-South divisions arose over the Lodge elections bill as well as over proposals to create a third party. Divisions between the radicals

The Committee on Demands presented its report to the assembled delegates at the morning session on December 7. After hours of some-times rancorous debate, the report was adopted by a vote of seventy-six to nine. Divisions emerged within the convention between large and small landowners, between radicals and conservatives and be-tween northerners and southerners. In the end, the Demands satisfied all but the most hardened opponents of the subtreasury, most signif-icantly the delegations from Tennessee and Missouri.

The subtreasury plan was the most controversial of the demands coming from the Ocala meeting. The Alliance demanded that Con-gress abolish all national banks and replace them with "subtreasuries" in each congressional district throughout the nation. These sub-treasuries would exist to loan money to "the people" at rates of in-terest not to exceed 2 percent per annum. Loans were to be secured by real estate and nonperishable farm products. For farmers this was a way to circumvent the usurious rates of the cotton merchant and to warehouse a year's crop until a high price could be gained. The aim, of course, was to lift the burden of the crop lien from the backs of farmers and to allow them to compete on national and world markets free from the inflexibilities of the cotton marketing practices that prevailed in the region.

Moreover, the subtreasury plan aimed at equalizing access to wealth-producing capital by eliminating price as a means of allocating loans. With interest rates fixed below 2 percent, individuals or enter-prises with a greater ability to pay would no longer be able to bid more for capital. Thus access to capital, the means of making money, was a primary goal of the subtreasury.

The subtreasury was focused upon cotton production. While this met the needs of most of the delegates, the representatives from Missouri and Tennessee argued that their constituents would reap few benefits from the subtreasury, as the bulk of their produce could not be warehoused and could not be classified as nonperishable. They urged, unsuccessfully, that the National Alliance eliminate the nonperishable restriction from the proposal. They were left with no option but to vote against the demands as a whole. Other demands were less controversial and received more universal support.

At Ocala, the delegates reaffirmed their support for currency reform, demanding that Congress increase the available stock of money in circulation to fifty dollars per person, through the free and

---

and the conservatives occurred over this last point, with the radicals urging a complete split from the democratic party and conservatives arguing the need to work for reform of the Democracy.

unlimited coinage of silver. Here too, the aim was to redress the financial disadvantage farmers suffered, indeed the disadvantage of all debtors in an era of steady deflation.[28]

Through the coinage of silver the Alliance, like the Greenbackers before them, intended to bring about a general inflationary trend in prices. Prices for farm produce would rise, as would wages and prices for manufactured goods. Perhaps most important of all, as prices inflated the value of debts declined. Farmers and others would pay back debts in dollars less valuable than those they borrowed. Through inflation and a general increase in the supply of money, the Farmers' Alliance wanted to reverse the power relationships incumbent in the lending of capital. Problematic, though, in this logic was the fact that incentives for capital owners to lend would decline under inflationary pressure. In any case, the Alliance was never to see either the intended or the unintended consequences of their demand for free silver.[29]

From Ocala the Farmers' Alliance also demanded that laws be passed to "prohibit the foreign ownership of land" and to reclaim "all lands now owned by railroads and other corporations in excess of such as is actually needed and used by them."[30] There was a common understanding among the leaders of the Alliance that land grants to railroads and land grabbing by foreign and domestic investors forced farmland to remain idle and put "actual tillers of the soil in the role of trespassers."[31] Like their financial demands, their land use demands reflected a desire to facilitate economic advancement among producers, to remove what they saw as impediments to their honest efforts to secure economic rewards through hard work.

The economic programs of the Alliance, as articulated in the 1890 Ocala Demands, were at the root of DeLeon's and Gompers' mistrust of the movement. The Alliance monetary planks of 1890 drew upon the premise that more money in circulation meant higher prices for

28. See chap. 1 of this volume.

29. The silver issue was for a generation the focus of historical attention when it turned to the Farmers' Alliance. John Hicks, *The Populist Revolt* is the paradigmatic work of that era. Contemporary accounts of the silver problem abound. Two written on the side of unlimited silver were James Weaver's *A Call to Action* (1892), and William Harvey's *Coin's Financial School* (1895). Both emphasized the conspiracy they saw between gold bug bankers and businessmen. More recent treatments of the silver problem have demonstrated the favorable terms of trade faced by farmers, even at the height of silver fever. See Milton Friedman and Anna Schwartz, *A Monetary History of the United States, 1867–1960.* (Princeton: Princeton University Press, 1963), 104–137 and Douglass North, *Growth and Welfare in the American Past* (Englewood Cliffs, N.J.: Prentice-Hall, 1974), 130–140.

30. Dunning, *Farmers' Alliance History,* 165.

31. Dunning, *Farmers' Alliance History,* 165; Weaver, *A Call To Action,* 347.

their products and for the products of all producers. This was of course true, but only for producers who owned what they produced. For the millions of industrial workers who labored for a wage rather than for title to their produce, higher prices meant only higher prices. Unless changes in the distribution of profits accompanied inflation, higher market prices for agricultural produce, for all consumer goods, simply meant that workers' wages would buy less. For workers to benefit from the inflationary program of the Alliance, wages would have to rise at least in step with inflation. The Alliance position held that more money in circulation would result in more spending and would translate into higher wages for workers.[32] This comfortable assurance was reinforced by a lack of knowledge about the nature of the relationship between capital and labor outside of the rural countryside, and an acceptance of the very economic logic Alliance leaders decried.

Despite their clear understanding that the laws of supply and demand did not apply in agriculture so long as distribution was controlled by a few large factors, the leaders of the Alliance did not transfer that understanding to the urban economy. As long as managers and owners directly controlled wages, and as long as a steady supply of surplus labor was available from which to replace workers who quit or who were fired, there was no evidence to suggest that increased spending, higher prices, or even increased profits in manufacturing would lead to real or nominal wage increases for urban workers. Indeed, without such evidence, there was little for labor to like in the Alliance monetary program.

The inability of the Alliance to come to grips with the economic problems facing industrial workers resulted not so much from ignorance as from an unwillingness to apply the same rigorous analysis to industrial labor that they so readily applied to their study of agricultural labor. The major flaw in Alliance thinking was a blindness to the fact that workers' wages were controlled by management and not by the market. Yet leaders of the movement understood that in agriculture "the law of supply and demand becomes an absurdity when it is comprehended that capital controls both."[33] Only the farmers' exclusive attention to small-scale agriculture and to the moral economy of the yeoman farm can explain this inattentiveness to other producers. Rather than follow their own rhetoric and assess the needs of all producers, Alliance leaders simply extrapolated from their own experience. The moralism of the Alliance ideology goes a long way in

32. *Southern Mercury,* January 21, 1892.
33. *National Economist,* June 15, 1889; *Southern Mercury,* August 9, 1894.

explaining, as well, the Order's peculiar and otherwise inexplicable position regarding the labor unrest of the 1890s.

4

Specifically, the Alliance opposed strikes of any kind, from Pullman to Homestead, and all others in between. The Alliance leadership did not understand what the labor leaders realized, namely that remedying the condition of labor was not possible through legislation, that changes in working conditions had to occur in the workplace through demands supported by direct action. White farmers, in contrast, were only beginning to feel the kind of direct control of their labor power that was common in the factories, mines, and mills of the North. Many Alliancemen and most of the leadership owned land, even if it was mortgaged. The Alliance reform ideology and reform program reflected the relationship of its leaders to the land. What these leaders opposed was the existence of monopolies that constricted their ability to carry on economic lives as small producers. They campaigned for legislation that would protect and preserve their position as landowners selling the fruits of their toil. In this, they seem to justify Gompers' portrait of the Alliance as a bourgeois organization of petty landowners.

This kind of legislation, designed to extend protection to independent producers, did not apply to industrial labor precisely because laborers sold their labor and not its products. This fundamental difference in perspective accounts for the inability of the two groups to agree on the source of their ills or on a site in which to wage the battle for reform. Here, Alliance ideas simply were not sophisticated enough to confront the problems facing urban workers.

For farmers, economic problems were rooted in unjust laws that gave preferential treatment to capital. These laws were easily overturned by taking control of the legislative mechanism. For workers, the central economic problem was lack of daily control over their labor and powerlessness in their relationship with managers and owners. These problems were rooted in the very structure of enterprise organized on the basis of wage labor. It was here, at the disjuncture between the Alliance plan to reform the state and labor's understanding of the need to restructure the workplace, that the Alliance's traditional understanding of democratic politics failed to provide even the hope of effective reform. Alliance leaders told their followers that politics guided economic activity. They failed to understand that economic structures, once in place, limit the efficacy and scope of political reform. The system of wage labor, combined with the sovereignty of private property, which the Alliance supported, virtually eliminated political solutions to the problem of an uneven division of surplus from industrial production. Moreover, no group in nineteenth-century America, with the possible exception of the early Knights of Labor, and later DeLeon's Socialists, was willing to address political change at the depth required to alter the fundamental values that supported capitalism. Certainly the Alliance's devotion to the traditions of small-scale capitalism prevented its political or educational apparatus from questioning its virtue. Balking at this more fundamental kind of questioning, the Alliance's dedication to the cause of "producer unity" became more rhetorical than real.

Alliance reaction to strikes captured this reticence to pursue the logic of "equal rights to all" to its conclusion. Pullman and Homestead, in particular, provide a glimpse of the tension between support for labor solidarity and repudiation of radical action.

On July 12, 1894, the *Southern Mercury* ran a banner headline that read: "PRESIDENT CLEVELAND HAS AGAIN VIOLATED THE CONSTITUTION AND LAIN HIMSELF LIABLE TO IMPEACHMENT BY ORDERING U.S. TROOPS TO SHOOT DOWN THE STRIKING RAILROAD MEN IN ILLINOIS."[34] Below the headline was a drawing of troops firing upon a mob and an article on the strike. Until Cleveland's order to the Army, the Alliance press had paid little attention to the strike, reporting only that it was going on and that as a note to Alliance members, electoral reform was more effective than strikes. Two years before, the *National Economist* had raised the cry, with "THE HOMESTEAD HORROR" as its front-page editorial.[35] What makes these articles interesting is their focus on the responses of Cleveland and the "Pinkerton Army" and not on the actual labor conflict. For the Alliance editors, the strikes, which they could not understand or support while they were simply battles between the workers and the railroads, became intelligible with the entry of government on the side of capital. In protecting the Pinkertons and taking an active role in stopping the strike, Cleveland's actions were parallel, in the writing of Alliance editors, to the passage of legislation favoring organized capital against the independent farmer. The *Economist* ended its editorial with the rather flat admonition that "the division of the people into plutocrats and paupers must be changed."[36]

At the local level, both strikes brought responses from suballiances

34. *Southern Mercury,* July 12, 1894.
35. *National Economist,* July 16, 1892.
36. *National Economist,* July 16, 1892.

throughout the South. One Alliance collected corn, wheat, and beef to send to the strikers in Homestead, wishing them "Godspeed in their struggle against monopoly and the Pinkerton thugs."[37] The Williamson County, Texas, Alliance passed eight separate resolutions at its July 20 meeting in support of the strikers in their "struggle for freedom for themselves and their posterity."[38] But despite this outward show of solidarity, the Alliance position remained that "strikes are not the methods (of the Alliance)." When the unions "find out for the hundredth time that strikes, even when successful, do not reach the root of the disease," the Alliance offered, "we will argue with them for the substitution of a better and more effective method."[39] The Alliance repeatedly argued their version of a better and more effective method, but that method was suited to their interests and their condition, not those of the mass of urban laborers whom they sought to bring into the producers' crusade.

Thus the traditions that empowered farmers within the movement also constrained them. Lurking not far from the noble vision of the independent yeoman farmer was a pervasive racism; under the idea of the sanctity of labor was a mistrust of wage labor and a misunderstanding of its demands. In the kind of education it promoted, the Alliance vision was limited by the blind spots of its traditional ideological base. Where there was common ground between blacks, white farmers, and urban workers, the three worked together; where common ground did not exist, farmers acted in their interests alone.

Yet, there were those in the movement who worked to expand the mutual aims of blacks, workers, and farmers. As their critique of capitalism deepened and became more sophisticated, some leaders approached the development of a theory of production and distribution that explained the plight of workers and farmers and that saw the perpetuation of racism as a tool for the continued fragmentation of the working class.[40] Scott Morgan, Evan Jones, Ben Terrell, and Charles Macune hoped that the campaign of education among the farmers of the South could in fact break down some of the barriers that divided these groups. In the texts of their curriculum, more serious attention was paid to the nature of industrial labor, to racial issues, and to broad and telling criticisms of the structures of capitalist enterprise than anywhere else in the movement. But in education as in political

37. *Southern Mercury,* July 12, 1894.
38. *Southern Mercury,* August 2, 1892.
39. *Southern Mercury,* August 2, 1892.
40. Morgan, *History of the Wheel,* 22–47. His explanation is very Marxian in its parallels to ideas of exploitation, surplus value, and control of labor power.

action for economic change, the legacy of the Alliance was muted by internal divisions and external oppositions.

5

Macune's withdrawal from the movement in 1892 left the national leadership without its most powerful educational spokesman and signaled a marked shift in the strategic priorities of the National Alliance. At the same time that Edgecombe's local leaders took up the educational standard, the Supreme Council was putting aside its educational efforts in favor of partisan political campaigning. Ironically, political education ended up competing for resources with political action. The headlong rush of the Alliance into third-party politics, and the rise to power of leaders like Tom Watson in Georgia and Lon Livingston in North Carolina, ended the movement's explicit concern with political education and began its partisan campaigning for People's party candidates. The shift in priorities involved a long and bitter struggle within the movement.

For years editors and local Alliance officials had argued that only by breaking ties with the Democrats could the farmers destroy the corruption that was destroying politics. Third-party agitation within the Alliance waned during the successful elections of 1890, when Democratic candidates pledging support of Alliance principles, notably support of the Ocala Demands, carried hundreds of seats in state legislatures and captured several southern governorships. Soon after the election, though, many of these candidates, now officeholders, repudiated their pledges to the Alliance, and to the principles for which the Alliance stood.[41] This double-dealing reinforced the image of the Democrats as corrupt and unscrupulous and delivered a telling blow to the idea of internal reform. Direct rejection of the Alliance by the Democrats after 1890 also breathed new life into the third-party movement.

On October 5, 1891, the Executive Committee of the Democratic party in Texas voted to expel from the party any individual who refused to publicly repudiate Macune's subtreasury plan.[42] In a stroke, the Texas Democrats alienated several of the loudest voices in the national leadership of the Alliance. In a searing editorial, Milton Park

41. Paper presented by Bruce Palmer on the voting records of Populist Congressmen at the Annual Meeting of the Organization of American Historians, Indianapolis, Indiana, April 1982. See also McMath, *Populist Vanguard,* 94–96, and Goodwyn, *Democratic Promise,* 213–224, 234.
42. *Southern Mercury,* October 8, 1891; December 31, 1892.

swung the *Mercury* into the third-party camp, and lecturer Stump Ashby began an odyssey across the South in support of independent partisan action. Somewhat ironically, given the demands of the Texas Democracy, the one steadfast voice in the councils of the Alliance favoring holding a course within the old Party was that of C. W. Macune.[43]

Matters came to a head at the 1892 convention of the Alliance in St. Louis. There, reform organizations from every section, representing every political persuasion, gathered under the banner of the Alliance for a unified assault on entrenched power and privilege. From the beginning, infighting plagued the convention. In 1891, Macune, as head of the National Executive Committee, made a formal agreement with Knights of Labor leader Terrence Powderly to hold a convention of reform organizations in Washington, D.C., in 1892, to coincide with the Alliance convention there. Washington was Macune's turf, but more important, it was a safe distance from the western strongholds of the most ardent third-party advocates. Soon thereafter, Alliance President Polk and his newly created Legislative Council overruled Macune and established St. Louis as the site of the 1892 gathering. It seems clear that Polk's decision aimed at increasing the representation of third-party men and at challenging Macune's power within the movement.[44] Macune fought the decision to move the convention, but this time the tide of opinion flowed against him.

Macune also fought Polk's leadership of the convention, nominating Ben Terrell as chairman in a last attempt to guide the Alliance from what he saw to be dangerous waters. In a decisive vote, Polk defeated Terrell, and so too, Macune. Stirring speeches, first by Polk and then by Minnesota's Ignatius Donnelly, fired the momentum for radical action and with a rousing ovation, the delegates voted to create

43. It is interesting that Macune's own account of the history of the Alliance ends at this point. For a man so concerned with history it is certainly dismaying to find that he left the history of the intense political struggle that followed to his enemies. For an account see Goodwyn, *Democratic Promise*, 265–270.

44. The Polk/Macune battle for control of the Alliance was personal and ideological. Both resorted to rather unscrupulous maneuvering in attempts to discredit and unseat the other, although Polk's manipulation of rumors about Macune's finances seem to make him the muddier of the two. Macune's attempts were largely focused on creating reform networks with himself or his lieutenants at the center. The National Reform Press Association was led by Macune, the Council of Industrial Organizations was headed by Ben Terrell. Macune tried to surround Polk with organizations all pressing in on the Alliance. Polk, meanwhile, sought to destroy Macune's credibility within the movement through challenges issued by his lieutenants regarding Macune's conduct in receiving loans from political candidates while he edited the *Economist*. For more detail see McMath, *The Populist Vanguard*, 90–95, 110–115.

the People's party and hold a presidential nominating convention on July 4, 1892.

The vote was, of course, a personal defeat for Macune and appeared to repudiate the slow course of reform through education advocated by Macune and his supporters. But Macune, who had captured and held the imagination of the membership for nearly four years, was not easily daunted. As the convention closed, he strode to the podium and called the delegates back to order. Never one to dally, Macune announced his support for the People's party and urged the convention to appoint a special committee to coordinate the efforts of the various assembled reform organizations with those of the new party. The convention agreed and appointed a committee of fifteen to oversee the impending campaign. Included at the last minute as a member of the committee was one Charles Macune from the state of Texas.[45]

As editor of the *Economist,* Macune still possessed significant leverage within the movement as the direct link between the membership and the leadership. Although personally distressed by the decision to enter the partisan fray, Macune worked during the winter and spring of 1892 to support the new party, uncharacteristically filling the role of good soldier under the command of Leonidas Lafayette Polk. Macune's editorials in the *Economist* crowed the impending success of the "people" in a final, titanic struggle against the "interests" with the People's party as the source of deliverance. In June, as the *Tarboro Southerner* celebrated another graduation in town, Macune suspended the publication of the *Economist* Educational Exercises "until after the Presidential election in November."[46] In their place, Macune gathered and published brief biographical sketches of Populist candidates and news of Populist campaigns throughout the country. Perhaps no other single act better captures the shifting priorities of the National Alliance than the substitution of campaign news for the Exercises. In a stroke, the national leadership moved political education, long the guiding star of the Southern Alliance, to the background, replaced by the tactical demands of winning an election. It is hard to imagine that Macune bore much enthusiasm for the change.

The election turned out to be far less than a victory for the people,

---

45. *St. Louis Republic,* February 24, 1892; Goodwyn, *Democratic Promise,* 267; McMath, *Populist Vanguard,* 130–131; Hicks, *Populist Revolt,* 205–238; Taylor, *Farmers' Movement,* 275–279.

46. The Democrat's nomination of Cleveland pushed Macune farther in his support of the third party, at least at the national level. See *National Economist,* May 28, 1892; July 2, 1892; June 20, 1892.

less, even, than a victory for the People's party. At the national level, Alliance leaders assumed that Polk would head the ticket. A southern unionist, his leadership would minimize the inevitable braying of sectional interests and would keep the farmers together as a block. Polk's sudden death on June 11 at the age of fifty-five threw the People's party into chaos just weeks before its convention. The eventual presidential nominee, James Weaver, a former Union general, generated no enthusiasm in the South and only lukewarm support. In August, defeats in the state elections in Georgia and Alabama made it clear that the People's party had not tapped even half the potential voting strength of the Alliance. The membership had not followed the leadership into the third party.[47]

In the fall, Macune changed course, feverishly attempting to disassociate the Alliance from the party. "It is no use now to calculate and discuss whether it was a mistake for the People's party to make a start this year," he wrote, but he urged his readers to remember that "the Alliance is not responsible for the starting or the success of the People's party."[48] Macune foresaw the party's disastrous defeat and worked to keep the Alliance from being dragged down with it.

His efforts failed to persuade the membership of the difference between the Alliance organization and the People's party, and those same efforts alienated him from more ardent third-party advocates within the Order's leadership. Estimates from Georgia suggest that up to 80 percent of the suballiances disbanded following the 1892 election. Similar reports from throughout the South paint a picture of a demoralized and dispirited membership, a membership that had forsaken party, section, and in some cases friends and family to answer the call for a new political order. The Populist defeat broke the spirit of the Alliance movement. It remained only for the leadership, in its bitterness, to devour itself.

The Supreme Council of the National Farmers' Alliance and Industrial Union gathered in Memphis soon after the November elections in an attempt to rebuild and regroup. The meetings barely started before the Populist hard-liners launched their attack on Macune. Macune, it seems, had hedged his bets in the November contest. He campaigned vigorously through the summer on behalf of Populist candidates. But in the early fall the returns from Alabama and Georgia convinced Macune that the third party would fail. In addition to trying to disassociate the Alliance from the People's party in

47. See McMath, *Populist Vanguard*, 142, 143; Hicks, *Populist Revolt*, chap. 9.
48. *National Economist*, November 5, 1892.

Economist editorials, Macune personally took action on behalf of Democratic candidates in an effort to restore relations with the Democratic party.

U. S. Hall, a member of the Supreme Council from Missouri and no friend of Macune, rose at the Memphis meeting with a startling accusation: that Macune had used the offices and presses of the *National Economist* to prepare and distribute campaign literature for the Democrats. Macune freely admitted supporting local and state Democratic candidates in November, although he never wavered in his opposition to Cleveland. In the days that followed, Macune and Henry Loucks, an ardent Populist from South Dakota, struggled for the presidency of the order and for leadership of the farmers' movement.

The two men represented two divergent paths down which lay two different futures for the Alliance movement. With Macune lay a retreat from the third party and retrenchment with education as the basis of a unified activism on the part of all producers. With Loucks lay closer ties with the People's party, the development of a national party hierarchy, and the mobilization of the organizational apparatus of the Alliance for political campaigning.

Following a barrage of charge and countercharge between the two camps. Macune had his name withdrawn from nomination, perhaps in an attempt to stir up a storm of protest among the delegates that could lead to his election by acclamation.[49] If that was Macune's plan, it backfired. Seconds after Ben Terrell withdrew Macune's nomination, a motion to close nominations passed, and Loucks stood as the only remaining candidate. The future of the Alliance lay along the path of the People's party, and its fortunes would henceforth rise and fall with the Populists.

With the leadership issue decided, Loucks attempted to build on his victory by attacking Macune's one remaining power base, the *National Economist*. Loucks complained that the *Economist* had been lukewarm in its support of Populist candidates and that its southern focus alienated midwestern and western readers. He urged the Council to withdraw its support of the journal and to create a new party organ under new editorial guidance. The council instead launched an inves-

49. Macune's own history is mute on the issue. Goodwyn subscribes to this theory and goes further to suggest that Macune's old nemesis, William Lamb, pulled the rug out from under him by jumping up to close nominations before any protest from the floor could materialize. For this and other accounts of the Memphis meeting see Goodwyn, *Democratic Promise,* 344–345; McMath, *Populist Vanguard,* 144–145. The closest Macune ever got to a discussion of the events in Memphis was an explanation of his resignation in the *Economist,* December 3, 1892.

tigation of the paper and of Macune, in an effort to uncover the truth of claims that Macune had "sold out" to the Democrats.

They need not have bothered. On December 3, 1892, Macune announced in the *National Economist* his resignation from all "offices and positions in the National Farmers' Alliance."[50] In 1891, Macune had written of the Alliance:

> let its earnest aim be first to educate the people, and when that is done, have an abiding faith in . . . the integrity of the people in living up to the full measure of the light as they see it.[51]

In Macune's eyes, the Supreme Council rejected these principles in Memphis. "There is a class of men," he wrote in his *nunc dimitis,* "who pose as reformers who seem to think that the formation of a new political party is of first importance." In their search for partisan support, Macune worried, "they are willing to accept any principles that may have local popularity."[52] To his horror, the People's party succumbed to the very demagoguery, the very partisan gamesmanship, the very elevation of party over principle that the Alliance fought in its struggle against the Democrats.

Macune was not alone in his fears, nor in his assessment of the failure of the venture into third-party politics. D. D. Langford, an organizer and lecturer in Kentucky, wrote to Macune after the election:

> I wish to say to the brotherhood that the battle is fought; the smoke has cleared and we can see clearly what has been done and the mistakes we have made . . . we have let partyism, in many instances, get the better of our judgment by making a great effort to get our demands before we have gotten the people educated up to the point that principle is above parties and men.[53]

Langford pleaded for a period of reflection and reunification. "Let us all go to work," he urged, "and build up the Order, make it stronger and better by making it an educational and cooperative movement, as that is our only hope for independence and freedom." For Langford

50. *National Economist,* December 3, 1892. It appears that Macune continued to write in the paper through February 1893.
51. *National Economist,* September 5, 1891.
52. *National Economist,* December 24, 1892.
53. *National Economist,* December 24, 1892.

and Macune, indeed for the movement as a whole, the time for such work had passed; it was too late.

Macune had argued that the fate of the Alliance was linked to the creation and maintenance of a strong campaign of political education. Perhaps his vision of an informed and critical citizenry supplanting parties was naive. Perhaps his faith in the ability and willingness of individuals to break the bonds of traditionally held views was utopian. Still, his understanding of the nature of southern politics led him to correctly predict the failure of a third party there. Education— political education—was not just the best means of unlocking the political potential of southern producers; it was the only way.[54]

In the years that followed, the Alliance rapidly forfeited any identity independent of the People's party. Party leaders, for their part, led their membership on a political roller coaster ride, uniting with first one, then the other, major party. Such marriages, as Macune feared, were marriages of convenience made on the altar of local issues. Not even these efforts sufficed. Alliance membership plummeted in the years after 1892 in virtually every southern state. Even the currency crisis of 1893 did not bring farmers back into the fold. Despite efforts by Park and a few others, independent Alliance leadership never re-emerged.

None can say whether the fate of the Alliance would have been different if it had decided to stay Macune's course. Certainly third-party leaders overestimated the ability of southern farmers to escape traditional partisan ties. Whether, over time and through the process of political educating, that ability would have been enhanced is a matter for speculation. It is clearer that the leadership and the membership could not move easily or simply from general consensus on broad principles to specific policies. It is clear, as well, that the same traditions that gave the Alliance strength in the South limited its ability to reach its stated aims. Finally, regarding education, it is clear that the membership did not fully appreciate the fine distinctions that the leadership made between different kinds of education and indeed between different kinds of knowledge. These distinctions did not seem

54. Goodwyn has argued that because of his allegiance to the Democrats, Macune was somehow less radical politically than his contemporaries or than his own economic ideas would suggest. One may look at Macune's politics in still another way. By asserting that political decisions should be made on the basis of discovered class interest, with parties merely as instruments for the execution of class politics, Macune articulated a kind of politics certainly bolder and newer in conception than many of his contemporaries. More, it is a kind of politics congruent with the development of producer and consumer cooperatives.

immediately germane to life in educationally underdeveloped southern communities like Tarboro. In those communities and in the South in general, the Alliance legacy produced consistent support for education and for the expansion of public schooling. Gone, though, was the kind of critical perspective on education promised at that first gathering of the Alliance in 1889 and articulated again in Evan Jones's comments on agricultural education:

> . . . the object of organization among agriculturalists is not only to teach our people how to produce larger crops . . . it is of vital importance that [they] have a well-defined system of organizations, educational and cooperative, through which they can again obtain control of the products of the farm and prevent their passing into the hands of the corporations.[55]

Support for this broad configuration of educational enterprises quickly decayed into traditional channels: support for more years of schooling, more days in the school calendar, and more and better schoolhouses. These were, there can be no doubt, important goals in the South, but in their pursuit, much of the subtlety, the creativity, and the power of the Alliance critique of education and society was lost. The Alliance did leave among its members a broad faith in education in all its dimensions. This legacy forged an ironic link between the educational efforts of the Alliance and the efforts of the self-proclaimed educational crusaders of the New South.

6

Alliance educational leaders attempted to alter the nature of political discourse among farmers and other producers in the region. Their central argument claimed that politics engaged class against class, each struggling for the protection and extension of class interests and economic power. Leaders like Macune tried to arm farmers for the struggle. They helped farmers shield themselves individually with basic literacy and numeracy and with an understanding of the nature of economic relations. They taught the members a sense of common purpose and common interest different from the purposes and interests of other groups in society. The leadership developed programs and ideas, like the exchange and the subtreasury, that helped producers attack

55. Evan Jones, *National Economist,* March 14, 1889.

entrenched power and privilege. The members themselves, through their meetings and gatherings, reached out to each other in social ways, creating communities among isolated rural populations.

Amidst the many struggles waged by the men and women of the Alliance for individual dignity and collective power, none was more important than their struggle to learn. One idea stood out clearly as the basis for their struggle, their sacrifices, and their dreams, that "education of the masses is the hope of the world,"[56] It is still so today.

56. Betty Gay, in Dunning, *Farmers' Alliance History,* 312.

Epilogue
The Progressive Response to Populist America

General intelligence reduces the need of harsh and external
government, it makes the protection of person and property
easier, surer, and more economical, and substitutes the teacher
for the sheriff, the workshop for the poorhouse, the school-
house for the prison.
—J. L. M. Curry, General Agent of the Peabody Fund, 1884[1]

1

Jabez Lamar Monroe Curry, the standard-bearer of southern school reform in the 1880s and 1890s, called the leaders of the Alliance "a good many fools" and condemned the People's party for "trying to find a shortcut to individual and national prosperity."[2] Curry and other educational leaders of the rising New South saw only one bright spot in the agrarian movement: its broad and longstanding support for education. Throughout the last decade of the century, the group of educational reformers made the most of this support in its efforts to bring a northern-style common-school system to the South.

Curry made direct appeals to Alliancemen and later to Populists. He spoke to Alliance groups and corresponded with Alliance leaders at length about how to raise support in the South for public education. The Alliance returned his attention by publishing Curry's speeches in favor of expanded educational opportunities.[3] The basis of the agreement between Curry and the Alliance lay in their shared desire for more schools and better schools in the region. But while the improvement of schooling was only one aspect of the Alliance's educational plan, it was the focal point of the crusader's attention.

1. *U.S. Bureau of Education Circular of Information,* no. 3, 1884; Charles Dabney, *Universal Education in the South,* 2 vols. (Chapel Hill: University of North Carolina Press, 1936), 2:120.
2. Quoted in D. Spivey, *Schooling for the New Slavery: Black Industrial Education, 1868–1915* (Westport, Conn.: Greenwood Press, 1978), 80.
3. Merle Curti, *The Social Ideas of American Educators* (Totowa, N.J.: Littlefield, Adams, 1974), 275; Rice, *The Negro in Texas,* 167–168.

The Crusade for Education in the South brought together educational professionals, laymen, and philanthropists interested in the related problems of unrest and development in the South. Where the Alliance saw education as an instrument of liberation and empowerment, crusaders generally saw schooling as a means of social control. Curry echoed the views of most of his peers when he wrote that

> General intelligence reduces the need of harsh and external government, it makes the protection of person and property easier, surer, and more economical, and substitutes the teacher for the sheriff, the workshop for the poorhouse, the schoolhouse for the prison.[4]

It is not surprising, given this notion of the proper function of education in society, that Alliance leaders were wary of contemporary schooling. Schooling for control embodied a set of values inimical to those at the center of the Alliance campaign for education. Yet the idea of schooling as a means of control fit well with the background, expectations, and aspirations of the crusaders.

Curry bridged the Old South and the New. He spent a leisured and privileged youth on his family's Alabama plantation. Tutors prepared the young Curry for college and he enjoyed a successful undergraduate career at the University of Georgia. After graduation in 1843, Curry moved north to study law at Harvard. While in Cambridge, Curry watched with interest the process of common school reform articulated by Horace Mann and his successor, Barnas Sears. With Sears, Curry developed a friendly and longlasting relationship.

Curry returned home in 1846 and in 1848 ran for a seat in the Alabama legislature. His skill as an orator, and a political position closely aligned with John Calhoun, made Curry popular with the voters. He worked hard as a legislator and quickly achieved prominence. His peers in the statehouse chose Curry to represent Alabama in the secession Congress and throughout the war as a member of the Confederate Congress. After Appomattox, Curry was pardoned along with Jefferson Davis and other high-ranking rebels; he again returned home, retreating into his deep Baptist faith. For several years, Curry presided over a small Baptist college in his home state, leaving only when his disgust for Reconstruction policies drove him away. He moved to Richmond and until 1873 lectured intermittently at the university there.

4. *U.S. Bureau of Education Circular of Information,* no. 3, 1884; Dabney, *Universal Education in the South,* 2:120.

In 1873, Barnas Sears, now general agent for the Peabody Fund, invited his friend Curry to serve as his lieutenant in the fund's effort to support black schooling in the South. For a decade, Curry labored to build support among southern legislatures and southern citizens for the idea of black education. His message was consistent: educate blacks to take their proper roles in society or suffer the consequences of massive social unrest.

In 1881, Sears fell ill and found he could not carry out his role as Agent for the Peabody trustees. Sears urged the trustees to select Curry as his successor, arguing that the cause of black education in the South needed a southerner in its vanguard. Others applied for or were nominated for the post. Commissioner of Education John Eaton expressed interest, Henry Barnard and Amory D. Mayo attracted the notice of the trustees, and William Ruffner's name matched and perhaps exceeded Curry's own in terms of his Bourbon pedigree. Yet in the end, Sears's urgings and Curry's own record won the day. Curry took the reins of the two million dollar fund in late 1881 and held the position of general agent, with a brief hiatus, until his retirement from public work in 1902.

As agent for the Peabody Fund, Curry managed the distribution of money to struggling black schools as well as a campaign for state funding of black education. Curry canvassed the South speaking in support of industrial education and training for blacks. He backed up his urgings with cash. It proved a persuasive combination. In 1889 Curry's power over the development of black schooling multiplied when he was named general agent of the John F. Slater Fund, another philanthropic trust aimed toward educating blacks for useful roles in southern society. By 1895, Curry was by all accounts the most powerful man in southern education. Yet for his power, Curry remained dissatisfied with the progress made by blacks or whites. In particular, he tired of sprinkling money on individual schools in the hope that they would grow and prosper on their own. He reported to the Slater Board in 1897 that "tinkering" would not address the root of the problem, that real "uplift" of the blacks, could come only "through the class, as a whole that requires it."[5] This implied a broader involvement of blacks in their own training as well as broader support from whites throughout the South.

Amory D. Mayo had come to a similar conclusion. Mayo was a northerner, a Unitarian-Congregationalist minister for whom educa-

5. Curry's report in *Proceedings of the Trustees of the John F. Slater Fund for the Education of Freedmen,* 1897 (Baltimore, 1897), 11.

tion became a central element in his "calling" during two terms on the Cincinnati school board. After Cincinnati, Mayo chose a new ministry, to travel the length and breadth of the South, observing educational conditions and witnessing in support of public schooling.[6]

Like Curry, Mayo held the farmers' movement in contempt, calling its efforts to reform politics "wild and dishonest schemes," that would "leave multitudes of these honest and credulous people worse off than before," and would eventually "scuttle the American state."[7] Mayo frankly doubted the people's ability to take correct action on their own behalf. He saw the plain folk of the South as "credulous," if honest. For him and for others in the crusade, hope lay in the leadership of an educated, semiprofessional cadre dedicated to implementing reform along lines of their own design. Mayo referred to this cadre as the "Southern Educational Public" and included in its membership not only men like Curry and the philanthropists who backed him, but also long-suffering fighters for southern schooling, like North Carolina Superintendent Calvin Wiley and the state superintendents who struggled to wrest even meager appropriations from southern legislatures.[8] It was a concept of *public* that would have been alien to Alliance leaders and members. One recent trend filled Mayo with hope for the reform cause: the rise to prominence of a small group of educational professionals in the region, a group that would be central to the success of the educational crusade.

Edwin Alderman and Charles McIver well represent this generation of educational professionals on the move. Both were born and spent their youth in North Carolina during the war and Reconstruction. The two young men met in college, at the newly revived University of North Carolina, through the debating society, of which both men were avid members. McIver, older by a year, was the more powerful orator, yet it was Alderman's grace and patience at one public debate that impressed Edward Moses, one of Curry's earliest disciples and principal of the Goldsboro Graded School. Moses was always on the lookout for articulate, energetic young men to teach in Goldsboro, and after the debate he approached Alderman with a proposal. Over the course of the next few days, Moses and Alderman talked often. In

6. There is no extant biography of Mayo. Biographical information compiled from Dabney, *Universal Education in the South,* 2:4, 6, 503; Edward Abbott, "The Conference at Capon Springs," *Literary World* 29, no. 14 (July 1898): 216.

7. A. D. Mayo, "Southern Women in the Recent Educational Movement in the South," *U.S. Bureau of Education Circular of Information,* no. 1, 1892, 132–133.

8. A. D. Mayo, "Overlook and Outlook in Southern Education," *U.S. Bureau of Education Circular of Information,* no.1, 1892, 285.

Edwin A. Alderman, 1923, founding member of the General Education Board and President of the University of Virginia

the end, Moses not only convinced Alderman to accept his offer of a teaching position, but managed to get McIver to give up his study of law to enter the field as well.

More than a decade later, Alderman tried to sum up the spirit at Chapel Hill that moved so many of his generation into positions of leadership in the New South:

> There was no better place, I think, for the making of leaders in the world than Chapel Hill in the late seventies. The note of life was simple, rugged—almost primitive. Our young hearts, aflame with the impulses of youth, were quietly conscious of the vicissitudes and sufferings through which our fathers had just passed. The unconscious discipline and tutelage of defeat and fortitude and self-restraint cradled us all.[9]

In teaching, Alderman and McIver found great satisfaction and a means of applying their "young hearts" to the rebuilding of their homeland.

Goldsboro became a heaven for the young men of Alderman's generation. The roster of teachers at Moses' school reads as a *Who's Who* of southern education. Alderman, who was to become the president of the University of North Carolina, Tulane, and the University of Virginia, was joined by Philander P. Claxton, future U.S. Commissioner of Education, James Joyner, future State Superintendent in North Carolina, and M. C. S. "Billy" Noble, future Dean of the School of Education at Chapel Hill. Joining the group in its frequent late-night discussions and revels was another college chum and debater, Charles Aycock, whose slow law practice gave him plenty of time for socializing and for dreaming of a future as the "education governor" he would become.

In 1885, Moses was transferred to Raleigh and Alderman moved into the superintendency of the Goldsboro schools. Although Moses' group had begun to disperse, Moses managed to bring them together, Aycock and all, for several days each holiday season. "We would have earnest discussions for two or three days and nights," wrote one of Moses' proteges, "and we always left these meetings with our ideals strengthened and our hearts aflame with the desire to accomplish

9. Dabney, *Universal Education in the South,* 1:198–210. Dumas Malone, *Edwin A. Alderman, a Biography* (New York: Doubleday, 1940), chaps. 1, 2. Edwin A. Alderman, "In Memoriam Charles Duncan McIver," Fiftieth Anniversary Volume, National Educational Association (Washington, D.C.: National Education Association, 1907), 311.

182   Epilogue

results."[10] Around the same time, Alderman attended a lecture Curry gave in Chapel Hill. Curry's vision, combined with Moses', directed Alderman to a life's work in "a cause to which a man might nobly attach himself."[11]

In 1889, Alderman and McIver reunited to direct a series of teachers' institutes throughout the state under the sponsorship of the state superintendent. "We were to start out on a new and untried experiment," wrote Alderman. On the night they received news of their appointment, the two men "talked about our plans and difficulties until the cocks began to crow." "I am inclined to think it," Alderman recalled later, "about the best night I ever spent, for an intelligent and unselfish idea held our youth under its spell."[12] McIver and Alderman canvassed the state by train and by wagon, setting up their mobile institute for a day or two in each county. They spoke often before Alliance and People's party audiences, and they always received warm approval for their stand in favor of higher school expenditures.[13] The work was draining, but it allowed the two a view of the state of education in North Carolina unmatched by any official's perspective.

In their reports, McIver and Alderman recommended that the state prepare a clear and comprehensive plan for teacher education, that it establish a teachers' library in every county, and that the state set a minimum length for school sessions. But all of these required substantially more money than was available. In order to address the financial problem, they urged the legislature to permit and even encourage local taxation for the benefit of schools. Such an act, as we have seen, passed the state legislature in 1891.

In 1892, as the Alliance collapsed, the North Carolina legislature appropriated funds for the creation of a Normal School for Women at Greensboro and named McIver its first president. He, in turn, appointed Alderman professor. After a year, Alderman left Greensboro for a post at Chapel Hill. Three years later, in 1896, Alderman succeeded George Winston as president of the University of North Carolina.

A chain of shared backgrounds and common mentors linked Curry, Mayo, Alderman, and McIver. As Charles Dabney, himself a crusader and historian of the reform movement, put it,

10. Dabney, *Universal Education in the South*, 1:195–197.
11. *Proceedings of the Sixth Conference for Education in the South, Richmond, Virginia, 1903* (Richmond, 1903), 266–267. Dabney, *Universal Education in the South,* 1:207–208.
12. Alderman, quoted in Dabney, *Universal Education in the South,* 1:208.
13. Louis Harlan, *Separate and Unequal* (Chapel Hill: University of North Carolina Press, 1958), 49.

. . . as Jefferson begat Curry and Curry begat Moses, so Moses begat Alderman, McIver, Joyner, and Aycock, who in turn begat hundreds of other workers who helped to build the present public schools of the South.[14]

Building schools in the South relied on building and extending this familial network of friends and acquaintances. It also depended on securing the support of the voters in southern states. In 1896 and 1897, the "family" of reformers in North Carolina turned to the People's party for help in securing legislation that would encourage local taxation.

2

Republicans joined Populists in the election of 1896 to capture the state legislature and major state offices in North Carolina.[15] Among those swept into office by the fusion victory was Charles Mebane, a Populist and former Alliance member, who became state superintendent of schools. During his brief tenure, Mebane worked closely with Alderman first, and later with the wider network of school reformers.

Alderman took on the presidency at North Carolina in part to push the school, its programs, and its graduates forward as examples of how the state could benefit from a vigorous system of education. He aimed, he said, to make the university the "chief public school."[16] He had in mind an ambitious program of expansion that needed the full support and financial backing of the legislature. Symbolic support came early. On January 27, 1897, the legislature adjourned so that its members might attend Alderman's inauguration. A huge delegation of politicians steamed into Chapel Hill on a special train. They listened attentively as Alderman argued the connection between educational and economic progress. At the end of his speech, the politicians joined the undergraduates, faculty, and guests in raising a loud cheer for the new president. It was the last cheer Alderman heard from the legislature for quite a while.[17]

The following week, Alderman made a slower and less showy journey in the opposite direction, to visit the legislators on their turf and to put before them his case for increased appropriations. The law-

14. Dabney, *Universal Education in the South,* 1:198.
15. For accounts of the 1896 election see Harlan, *Separate and Unequal,* chap. 2. Also Dabney, *Universal Education in the South,* 1:213–216.
16. Malone, *Edwin A. Alderman,* 80. Harlan, *Separate and Unequal,* 33.
17. Malone, *Edwin A. Alderman,* 80–84. "The Inauguration of Edwin A. Alderman, D.C.L., President of the University of North Carolina, January 27, 1897." Pamphlet in the Southern Historical Collection, University of North Carolina, Chapel Hill.

makers once again listened to him with respect. But this time, instead of an ovation, Alderman faced a barrage of questions, from Populists concerned with the expenditure of state funds (twenty thousand dollars per year) on an institution that benefited a small, and by some accounts, elite group. Alderman answered that "over one-half of our students are the sons of farmers."[18] While that answer may have persuaded some, behind-the-scenes negotiations between Mebane, Alderman, and Populist leader Marion Butler probably had a larger effect on the outcome of the hearings. After haranguing Alderman, the legislature voted to increase his appropriation by 25 percent, to twenty-five thousand dollars.[19]

With the university's budget under as much control as possible, Alderman went to work with Mebane and McIver to champion the cause of public schooling in general. Together they wrote a bill that required each local district to hold an election every other year until a school tax proposal passed. Opposition came from Democrats who feared political losses should the fusionists actually make progress in education, from conservatives who still feared an overeducated class of blacks and poor whites, and from planters who objected to any action that could reduce the amount of labor available to them within a family under contract. But that opposition was not enough in the fusion legislature. The bill passed in the winter and as law, demanded that the first elections be held in late summer. That gave Alderman and McIver little time to organize and carry off a successful campaign in support of local taxation.

In the battle for North Carolina's schools, the reform network coalesced and became more focused. Mebane continued to work with Alderman, but gradually throughout the spring and summer, Alderman's efforts came to depend less and less on the official head of the state's schools and more and more on the informal family of which he was a part. Drawing from their own experience, McIver and Alderman built their campaign strategy around a sustained flow of lectures and rallies in as many localities as possible. McIver took the lead in the orchestration of the campaign, recruiting speakers, planning itineraries, and briefing lecturers on the kind of opposition they were likely to face.[20]

18. Quoted in Bode, *Protestantism in the New South,* 83. Other arguments against state aid came from supporters of denominational colleges who worried that a fully revived university would lure away tuition-paying students. For the subtlety of their argument, see Bode, chaps. 2 and 5, and Harlan, *Separate and Unequal,* 52–54.

19. Alderman to Butler, December 17, 1896. In Marion Butler Papers, Southern Historical Collection, University of North Carolina, Chapel Hill.

20. Dabney, *Universal Education in the South,* 1:197–206, 214–215; Harlan, *Separate and Unequal,* 57–58.

Curry put aside his work with the Peabody Fund for a time to devote himself to public speaking in North Carolina. Mayo gave up his wanderings to participate and observe. He was the first to call the efforts a crusade; the name and the image stuck. Moses moved from his accustomed place behind the scenes into the public eye. Among the university crowd, Joyner, Noble, Claxton, and Aycock all delivered speeches on behalf of local taxation, all became part of the crusade.

At the beginning of April, McIver took stock and admitted that the campaign was not doing well. Democrats, like Josephus Daniels of the *Raleigh News and Observer,* took advantage of ambiguous portions of the proposed tax bill to raise the spectre of black rule. They accused the reformers of attempting to steal money from whites to educate blacks. They were at least accurate, if not right. The proposed tax would distribute tax dollars raised from whites to black schools. This became a focal point for the debate.

McIver attempted to meet the problem head-on. In April he invited Walter Hines Page, editor of the *Atlantic Monthly* and one of the most respected southerners of the era, to return home and deliver an address that would once and for all quiet those who attempted to reduce the school issue to a simple racist equation. Page agreed to try, and in May he delivered an address that galvanized the crusade for a generation to come.

He called his talk "The Forgotten Man" and in it argued that the real victim of southern underdevelopment was the poor white woman and man, boy and girl. "The only effective means to develop the forgotten man" was "a public school system."[21] The speech provoked Daniels' ire and probably did little good to the electoral efforts of the campaign. Of thirteen hundred districts in the state, only twelve voted to tax themselves for schools.[22]

But Page did have an effect, not in his native South but in his adopted North, where men including merchant Robert Ogden and railroad man William Baldwin read of and understood the importance of lifting up "the forgotten man." Defeat at the polls discouraged the reformers in North Carolina regarding the utility of attempting to mobilize the common people directly. They became disillusioned with politics and the political process. As one reformer wrote in the margins of a notebook, "I lose faith in the political machinery of education . . . if we could only do something that would enable men to

21. Walter Hines Page, "The Forgotten Man," in *The Rebuilding of Old Commonwealths* (New York: Doubleday, Page, 1902), 26; Dabney, *Universal Education in the South,* 2:238–240; Harlan, *Separate and Unequal,* 59; Woodward, *Origins of the New South,* 401.

22. Harlan, *Separate and Unequal,* 59.

keep in the field without regard to politics."[23] Curry and Mayo, whose perspective went beyond North Carolina, saw that reformers in every southern state inevitably came up against intransigent legislatures and unenthusiastic citizens. Their solution was to bring together a broad private network of reformers, philanthropists, and educators, whose support for education could be assumed and, more importantly, built upon.

In their attempt to avoid politics, the crusaders tried to make southern educational leaders less vulnerable to pressure from the electorate. This they accomplished in great part by creating an independent and private financial base in the form of several interlocked organizations endowed, mostly by northern industrialists and merchants, for the purpose of aiding southern schools. Nothing could have been more different from the Alliance vision, from the demands of Alliance leaders that public officials and institutions be made more accountable to the common citizen. As the Crusade widened its network to include northern businessmen interested in southern economic development, it also drew decision making about public schools farther away from the arena of public control.

3

The first attempts to draw like-minded reformers together, outside of Moses' small gatherings in Raleigh, came from the gadfly, Mayo. Together with several fellow clergymen from the North, Mayo organized a Conference for Christian Education in the South, at the resort hotel in Capon Springs, West Virginia in 1898. Edward Abbott and Hollis Frissell, director of Hampton Institute, headed the program committee consisting of religious and educational leaders whose primary concern was the education of blacks.[24] For four days, the conferees explored their common interests and common problems, resolving in the end that they should support black education that combined piety and industrial training, based on the Hampton model. The conferees also resolved to expand the Conference in the following year.

In 1899 a second Conference for Education in the South convened at Capon Springs. An impressive collection of private railcars

23. Dabney, *Universal Education in the South,* 2:300-301. G. S. Dickerman notes on Ninth Conference for Education in the South, in G. S. Dickerman Papers, SEB Papers, Box 6: Southern Historical Collection, University of North Carolina, Chapel Hill.

24. Dabney, *Universal Education in the South,* 2:3-5. *Proceedings of the First Conference for Christian Education in the South* (Capon Springs, 1898), 2-6. See also Abbott's account in "The Conference at Capon Springs," 216.

Robert Curtis Ogden, 1891, founder of the Southern Education Conference, and its president for thirty years, chairman of the Southern Education Board, and member of the General Education Board gathered at the station gave the scene a new texture, and a texture decidedly different from that of the conferences and rallies of farmers. One of the coaches belonged to Robert Ogden, New York businessman, philanthropist, and as he put it, "business-man of ideals."[25] Ogden's connection to southern education began with a chance meeting with Samuel Armstrong, the founder and guiding hand of Hampton Institute. Armstrong's experiment at Hampton captured Ogden's imagination. Ogden became a frequent visitor to the school, a generous supporter, and, by 1899, chairman of its Board of Trustees. In Ogden's car traveled Mayo, Curry, and Reverend George Dickerman from New Haven.

Another of the luxury cars belonged to George Peabody, founder and guiding influence of the Peabody Fund. With a slightly different, but certainly complementary, agenda in mind, Peabody entertained the New York press corps on the journey south. Aboard were Albert Shaw, editor of the *Review of Reviews,* St. Clair McKelway of the *Brooklyn Eagle,* Clark Firestone of the *Evening Mail,* and Stanhope Simms of the *Times.*[26]

At its opening session, Curry was elected president of the conference, and Ogden, vice-president. Discussions of Hampton and black education again dominated the conference, but Ogden reminded the members and guests that the "forgotten man" should not remain forgotten by the group.

At the third Conference in 1900, Ogden took over the presidency from an ailing J. L. M. Curry. As president of the conference and now a leader in the crusade in his own right, Ogden redoubled his efforts to recruit other men of ideals, power, and wealth. To the cause he drew businessmen, like William Baldwin, longtime railroad man and president of the Union Pacific and Southern lines. Of Baldwin, Dabney wrote, "he went South as a business-man whose responsibilities compelled him to take account of the question of negro labor; he needed the cooperation of thousands of trained negroes."[27] For Baldwin, as for so many of his contemporaries, support of southern education protected and extended his interests in the economic development of the region. In addition to Baldwin, the ranks of the crusaders swelled with the likes of Morris Jessup, Everit Macy, Frank Doubleday, and John D. Rockefeller.

Ogden used the occasion of the fourth Conference in 1901 to create

25. Quoted in Dabney, *Universal Education in the South,* 2:23–24.
26. Dabney, *Universal Education in the South,* 2:7–8; *Proceedings of the Second Conference for Education in the South* (Capon Springs: 1899), 40–41.
27. Dabney, *Universal Education in the South,* 2:149.

an executive body to oversee the efforts of the conference between sessions and to serve as a clearinghouse for information regarding southern educational reform: a kind of chamber of commerce for southern
schools. He wanted the executive body, as well, to channel various
kinds of support directly to southern schools. The minutes record that
this group, the Southern Education Board, met for the first time in
Ogden's private office in New York on November 4, 1901. Its membership gave structure to the loose network of reformers who had
labored on behalf of southern education for a decade. The board
brought together Curry, Ogden, McIver, Alderman, Frissell, Charles
Dabney, Peabody, Walter Hines Page, Albert Shaw, and Wallace
Butrick, and it legitimated their claim, as a group, to the leadership of
the crusade to bring public education to the South.[28]

Ogden celebrated the birth of the Southern Education Board with a
fete at the Waldorf-Astoria on the evening of November 8. Besides the
board members and the members of the Conference, the Ogden party
drew many of the educational, social, and industrial leaders of the era.
Woodrow Wilson, president of Princeton, arrived with Daniel C.
Gilman. Nicholas Murray Butler attended as did William Dodge and
John D. Rockefeller, Jr. After a meal of *filet de bass à la moran,
mignons d'agneau a la Dager, sorbet crème Yvette, and grouse rôti,*
the speeches began. Ogden started with the happy announcement that
an anonymous donor (Peabody) had given forty thousand dollars to
support the board's work, which was to campaign vigorously in the
South for the establishment of a system of public schools for black
and white children.

Alderman, McIver, and Dabney all reinforced this message in their
talks, arguing that it was time for men of affairs to take the initiative
in bringing enlightenment to the benighted South. Dabney summed up
the board's view of matters, saying simply that "the people are poor
because they are ignorant and they are ignorant because they are
poor."[29] The aim of the board was to break this circle of poverty and
ignorance through firm, expert leadership and a hearty dose of
money.

28. *Southern Education Board Minute Book,* undated, Southern Education Board
(SEB) Papers, Southern Historical Collection, University of North Carolina, Chapel
Hill.
29. Originals of the invitations and the guest list in Ogden's hand remain in the SEB
Papers, MS, vol. 1, Southern Historical Collection, University of North Carolina,
Chapel Hill. The dinner was covered by the major New York dailies, perhaps the only
time an educational conference has made the society pages. For Dabney's quote, see
New York Times, November 12, 1901; *New York Tribune,* November 11, 1901.

At one level, the creation of the Southern Education Board solidified connections within a network of individuals who had labored in different arenas for educational reform in the South (see Scheme). At another level, the board, by taking center stage, reified a set of ideas about education that became the guiding ideas of southern educational reform. These ideas bound the reformers to one another as expressions of a common ideology.

First, whether businessmen, churchmen, or educational professionals, the reformers agreed that their understanding of the needs of society, their success within that society, gave them legitimate claims to leadership. "The people," wrote Dabney, "need leaders to show them the way." If public opinion was the raw material of educational expansion, expertise exercised by the reformers was its architectural plan. The reformers saw public opinion as a mass to be shaped and molded, convinced to accept their notions of education and schooling.[30]

Second, those notions were clear and unequivocal. "Learning for its own sake debases," said Ogden in his opening remarks to the third Conference on Education in the South. Drawing their basic plans for universal education from the program already in place at Hampton and Tuskegee, reformers argued that schooling must suit individuals "to work under the conditions in which they must farm their livelihood." Their ideas and their programs insisted on the schools fitting people into the matrix of social and economic structures.[31] Schools for whites or blacks served no positive social function, wrote one conferee, "unless they educate the children to be law abiding citizens. The importance of developing a broad and efficient system of drilling the children in the public school to the habits of discipline and the customs of obedience which make for public order," he continued, "cannot be overemphasized." Along with Curry's declaration that teachers could replace sheriffs as keepers of the peace, these declarations paint a clear picture of the idea of social control that lay at the base of the reform creed.[32]

Third, reformers agreed in their vision of the South to which education would reconcile southerners. That South grew economically through industrialization managed by "trained commanders of industry." They shared a belief that prosperity could best be achieved

30. *Proceedings of the Fourth Conference for Education in the South* (Capon Springs, 1901), 30. See also Dabney, *Universal Education in the South,* 2:chap. 1.

31. *Proceedings of the Third Conference for Education in the South* (Capon Springs, 1900), 27; Dabney, *Universal Education in the South,* 2:300–301.

32. *Proceedings of the Eighth Conference for Education in the South* (Columbia, S.C., 1905), 117–118. Curry, see above.

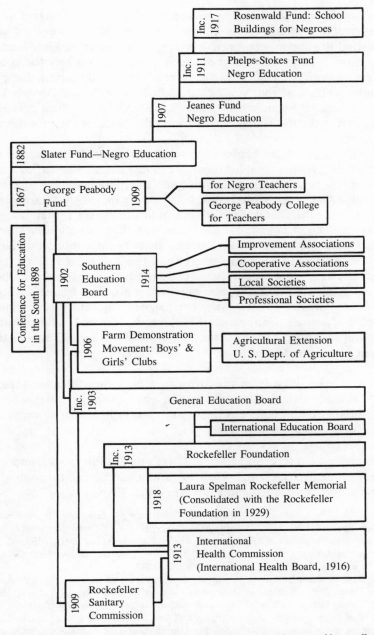

Scheme: The Southern Education Board and the agencies growing out of it or collateral with it. (Charles W. Dabney, *Universal Education in the South* [Chapel Hill: University of North Carolina, 1936], 2:514.)

by growth and growth by increasing the technical training of the southern population. McIver argued that "machinery has entered all industrial life and modern machinery calls for trained and intelligent operatives." In properly trained black labor Baldwin saw the producers of "infinite wealth for the South." In just this spirit, Henry Grady, prophet of the New South, called for a "white Booker T. Washington,"[33] Sound moral training, the tenets of obedient citizenship, and industrial training: these were the bases of the crusaders' pedagogy.

Finally, the private network of reformers secured support from wealthy backers that enabled them to conduct a campaign for education in the South independent of political parties and politics in general. With gifts from Rockefeller, Morgan, Macy, Carnegie, Ogden, and others, and with the control of the Peabody, Slater, and Jeanes funds in the hands of board members, the Southern Education Board managed a war chest of effectively fifty-three million dollars between 1903 and 1909.[34] The majority of funds disbursed served the needs of establishing programs and colleges for teacher training in the region. A sizable portion supported an active group of lecturers who, like their Alliance counterparts, campaigned vigorously for public support of schools. Until his death, McIver coordinated campaigns to encourage the passage of local tax measures. In March 1903 he sent an urgent request to Joyner to

> . . . send out a letter tomorrow to county superintendents that will secure immediate information as to all the points that will hold elections before June so that we may immediately provide speakers for those places.

Almanance County, North Carolina, was one of those places, and its superintendent, Dr. Long, "will have nine elections" to establish schools. "We must help him," McIver urged Joyner:

33. McIver in *Proceedings of the Fourth Conference for Education in the South* (Capon Springs, 1901), 57; Baldwin in *Proceedings of the Second Conference for Education in the South* (Capon Springs, 1899), 72; also SEB Papers, MS, vol.2, Southern Historical Collection, University of North Carolina, Chapel Hill; Grady quoted in Mayo, "The Third Estate in the South," 282.

34. The Southern Education Board had no endowment of its own and controlled money through the joint membership of its directors on other boards, including the Jeans Fund, Slater Fund, Peabody Fund, and the largest of them all, the General Education Board, incorporated by Ogden and Rockefeller in 1903 to raise and distribute money to southern schools. See *The General Education Board. An Account of its Activities, 1903-1912* (New York, 1915), passim. For the interlocks in directorates, see Harlan, *Separate and Unequal,* 86 and 86 n. 38.

we must come to the rescue of a county that is trying to establish nine graded schools within the next two months, and if necessary, you, Aycock, Winston, and I must make at least one speech for Long.[35]

Wherever they went, lecturers organized reform leagues around the central principles of the crusade. A smaller but significant portion of the board's attention and money aided individual schools.[36]

The unlikely center for these efforts was a small house at 140 Cottage Street in New Haven, Connecticut. There, George S. Dickerman ran a clearinghouse for channeling northern funds into southern schools. Dickerman's work began when a donor approached him, usually through the board, with a sum to be used in support of the cause of southern education. Dickerman then selected a school or schools whose program conformed to the goals and ideals of the crusaders.[37] He gathered his information in three basic ways.

First, Dickerman relied heavily on information from members of the reform network about the condition and program of specific schools. On several occasions, Dickerman asked John McMahon, state superintendent in South Carolina and member of the Conference for Education in the South, to check out individual schools in the state. That McMahon complied speaks to the way the network of reformers subdued and appropriated even the more political apparatus of school governance.[38]

Second, Dickerman traveled extensively in the South for the purpose of visiting prospective recipients of his largess. Through Baldwin's influence Dickerman enjoyed free transportation on the rail lines in the South and in 1900 and 1901 spent several months on the road, "getting on the track of superior public schools under superior teachers as points of influence for white pupils as well as colored

35. McIver to Joyner, March 13, 1903. SEB Papers, Southern Historical Collection, University of North Carolina, Chapel Hill.

36. McIver and later A. C. Bourland managed the campaigns in southern localities. His papers in the Southern Historical Collection consist mostly of requests from local reform groups, Bourland's requests to the lecturers, and schedules, McIver, Alderman, Page, and the whole panoply of reform leaders worked as much as they could under Bourland's logistical guidance.

37. Dickerman's work is amply recorded in his account books and correspondence ledgers. See G. S. Dickerman Papers, SEB Papers, Southern Historical Collection, University of North Carolina, Chapel Hill.

38. Dickerman to McMahon, November 12, 1900 and January 19, 1901, in G. S. Dickerman Correspondence, SEB Papers, MS, vol. 28. Southern Historical Collection, University of North Carolina, Chapel Hill.

pupils in the rural parts of the South.''³⁹ Thus these private dollars for public schools were to support in practice the educational ideals of the reformers and to make examples of those practices. As the flow of funds into the network increased, Dickerman refined and formalized his information-gathering apparatus. He began to send questionnaires to schools that had been recommended to him as likely recipients of financial assistance. The questionnaire gives us some insight into the features reformers looked for in a school before they took it under their wing. Moreover, by labeling these schools as superior and deserving of support, Dickerman and his colleagues in fact defined what was superior in education, and, by negation, what was subpar. In this way the Crusade embedded its ideas about what was right and wrong in education into the structure of southern schools.

Dickerman asked that schools submit to him a detailed financial statement, a list of trustees, an account of property owned by the school, enrollment figures, and a list of faculty. Dickerman requested only two pieces of information regarding curriculum: a list of industrial courses taught and an inventory of the tools used in industrial classes. This narrow emphasis suggests the persistence of the crusader's almost millennial faith in industrial education for both blacks and whites.⁴⁰ In his search for excellent schools to support and publicize, Dickerman searched for schools with developed programs of industrial training. So in New Haven, rather than in Atlanta, Richmond, or even Tarboro, the model of the excellent southern school took shape, without public debate. While there is no direct evidence that any school changed its curriculum in order to meet Dickerman's criteria, it stands to reason that the questionnaries offered schools and school officials a vision of the new orthodoxy and a gilt-edged invitation to join the party.

4

In 1902, Milton Park looked with regret at the educational changes that had followed the demise of the Alliance:

> Mark Hanna said that the two great conservative forces in American Society were the Public Schools and the Romish

39. Dickerman to Rev. D. C. Lilly, January 25, 1901, in G. S. Dickerman Correspondence, SEB Papers, Southern Historical Collection, University of North Carolina, Chapel Hill.

40. Questionnaire in SEB Papers, Box 29, Southern Historical Collection, University of North Carolina, Chapel Hill. Dickerman's files were so widely known that in 1902,

Church. He is quite right. The Public Schools, and in fact, all the departments of college education are as much in the hands and under the control of the plutocracy as ever the Jesuit schools were under the control of that order.[41]

In 1903 John D. Rockefeller created the General Education Board to finance educational progress in the South and celebrated its birth with an endowment of fourteen million dollars. Few members of the old Alliance crusade took notice. Their time, perhaps their chance, had passed. They fought against the centralization of wealth and power in the hands of the few. They struggled to make citizens masters of their institutions. They battled to bring common people into the process of political discourse. Ultimately, they sought to widen the scope of politics. In these ways the educational crusade mounted by the businessmen, philanthropists, and educators of the New South stood against all the Alliance had once stood for. The crusade was a campaign coordinated, funded, and conceived by a small and exclusive network of self-proclaimed experts whose decisions could not be appealed, fought, nor even debated. Yet those decisions held great consequences for the educational development of the South.

In the twentieth-century South, education—like politics, economics, and science—came to be dominated by the professionals the Alliance had opposed in every guise. Questions of how best to train became technical puzzles, and their connection to broader issues was lost. Schools reified one set of values and ideals while excluding other, competing values, yet history soon forgets the struggle. It is a feature of the dialectic of educational change, in particular, that as one set of values becomes dominant, the very nature of the struggle by which they came to dominate becomes obscured by the teaching and the texts of the dominant culture. Even the dominant ideology is thus deprived of a history and, being ahistorical, appears universal and immutable. Just as Macune feared, as the values of the crusaders became dominant, challenges to the traditional story of history waned, leaving schooling aligned with dominant values. In this way, alternatives (both social and educational ones) were obscured. Indeed, in the new history, they never existed. To the leaders of the Alliance, such a statement would rightly sound ludicrous; theirs was a part of the historical struggle.

---

banks, credit agencies, and other nonallied philanthropies began paying Dickerman for copies of his reports on individual schools.

41. *Southern Mercury,* February 6, 1902.

It is ironic, at least, that two such dissimilar movements could both have as their goal the education of the common people of the South. But, for the South, for the common people, and for education, Charles Macune and Robert Ogden had vastly different dreams.

Appendices

Bibliography

Index

Appendix A
The Alliance as History

An Essay on Sources

Analyses of populism, of both the Alliance and the People's party, have passed through four major phases. Each has defined populism differently, often in terms consonant with the texture of contemporary political or social events. Each has interpreted the essence of the movement differently, often in ways that are dependent upon the kind of evidence drawn upon. And each has held, implicitly or explicitly, a different normative evaluation of the farmers' movement.[1]

The first analyses of the agrarian revolt appeared hard on the heels of the downfall of the People's party. Frank McVey's *The Populist Movement* appeared in 1896 and chronicled the rise and fall of the People's party through an examination of its platform, its leaders, and its electoral battles.[2] McVey and this first generation of scholars

1. The farmers' movement captured the interest of the readers of popular urban magazines from the start. Journals including *Forum, Harper's, Arena,* and *The Nation* often ran stories on the Alliance or the general issue of agrarian discontent. Stories in the northern literary magazines were of a generally deprecating nature. See, for example, "Farmers' Alliance in the Southeast," *Harper's Weekly* 34 (December 13, 1890): 968; J. R. Dodge, "Discontent of the Farmer," *Century Magazine* 43, n.s., (June 1892): 447–456; J. T. Morgan, "The Danger of the Farmers' Alliance," *Forum* 12 (November 1891): 399–409. More scholarly journals also took an interest in the farmers' movement. See Frank Drew, "The Present Farmers' Movement"; Edward W. Bemis, "The Discontent of the Farmer," *Journal of Political Economy* (March 1893): 193–219. The Alliance's first historian was the sympathetic Frank McVey. See McVey, "The Populist Movement," *Economic Studies* 1, no. 3 (New York: Macmillan, 1896).

2. Frank McVey, *The Populist Movement* (New York: Macmillan, 1896). See also McVey's "Cooperation by Farmers," *Journal of Political Economy* 6 (June 1898): 401–403; and "Our Next Money Controversy," *Journal of Political Economy* 10 (December 1901): 119–126. In addition to McVey, several others made contemporary

seemed most interested in exploring what we might call today "special interest politics" in the third party. What they saw, and criticized, was the third party's exclusive devotion to the needs and demands of farmers. McVey, Solon Buck, and even John Hicks, branded the party a failure and blamed that failure on the inability of Populist leaders to develop a national reform program that reached outside the special interests of farmers in an era when farm interests were becoming less important, politically, economically, and culturally.[3] To support their thesis, all three pointed to the Populist support for the unlimited monetization of silver to increase the amount of currency in stock. The "free silver" campaign of the Populists in 1895 and 1896 did indeed capture much of the populist ethos. Concerned with low prices for agricultural output, some Populist leaders found both an explanation and a remedy in the monetary theories of the "free silver" and "greenback" economists. Simply stated, greenbackers and free silverites argued that low prices resulted from an inadequate flow of currency. More circulating currency, either silver or greenbacks backed by silver would, they maintained, raise prices and stimulate economic activity. Critics, including later historical analysts, pointed out that while an inflationary increase in prices would benefit those with substantial debt (who would pay back debts in money worth less than that borrowed) and those who sold goods in the marketplace, that same rise in prices would only hurt individuals who bought goods in the market and those whose income was determined by proprietor-controlled salary scales. In other words, the inflation occasioned by unlimited coining of silver might have helped farmers who were both debtors and sellers, but would have put pressure on the economic position of most wage workers and all net creditors. This struggle over monetary policy, set in the historical imagination by William Jennings Bryan's famous "Cross of Gold" speech in 1896, came to stand for the parochial interests of the farmers and to symbolize the entire agrarian movement.

Thus, McVey, Buck, and Hicks defined populism as a political movement advancing narrow economic goals. This perspective focused subsequent attention in several other ways. First, and most important,

---

analyses. See J. Laurence Laughlin, "The Causes of Agricultural Unrest," *Atlantic Monthly* 78 (November 1896): 577–585; Matthew Hammond, "The Southern Farmer and the Cotton Question," *Political Science Quarterly* 12 (September 1897): 450–475.

3. Solon Buck, *The Agrarian Crusade: A Chronicle of the Farmer in Politics* (New Haven: Yale University Press, 1920); John Hicks, *The Populist Revolt* (Minneapolis: University of Minnesota Press, 1931). Buck and Hicks made the political interpretation the standard interpretation of the farmers' movement for a generation of historians.

the lens of the People's party focused historians' attention upon the geographic strongholds of the third party—on Kansas, Minnesota, North Dakota, and to a far lesser degree, on Texas. It was Ambrose Bierce who, although no historian, captured this centering of the populist movement in the Midwest with his Devil's definition of populism as "what is wrong with Kansas."[4] Second, the political focus also shined the spotlight of historical fame or infamy on the political figures among the Populist leaders. In the hands of the early historians, officeholders, like Watson, Simpson, Marion Butler, and candidates for office, led by William Jennings Bryan, comprised the pantheon of Populist heroes. Few lecturers or Alliance leaders were recognized in the early histories. There is no better example of the anonymity of the Alliance leader than Charles Macune, whose importance as an organizer and theoretician of the movement has only recently been recognized. The exception seems to be Mary Lease, whose eloquence and power as a spokeswoman for equality made her a symbol of the party to both supporters and critics alike. The limitations to the political approach to the study of populism became apparent only slowly, led in part by a set of state studies that still accepted the basic premise of the Hicks "school," namely that populism was first and last a partisan political movement.

Alex Arnett, John B. Clark, and Roscoe Martin broke through the Mason-Dixon line with a set of detailed monographs examining third-party politics in Georgia, Alabama, and Texas, respectively.[5] In some ways these state analyses achieved a greater degree of sophistication than did the more national studies. Arnett and Martin both devoted considerable attention to the material changes that underlay the political agitation and John Clark drew attention to the emergence of a producer ideology in the South that threatened the basic assumptions upon which southern society had operated for generations.

It is no coincidence that attention to the southern wing of the farmers' movement would shift attention gradually from the partisan politics of the People's party to the economic and ideological struggles of the Alliance, for in much of the South, Alliance members did not automatically support the third party. When the time came to break with the Democratic party many southerners balked at severing traditional ties so completely. It was one thing to demand that the Demo-

4. Ambrose Bierce, *The Devil's Dictionary* (New York: Dover, 1958), 177.
5. A. M. Arnett, "The Populist Movement in Georgia," *Columbia University Studies in History* 104 (1922); John B. Clark, *Populism in Alabama* (New York: Columbia University Press, 1928); Roscoe C. Martin, *The People's Party in Texas: A Study of Third Party Politics* (Austin: University of Texas Press, 1933).

cratic party change and another entirely to forsake it. These state histories of populism introduced a great deal of subtlety and complexity into the study of the agrarian movement and mark a point of transition from the political history of the early years to a more intellectual and economic analysis in midcentury.

Writing in the 1950s, a second generation of scholars brought the farmers' movement under scrutiny, this time paying special attention to ideology and to the ideocultural roots of populism. This group of historians and political scientists suggested that the articulation of agrarian interests in the face of industrialization, urbanization, and the commercialization of society reflected a typical, if lamentable, atavism of the countryside. Richard Hofstadter, looking at the populists against the backdrop of the McCarthyism of his own age, labeled the populists protofacist for the streaks of nativism, anti-Semitism, and, ultimately, racism that clung to the edges of the farmers' movement and that dominated the later careers of Populist leaders like Tom Watson and Cyclone Davis.[6]

In the fifties' iteration of populism, historians removed the third party from center stage, to be replaced by the darkening shadow of "the mass," mobilized by demagogues for the purpose of throttling social change and suffocating the growing pluralism of American culture. The fear of the mobilized mass is palpable in the writing of Oscar Handlin, Peter Vierick, and Daniel Bell, all of whom saw in the southern populism of the 1890s the seeds of the McCarthyite populism of the 1950s. More broadly, they came to use populism as a term to describe the generic result of the unprincipled application of demagoguery on untutored masses, with a universally negative meaning. The farmers' movement had its defenders against this critique. Theodore Saluotos placed the movement of the 1890s into a broader context to show the continuity of farmers' concerns and the persistence of rural agitation. The title of Walter Nugent's *The Tolerant Populists*

6. Richard Hofstadter, *The Age of Reform* (New York: Vintage Books, 1955). See also Daniel Bell, ed., *The New American Right* (New York: Criterion Books, 1954); Viereck, Peter, "The Revolt Against the Elite," in *The Radical Right,* ed. D. Bell (New York: Criterion Books, 1954); Ferkiss, Victor, "Populist Influences on American Facism," *Western Political Quarterly* 10 (June 1957): 350–373; S. M. Lipset, *Political Man: The Social Basis of Politics* (New York: Doubleday, 1959). Oscar Handlin focuses specifically on the relationship between populists and Jews in his "American Views of Jews at the Turn of the Twentieth Century," *Publications of the American Jewish Historical Society* 40 (June 1951): 323–344 and "Reconsidering the Populists," *Agricultural History* 39 (April 1965): 68–74. An excellent summary and analysis of the conservative attack is C. Vann Woodward's "The Populist Heritage and the Intellectual," *American Scholar* 29 (1959–60): 55–72.

speaks for itself as a defense of the "soft" side of the farmers' attempts to reconcile social change with traditional values.[7]

If McCarthyism shaped historians' views of populist agitation during the 1950s, the social movements of the 1960s and the concomitant public expression of radical views and radical analysis strongly influenced historical interpretations of the Populists. Norman Pollack, reworking the evidence cited by Hofstadter, found in populism not only a reform movement with specific objectives, but a substantial and sustained cultural critique of laissez-faire capitalism. Pollack's *The Populist Response to Industrial America* concluded that populism represented an authentic form of American socialist thinking, brought into existence by material changes in the lives of countless rural producers and given voice by Alliance organizers. In the 1970s, James Green has carried on Pollack's work, seeing the Populist movement as protosocialist, citing the organic connection between much of the ideology subsumed in the populist rhetoric with that of the early Marx.[8]

In the last decade, historians have begun to look at the Alliance, the Populists, and the farmers' movement in general not as "like" anything else, facist or socialist, but as particular organizational responses to particular economic and social circumstances. This has been to the good. Most recently, in works that have been provoked by Lawrence Goodwyn's *The Democratic Promise,* historians have begun to look at the agrarian movement as a culture and in its own cultural terms.[9]

Goodwyn's efforts to recover the "movement culture" of populism has enabled historians to see beyond the electoral successes and failures of the Peoples' party and beyond the speeches and stump talks of the movement's most famous, colorful, and perhaps least representative individuals.

Attuned to this new challenge, Bruce Palmer has written an excellent history of Alliance ideas as they were expressed in populist journals and newspapers. Palmer's work is particularly useful in demonstrating the important tension between radicalism and con-

7. Theodore Saluotos, *Farmer Movements in the South;* Walter K. Nugent, *The Tolerant Populists* (Chicago: University of Chicago Press, 1963).

8. Norman Pollack, *The Populist Response to Industrial America* (New York: Norton, 1962).

9. This new generation took its cues from the pathbreaking work by Robert McMath, Jr., in his *Populist Vanguard: A History of the Southern Farmers' Alliance* (Chapel Hill: University of North Carolina Press, 1975) and Rogers, *The One-Gallused Rebellion.*

servatism in populist thought. Thus, for example, Alliance President Leonidas Lafayette Polk could argue that

> [w]e are rapidly drifting from the moorings of our fathers, and stand today in the crucial era of our free institutions, our free form of government, and of our Christian civilization. To rescue these inestimable blessings and interests from the impending peril should be the self-imposed duty of all patriots throughout the land.[10]

In order to fulfill these tasks as patriots, leaders like Polk and Macune urged the Alliance to undertake a radical restructuring of the nation's financial markets, to support a marked increase in government sponsorship and ownership of productive enterprise, and to make major moves away from sectional and racial prejudices.

Barton Shaw's work on the People's party in Georgia reexamines the rise and fall of the third party through an analysis of the political demography and political culture of the farmer's movement. Looking closely at available information regarding People's party membership in Worth County, Shaw builds his analysis of the party from the bottom up rather than from the top down as the early Hicks school had done. Through such an analysis, Shaw is able to add to a growing consensus among historians that populists were likely to own land rather than rent or farm shares, but that the holdings of the populists were relatively small, in this case smaller than the county average. These small-hold farmers were more vulnerable to changes in input and output prices than were their neighbors and, as Shaw argues, more amenable to the approach of Alliance leaders and Populist organizers.

Most recently, Steven Hahn's prize-winning book, *The Roots of Southern Populism,* has addressed the kinds of economic changes that threatened small-hold farmers. These changes, he argues, did indeed place yeoman farmers at substantial financial risk. Moreover, the changes in the organization of markets threatened the traditional cultural norms of interdependence that obtained in the cotton South. Farmer activism, Hahn argues, was as much the result of this cultural disintegration as it was the result of immediate economic crisis.[11]

10. Polk, quoted in Dunning, *Farmers' Alliance History,* 141.

11. Hahn, *Roots.* Hahn's work is influenced by the earlier quantitative work done by Michael Schwartz in his *Radical Protest,* and by questions posed by earlier work on the role of planters in the postbellum South. See Sheldon Hackney, *Populism to Progressivism in Alabama* (Princeton: Princeton University Press, 1969); Weiner, *Social Origins of the New South;* and Dwight Billings, *Planters and the Making of the New South* (Chapel Hill: University of North Carolina Press, 1979).

Taken together, this latest generation of scholarship has made three major changes in our understanding of the agrarian movement.[12] First, it has moved our attention downward and inward by looking at the material and political culture of the movement in addition to the politics of the third party. Second, it has moved the geographical center of attention from the Midwest to the South, acknowledging the intellectual and organizational origins of the agrarian movement. Third, it has revived, in more subtle ways than before, the notion that there was something essentially dramatic about the movement, dramatic in the sense that it changed the lives of its members and dramatic also in the sense that it challenged the status quo in politics, in economics, and in the very image America held of itself during the Gilded Age.

12. For a recent attempt to synthesize this recent generation of work and to provide a systematic critique of Goodwyn's work, see James Turner, "Understanding the Populists," *Journal of American History* 67, no. 2 (September 1980).

Appendix B
The Ocala Demands

The following demands upon Congress were approved by the National Council of the National Farmers' Alliance and Industrial Union at its meeting in Ocala, Florida, December 2–9, 1890.

1. We demand the abolition of national banks.

   a. We demand that the Government shall establish sub-treasuries or depositories in the several States, which shall loan money direct to the people at a low rate of interest, not to exceed two per cent per annum, on non-perishable farm-products, and also upon real estate, with proper limitations upon the quantity of land and amount of money.

   b. We demand that the amount of the circulating medium be speedily increased to not less than $50.00 per capita.

2. We demand that Congress shall pass such laws as will effectually prevent the dealing in futures of all agricultural and mechanical productions; providing a stringent system of procedure in trials that will secure the prompt conviction, and imposing such penalties as shall secure the most perfect compliance with the law.

3. We condemn the silver bill recently passed by Congress and demand in lieu thereof the free and unlimited coinage of silver.

4. We demand the passage of laws prohibiting alien ownership of land, and that Congress take prompt action to devise some plan to obtain all lands now owned by aliens and foreign syndicates; and that all lands now held by railroads and other corporations, in excess of such as is actually used and needed by them, be reclaimed by the government, and held for actual settlers only.

5. Believing in the doctrine of equal rights to all, and special privileges to none, we demand:

a. That our national legislation shall be so framed in the future as not to build up one industry at the expense of another.

b. We further demand a removal of the existing heavy tariff tax from the necessities of life that the poor of our land must have.

c. We further demand a just and equitable system of graduated tax on incomes.

d. We believe that the money of the country should be kept as much as possible in the hands of the people, and hence we demand that all national and state revenues shall be limited to the necessary expenses of the government, economically and honestly administered.

6. We demand the most rigid, honest, and just state and national governmental control and supervision of the means of public communication and transportation; and if this control and supervision does not remove the abuse now existing, we demand the government ownership of such means of communication and transportation.

7. We demand that the Congress of the United States submit an amendment to the Constitution, providing for the election of United States Senators by direct vote of the people of each state.

—Moved by Brother Livingston that the report
be adopted as a whole.
Carried.

Bibliography

PRIMARY SOURCES

Newspapers (some runs only partial)

Alliance Weekly, Hillsboro, North Carolina: January through March 1896.
Farmers' Advocate, Tarboro, North Carolina: April 1891 through December 1892.
Jeffersonian, Troy, Alabama: November 1893 through October 1894.
Louisiana Populist, Natchitoches, Louisiana: August 1894 through December 1897.
National Economist, Washington, D.C.: March 1889 through December 1893.
News and Observer, Raleigh, North Carolina: January 1888 through December 1900.
People's Party Paper, Atlanta, Georgia: November 1892 through January 1897.
Southern Mercury, Dallas, Texas: August 1891 through December 1902.
Tarboro Southerner, Tarboro, North Carolina: January 1891 through August 1891.

Manuscript Collections

Edwin Alderman Papers. Southern Historical Collection, Chapel Hill, North Carolina.
Marion Butler Papers. Southern Historical Collection, Chapel Hill, North Carolina.
Caroline Buttrick Papers. Southern Historical Collection, Chapel Hill, North Carolina. (Contains an unpublished biography of her father, Wallace H. Buttrick.)
Jabez Lamar Monroe Curry Papers. Southern Historical Collection, Chapel Hill, North Carolina.

209

I. F. Lewis Plantation Records. Southern Historical Collection, Chapel Hill, North Carolina. (Lewis' granddaughter used one of the plantation record books as a notebook while attending McIver's summer school at the University of North Carolina in 1902.)

Charles Macune Papers, Barker Texas History Center, University of Texas, Austin. (Contains Macune's typescript: "The Farmers Alliance.")

M. C. S. Noble Papers. Southern Historical Collection, Chapel Hill, North Carolina.

Leonidas Lafayette Polk Papers. Southern Historical Collection, Chapel Hill, North Carolina.

Southern Education Board Papers. Southern Historical Association, Chapel Hill, North Carolina. Contains papers, letters, and diaries of many of the leaders of the Crusade for Public Education in the South including:

A. L. Bourland
Charles Dabney
George Dickerman
Charles Duncan McIver
Wycliffe Rose

Of particular importance are Dickerman's letter books in which he recorded correspondence as the field agent for the SEB and two typescripts: Rose's "The Educational Movement in the South," and Bourland's "The School and Industrial Progress."

Thomas Watson Papers. Southern Historical Collection, Chapel Hill, North Carolina.

School Texts

Gardiner, S. R. *English History for Schools.* New York: Henry Holt & Company, 1881.

Guereber, H. A. *The Story of the Greeks.* New York: American Book Company, 1896.

Lancaster, Edward M. *A Manual of English History for the Use of the Schools.* New York: American Book Company, 1877.

McMaster, John. *A School History of the United States.* New York: American Book Company, 1896.

Quackenbos, G. P. *Illustrated School History of the United States and Adjacent Parts of America.* New York: D. Appleton & Company, 1872.

Smith, William. *Smith's History of Greece.* New York: Harper & Brothers, 1897.

Thalheimer, M. E. *The Eclectic History of the United States.* New York: Van Antwerp, Bragg, and Co., 1881.

Other Primary Sources

Abbott, Edward. "The Conference at Capon Springs," *Literary World,* 9 July 1898, p. 216.

Alderman, Edwin A. "The Function and Needs of Schools of Education in

Universities and Colleges." *General Education Board Occasional Papers* 4. New York: 1917.

Alderman, Edwin A. "Higher Education in the South," *National Education Association Journal of Addresses and Proceedings for 1895,* pp. 479–489. Washington, D.C.: National Education Association, 1895.

Alderman, Edwin A. "In Memoriam: C. D. McIver." In *50th Anniversary Volume: National Education Association,* 1906, pp. 311–318. Washington, D.C.: National Education Association, 1906.

Alderman, Edwin A., and A. C. Gordon. *J. L. M. Curry: A Biography.* London and New York: Macmillan, 1911.

Beam, Lura. *He Called Them by the Lightning: A Teacher's Odyssey in the Negro South.* New York: Bobbs-Merrill, 1967.

Bergh, A. E., ed. *Grover Cleveland Addresses, State Papers, and Letters.* New York: Sun Dial Co., 1908.

Bingham, Robert. "Educational Status and Needs of the South." *NEA Journal of Addresses and Proceedings for 1894,* pp. 3–21.

Blood, F. G., ed. *Handbook and History of the National Farmers Alliance and Industrial Union.* Washington, D.C.: Alliance Publishing Company, 1893.

Buttrick, Wallace. "The Beginning and Aims of the General Education Board." *Journal of Addresses and Proceedings of the 42nd Annual Meeting of the N.E.A.* (1903), 116–123.

Cable, George W. "Does the Negro Pay for His Education?" *Forum* 13 (July 1892): 640–649.

Cable, George W. *The Negro Question.* New York: Scribners, 1903.

Calhoun, Daniel C. *The Educating of Americans: A Documentary History.* Boston: Houghton-Mifflin Co., 1969.

Chamberlain, H. R. *The Farmers' Alliance: What It Hopes to Accomplish.* New York: published by the author, 1891.

Coleman, Kenneth, ed. "How to Run a Middle George Cotton Plantation in 1885: A Document." *Agricultural History* 42 (January 1968): 55–60.

Curry, Jabez Lamar Monroe. *A Brief Sketch of George Peabody and a History of the Peabody Education Fund Through Thirty Years.* Cambridge, Mass.: Peabody Fund, 1898.

Curry, Jabez Lamar Monroe. "Education of the Negro." *U.S. Bureau of Education Circular of Information 1884,* no. 3. Washington, D.C.: Government Printing Office, 1885.

Curry, Jabez Lamar Monroe. "Speech to the Georgia Legislature." *U.S. Commissioner of Education Report 1894–5,* pt. 2 Washington, D.C.: Government Printing Office, 1896.

Dabney, Charles. "Education and Production," *U.S. Commissioner of Education Report 1900–1,* pt. 1. Washington, D.C.: Government Printing Office.

Dabney, Charles. "Ratio of Education to Production," *World's Work* 1 (April 1901): 587–588.

Dabney, Charles, *Universal Education in the South*. 2 vols. Chapel Hill: University of North Carolina Press, 1936.

Democratic Party Campaign Book for 1892. Washington, D.C.: Democratic Congressional Committee, 1892.

Diggs, Annie L. "The Farmers' Alliance and Some of its Leaders." *Arena* 5 (April 1892): 590–604.

Diggs, Annie L. "Women in the Alliance Movement." *Arena* 6 (July 1892): 160–179.

Dunning, Nelson A., ed. *Farmers' Alliance History and Agricultural Digest*. Washington, D.C.: Alliance Publishing Company, 1891.

"The Farmers' Grievance." *Nation*, 14 August 1873, p. 112.

Garvin, W. L., and S. O. Daws. *History of the Farmers' Alliance and Cooperative Union of America*. Jacksboro, Tex.: J. N. Rogers & Co., 1887.

General Education Board: An Account of Its Activities, 1902–1914. New York: General Education Board, 1915.

Gladden, Washington. "The Embattled Farmers." *Forum* 10 (November 1890): 315–322.

Gompers, Samuel. "Organized Labor in the Campaign." *North American Review* 155 (August 1892): 93–95.

Gompers, Samuel. *Organized Labor: Its Struggles, Its Enemies, and Fool Friends*. Washington: American Federation of Labor Bureau of Literature, n.d. [1923–25?].

Grady, Henry. *The New South*. New York: Robert Bonner's Sons, 1890.

Harris, W. T. "An Educational Policy for Our New Posessions." *NEA Journal of Addresses and Proceedings*, 1899.

Haygood, Atticus G. "The Church and the Education of the People." *Emory University Alumni Addresses*. Nashville, 1874.

Haygood, Atticus G. *Our Brother in Black: His Freedom and His Future*. New York: Phillips and Hunt, 1881.

Haygood, Atticus G. "The South and the School Problem." *Harper's New Monthly Magazine* 79 (July 1889): 225–231.

Journal of Proceedings and Addresses of the Ninth Annual Meeting of the Southern Educational Association. Published by the Association, 1899.

Knight, Edgar. *A Documentary History of Education in the South*. Chapel Hill: University of North Carolina Press, 1955.

Laughlin, J. Laurence. "The Causes of Agricultural Unrest." *Atlantic Monthly* 78 (November 1896): 577–585.

Lloyd, Henry Demarest. "The Populists at St. Louis." *Review of Reviews* 14 (September 1896): 265–266.

Mayo, Amory D. "The American Common School in the Southern States During the First Half-Century of the Republic." *U.S. Commissioner of Education Report, 1895–6*, pt. 1. Washington, D.C.: Government Printing Office.

Mayo, Amory D. "The Beginnings of the Common School System in the South." *U.S. Commissioner of Education Report, 1896–7*, pt. 2. Washington, D.C.: Government Printing Office.

Mayo, Amory D. "Building for the Children of the South." *U.S. Bureau of Education Miscellaneous Papers, 1884–1893*. Washington, D.C.: Government Printing Office, 1894.

Mayo, Amory D. "Common School Education in the South from the Beginnings of the Civil War to 1807." *U.S. Commissioner of Education Report 1901*, pp. 403–512. Washington, D.C.: Government Printing Office.

Mayo, Amory D. "The Common School in the Southern States Beyond the Mississippi River from 1830 to 1860." *U.S. Commissioner of Education Report, 1901*, 357. Washington, D.C.: Government Printing Office.

Mayo, Amory D. "The Educational Situation in the South." *U.S. Bureau of Education Circular of Information, 1892*. Washington, D.C.: Government Printing Office.

Mayo, Amory D. "Education in the South." *Journal of Addresses and Proceedings of the National Education Association, 1884*.

Mayo, Amory D. "The Final Establishment of the American Common School System in North Carolina, South Carolina, and Georgia, 1863–1900." *U.S. Commissioner of Education Report, 1904*, pp. 999, 1021. Washington, D.C.: Government Printing Office.

Mayo, Amory D. "The Final Establishment of the American Common School System in West Virginia, Maryland, Virginia, and Delaware, 1863–1900." *U.S. Commissioner of Education Report, 1903*, pp. 391–453. Washington, D.C.: Government Printing Office.

Mayo, Amory D. "Four Years Among the Children of the South: A Sermon Preached at the Church of Unity, Boston, December 12, 1884." *U.S. Bureau of Education Circular of Information 1884*. Washington, D.C.: Government Printing Office.

Mayo, Amory D. "Industrial Education in the South." *U.S. Bureau of Education Circular of Information, 1888*. Washington, D.C.: Government Printing Office.

Mayo, Amory D. "Is There a New South?" *Social Economist* 5, October 1893.

Mayo, Amory D. "Last Words from the South." *National Education Association Addresses and Proceedings for 1884*, pp. 117–124.

Mayo, Amory D. "The New Education—The Christian Education." *First Capon Springs Conference on Christian Education in the South, 1898*.

Mayo, Amory D. "The Organization and Development of the American Common School in the Atlantic and Central States of the South, 1830–1860." *U.S. Commissioner of Education Report, 1899–1900*, pt. 1. Washington, D.C.: Government Printing Office.

Mayo, Amory D. "Overlook and Outlook in Southern Education." *U.S. Bureau of Education Circular of Information, 1892*. Washington, D.C.: Government Printing Office.

Mayo, Amory D. "The Progress of the Negro." *Forum* 10 (November 1890): 335–345.

Mayo, Amory D. "Southern Women in the Recent Educational Movement in the South." *U.S. Bureau of Education Circular of Information, 1892*. Washington, D.C.: Government Printing Office.

Mayo, Amory D. "The South, the North, and the Nation Keeping School." *U.S. Bureau of Education Circular of Information, 1892.* Washington, D.C.: Government Printing Office.

Mayo, Amory D. "The Third Estate in the South." *U.S. Bureau of Education Circular of Information, 1890.* Washington, D.C.: Government Printing Office.

Mayo, Amory D. "The Training of Teachers in the South." *National Education Association Addresses and Proceedings for 1889,* pp. 597–609.

Mayo, Amory D. "A Tribute to J. L. M. Curry." *U.S. Commissioner of Education Report, 1903,* p. 480. Washington, D.C.: Government Printing Office.

Mayo, Amory D. "The Women's Movement in the South." *New England Magazine,* n.s. 5 (October 1891): 249–261.

Mayo, Amory D. "The Work of Certain Northern Churches in the Education of Freedmen." *U.S. Commissioner of Education Report, 1903,* pp. 285–293. Washington, D.C.: Government Printing Office.

Mayo, Amory D., and B. T. Washington. "Debate on the Future of Black Education." *U.S. Commissioner of Education Report, 1898–1899,* pt. 1. Washington, D.C.: Government Printing Office.

Morgan, T. W. Scott. *History of the Wheel and Alliance.* Published by the author.

National Economist Almanac and National Farmers' Alliance Handbook for 1890. Washington, D.C.: National Economist Publishing Co., 1890.

Page, Walter Hines. "Study of an Old South Borough." *Atlantic Monthly* 47 (May 1881): 643–638.

Powderly, Terence V. *The Path I Trod.* New York: Columbia University Press, 1940.

Powderly, Terence V. *Thirty Years of Labor, 1859–1889.* Philadelphia, 1890.

Proceedings of the Conferences for Education in the South 1898–1906. 9 vols. Executive Committee of the Conference, 1898–1906.

Republican Campaign Text Book for 1892. New York: Republican National Commmittee, 1892.

Rose, Wycliffe. "The Educational Movement in the South." *U.S. Commissioner of Education Report, 1903,* pt. 1. Washington, D.C.: Government Printing Office.

Root, George F., and Mrs. S. M. Smith. *The Trumpet of Reform: A Collection of Songs.* Cincinnati, 1874.

Tourgee, Albion. "Aaron's Rod in Politics." *North American Review* 132 (February 1881): 139–163.

Vincent, Leopold. *Alliance and Labor Songster.* New York: Arno Press Reprints, 1975.

Watson, Tom. "The Negro Question in the South." *Arena* 6 (October 1892): 540–550.

Watson, Tom. "Why the People's Party Should Elect the Next President." *Arena* 6 (October 1892): 201–204.

Winkler, E. W. *Platforms of Political Parties in Texas.* Austin: University of Texas Press, 1916.

SECONDARY SOURCES

Contemporary Accounts

Alexander, E. P. "Industrial Progress of the South." *Forum* 13 March 1892: 66–74.

Bacon, Mary A. "Industrial Education in the South." *Harper's* 107 (October 1903): 659–667.

Bailey, Josiah W. "The Case for the South," *Forum* 31 (April 1901): 225–230.

Barrows, Samuel June. "What the Southern Negro Is Doing for Himself." *Atlantic Monthly* 67 (June 1891): 805–815.

Bemis, Edward W. "The Discontent of the Farmer." *Journal of Political Economy* 1 (March 1893): 193–213.

Buckley, Rev. J. M. "Christianity and Socialism." *Harper's* 83 (March 1891): 185–190.

Cable, George. "Does the Negro Pay for His Education?" *Forum* 13 (July 1892).

Carlton, Frank. "The Relation Between Recent Industrial Progress and Educational Advance." *Popular Science Monthly* 72 (June 1908): 543–557.

"Crazes." *Nation* 53 (November 26, 1891): 403.

Davis, John. "Communism and Capitalism, the Real Issue Before the People," *Arena* 7 (1893).

Dodge, J. R. "Discontent of the Farmer." *Century Magazine,* n.s. 43 (January 1892): 447–456.

Drew, Frank M. "The Present Farmers' Movement." *Political Science Quarterly* 6 (June 1891).

Ellis, Lenora B. "A New Class of Labor in the South." *Forum* 31 (May 1901): 306–310.

Ely, Richard. "An American Industrial Experiment," *Harper's* 105 (June 1902): 39–45.

"Farmers' Alliance in the Southeast." *Harper's Weekly* 34 (December 13, 1890): 968.

Felton, Rebecca F. *Country Life in Georgia in the Days of My Youth.* Atlanta: published by the author, 1919.

Hamilton, S. A. "The New Race Question in the South." *Arena* 27 (April 1902): 352–358.

Hammond, Matthew. *The Cotton Industry.* New York: Macmillan, 1897.

Hammond, Matthew. "The Southern Farmer and the Cotton Question." *Political Science Quarterly* 12 (September 1897): 450–475.

Holman, Charles W. "Probing the Causes of Unrest." *Survey* 34 (April 12, 1916): 62–64.

Holmes, George K. "The Peons of the South." *Annals of the American Academy of Political and Social Science* 4 (September 1893): 265–274.

Jordan, D. S. "Agricultural Depression and the Waste of Time." *Forum* 22 (October 1891).

Kautsky, Karl. "Socialist Agitation Among the Farmers in America." *International Socialist Review* 3 (1902).

McVey, Frank. "Cooperation by Farmers." *Journal of Political Economy* 6 (June 1898): 401–403.

McVey, Frank. "Our Next Money Controversy." *Journal of Political Economy* 10 (December 1901): 119–126.

McVey, Frank. "The Populist Movement." *Economic Studies* 1 no. 3. New York: Macmillan Co. and the American Economic Assn., 1896.

Morgan, J. T. "The Danger of the Farmers' Alliance." *Forum* 12 (November 1891): 399–409.

"People's Party in the South." *The Outlook* 48 (December 30, 1893): 1253–1254.

Rubinow, I. M. "The Industrial Development of the South." *International Socialist Review* 3 (1902).

Scarborough, W. S. "The Negro and Our New Posessions." *Forum* 31 (May 1901): 341–349.

Simons, A. M. "Socialism and the American Farmer." *International Socialist Review* 3 (1902).

Simons, May Wood. "Education in the South." *American Journal of Sociology,* no. 10 (November 1904): 382–407.

Spahr, C. B. "Industrial America: Southern Farmers in Politics." *Outlook* 48 (August 12, 1893): 296–298.

Stahl, J. M. "Free Coinage and Farmers." *Forum* 22 (October 1896): 146–151.

Thomas, D. Y. "The Cotton Tax and Southern Education." *North American Review* 190 (November 1909): 688–692.

Thompson, William O. "The Economic Relations of Education." *National Education Association Proceedings for 1907,* pp. 87–94.

Tracy, Frank. "The Rise and Doom of the Populist Party." *Forum* 16 (October 1893): 240–250.

Other Secondary Sources

Abramowitz, Jack. "Agrarian Reform and the Negro Question." *Negro History Bulletin* 11 (March 1948).

Abramowitz, Jack. "The Negro in the Agrarian Revolt." *Agricultural History* 24:2 (April 1950): 89–95.

Abramowitz, Jack. "The Negro in the Populist Movement." *Journal of Negro History* 38 (July 1953): 257–289.

Alapuro, Risto. "On the Political Mobilization of the Agrarian Population in Finland: Problems and Hypotheses." *Scandinavian Political Studies* 11.

Alderman, E. A. and A. C. Gordon. *J. L. M. Curry: A Biography.* New York: 1911.

Althusser, Louis. *Lenin and Philosophy.* New York: Monthly Review Press, 1971.

Anderson, James. "Ex-Slaves and the Rise of Universal Education in the New South, 1860–1880." In *The Rise of Public Education in the New South,* edited by Ronald Goodenow. Boston: G. K. Hall, 1982, pp. 1–25.

Anderson, James. "The Historical Development of Black Vocational Education." In *Work Youth, and Schooling: Historical Perspectives on Vocationalism in American Education,* edited by Harvey Kantor and David Tyack. Stanford: Stanford University Press, 1982.

Anderson, James. "Northern Foundations and the Shaping of Southern Black Rural Education, 1902–1935." *History of Education Quarterly* 14:4 (Winter 1978): 371–396.

Anderson, James. "Philanthropy in the Shaping of Black Industrial Education Schools: The Fort Vaney Case, 1902–1938." *Review Journal of Philosophy and Social Science* 3:2 (Winter 1978).

Anderson, Perry. "The Antinomies of Antonio Gramsci." *New Left Review* 100 (January 1977): 5–78.

Anderson, Perry. *Considerations on Western Marxism.* London: New Left Books, 1976.

Apple, Michael, ed. *Cultural and Economic Reproduction in Education.* London: Routledge and Kegan Paul, 1982.

Apple, Michael. *Education and Power.* London: Routledge and Kegan Paul, 1982.

Apple, Michael. *Ideology and Curriculum.* London: Routledge and Kegan Paul, 1979.

Arnett, Alex. "The Populist Movement in Georgia." *Columbia University Series in History Economics and Public Law* 104 (1922).

Arnove, Robert. *Philanthropy and Cultural Imperialism.* Bloomington: Indiana University Press, 1982.

Bailey, Joseph C., and Seaman A. Knapp. *Schoolmaster of American Agriculture.* New York: Columbia University Press, 1945.

Bailey, Kenneth K. *Southern White Protestantism in the Twentieth Century.* New York: Harper and Row, 1964.

Bedford, Henry F. *Socialism and the Workers of Massachusetts, 1886–1912.* Amherst: University of Massachusetts Press, 1966.

Bell, Daniel, ed. *The Radical Right: The New American Right* New York: Criterion Books, 1954.

Benedict, Murray R. *Farm Politics of the United States, 1790–1950: A Study of Their Origins and Development.* New York: Octagon Books, 1966.

Berg, Ivar. *Education and Jobs: The Great Training Robbery.* Boston: Beacon Press, 1971.

Billings, Dwight. *Planters and the Making of a New South: Class Politics and Development in North Carolina, 1865–1900.* Chapel Hill: University of North Carolina Press, 1979.

Bledstein, Burton. *The Culture of Professionalism.* New York: W. W. Norton, 1971.

Bliss, William. *The Encyclopedia of Social Reform*. New York: Funk and Wagnalls, 1897.

Bode, Frederick A. *Protestantism in the New South: North Carolina Baptists and Methodists in Political Crisis*. Charlottesville: University Press of Virginia, 1975.

Bode, Frederick A. "Religion and Class Hegemony: A Populist Critique." *Journal of Southern History* 37 (August 1971): 417–438.

Bond, Horace Mann. *Education of the Negro in the American Social Order*. New York: Prentice-Hall, 1934.

Bond, Horace Mann. *Negro Education in Alabama: A Study in Cotton and Steel*. New York: Atheneum, 1969.

Bowles, Samuel, and Herbert Gintis. *Schooling in Capitalist America*. New York: Basic Books, 1976.

Breton, A. "An Economic Theory of Social Movements." *American Economics Review* 59 (May 1969): 198–205.

Bromberg, Alan B. "'The Worst Muddle Ever Seen in North Carolina Politics:' The Farmers' Alliance, the Sub-Treasury, and Zeb Vance." *North Carolina Historical Review* 56, no. 1 (January 1979): pp. 19–40.

Brooks, Robert P. *The Agrarian Revolution in Georgia, 1865–1912*. Madison: Bulletin of the University of Wisconsin, 1914.

Brown, William W., and M. O. Reynolds. "Debt-Peonage Re-examined." *Journal of Economic History* 33 (December 1973): 862–871.

Buck, Solon. *The Agrarian Crusade: A Chronicle of the Farmer in Politics*. New Haven: Yale University Press, 1920.

Buck, Solon. *The Granger Movement: A Study of Agricultural Organization, 1870–1880*. Cambridge: Harvard University Press, 1913.

Bull, Jacqueline. "The General Merchant in the Economic History of the New South." *Journal of Southern History* 18 (February 1952): 37–59.

Bullock, Henry Allen. *A History of Negro Education in the South*. Cambridge: Harvard University Press, 1967.

Burnham, Walter Dean. *Presidential Ballots, 1836–1892*. New York: Arno Press, 1976.

Callahan, Raymond. *Education and the Cult of Efficiency*. Chicago: University of Chicago Press, 1962.

Cameron, David R. "Toward a Theory of Political Mobilization." *Journal of Politics* 36 (February 1974): 138–171.

Campbell, Randolph B. "Population Persistence and Social Change in Nineteenth Century Texas: Harrison County, 1850–1880." *Journal of Southern History* 48 (May 1982): 185–204.

Campbell, Thomas. *The Movable School Goes to the Negro Farmer*. Tuskegee: Tuskegee Institute, 1936.

Canovan, Margaret. *Populism*. New York: Harcourt, Brace Jovanovich, 1980.

Carnoy, Martin. *Education as Cultural Imperialism*. New York: David McKay, 1974).

Carnoy, Martin. "Education and Theories of the State." Typescript, 1987.

Carnoy, Martin. "Marxian Approaches to Education." *Institute for Finance and Governance Project Report,* 80-B13. Stanford University (July 1980).

Carnoy, Martin, and Derek Shearer. *Economic Democracy: The Challenge of the 1980's.* White Plains: M. E. Sharpe, 1980.

Carlton, David. *Mill and Town in South Carolina, 1880–1920.* Baton Rouge: Louisina State University Press, 1982.

Carlton, Frank. *Economic Influences Upon Educational Progress in the U.S., 1820–1850.* New York: Teachers College Press, 1966.

Cash, Wilbur. *The Mind of the South.* New York: Vintage, 1941.

Chalmers, David M. *Hooded Americanism: The History of the Ku Klux Klan.* New York: Franklin Watts, 1976.

Chambers, William N., and W. D. Burnham. *The American Party: Party Systems.* New York: Oxford University Press, 1967.

Clark, Christopher. "Household Economy, Market Exchange, and the Rise of Capitalism in the Connecticut Valley." *Journal of Social History* 8, no. 3 (Summer 1979): 169–189.

Clarke, John, Chas. Critcher, and Richard Johnson, eds. *Working Class Culture: Studies in History and Theory.* London: Hutchinson, in association with the Centre for Contemporary Studies, University of Birmingham, 1979.

Clark, John B. *Populism in Alabama.* New York: Columbia University Press, 1928.

Clark, Thomas D. "The Country Newspaper: A Factor in Southern Opinion, 1865–1930." *Journal of Southern History* 14 (February 1948): 3–33.

Clark, Thomas D. *The Emerging South.* New York: Oxford University Press, 1961.

Clark, Thomas D. "The Furnishing and Supply System in Southern Agriculture." *Journal of Southern History* 12 (July 1946): 24–44.

Clark, Thomas D. *Pills, Petticoats, and Plows.* Indianapolis: Bobbs-Merrill, 1944.

Clark, Thomas D. *The Rural Press in the New South.* Baton Rouge: Louisiana State University Press, 1948.

Clark, Thomas D. *The Southern Country Editor.* Indianapolis: Bobbs-Merrill, 1948.

Clark, Thomas D., ed. *The South Since Reconstruction.* Indianapolis: Bobbs-Merrill, 1973.

Clevenger, Homer C. "The Teaching Techniques of the Farmers' Alliance." *Journal of Southern History* 11 (February 1945): 504–518.

Cohn, Elchanan. *The Economics of Education.* Cambridge, Mass.: Ballinger, 1979.

Cook, John H. *A Study of Mill Schools in North Carolina.* New York: Columbia University Press, 1925.

Cooper, William J., Jr. "The Cotton Crisis in the Antebellum South: Another Look." *Agricultural History* 49, no. 2 (April 1975): 381–391.

Cox, LaWanda. "The American Agricultural Wage Earner." *Agricultural History* 22 (1948): 95–114.

Cox, LaWanda. "Tenancy in the U.S., 1865–1900." *Agricultural History* 18, no. 2 (April 1944): 97–105.

Cremin, Lawrence A. *American Education The National Experience, 1783–1876*. New York: Harper and Row, 1980.

Cremin, Lawrence A. *Traditions of American Education*. New York: Basic Books, 1977.

Cremin, Lawrence A. *The Transformation of the School: Progressivism in American Education, 1876–1957*. New York: Vintage, 1964.

Crofts, Daniel W. "The Black Response to the Blair Education Bill." *Journal of Southern History* 37 (February 1971): 41–65.

Crowe, Charles. "Tom Watson, Blacks, and Populists Reconsidered." *Journal of Negro History* 55 (April 1970): 99–119.

Curti, Merle. *The Social Ideas of American Educators*. Totowa, N.J.: Littlefield, Adams, 1974).

Dahl, Robert A. *Political Opposition in Western Democracy*. New Haven: Yale University Press, 1966.

Dale, Roger. *Schooling and Capitalism*. London: Routledge and Kegan Paul, 1976.

Danbom, David. "Rural Education Reform and the Country Life Movement." *Agricultural History* 53 (April 1979): 462–474.

Dann, Martin. "Black Populism: A Study of the Colored Farmers' Alliance through 1891." *Journal of Negro History* 57 (October 1972).

David, Miriam. *The State, Family, and Education*. London: Routledge and Kegan Paul, 1980.

Davis, John W. "The Negro Land Grant Colleges." *Journal of Negro Education* 2 (July 1933).

Dawley, Allan, and Paul Faler. "Working Class Culture and Politics in the Industrial Revolution." *Journal of Social History* 9 (Summer 1976): 466–480.

DeCanio, Stephen. *Agriculture in the Post-Bellum South*. Cambridge: Harvard University Press, 1974.

DeCanio, Stephen. "Cotton 'Overproduction' in Late Nineteenth Century Southern Agriculture." *Journal of Economic History* 33 (September 1973); 608–633.

Degler, Carl N. *The Other South: Southern Dissenters in the Nineteenth Century*. New York: Harper and Row, 1974.

Degler, Carl N. *Place Over Time: The Continuity of Southern Distinctiveness*. Baton Rouge: Louisiana State University Press, 1977.

Delap, Simeon, "The Populist Party in North Carolina." *Trinity College Historical Society, Historical Papers* 14 (1922).

Dollar, C. M., and R. J. Jensen. *Historian's Guide to Statistics*. New York: Holt, Rinehart, and Winston, 1971.

Dreben, Robert. *On What Is Learned in Schools*. Menlo Park, Calif.: Addison-Wesley, 1968.

DuBois, W. E. B. *Black Reconstruction in America 1860–1880*. New York: Atheneum, 1975.

Durkheim, Emile. *The Division of Labor in Society.* New York: Macmillan, 1933.

Easterlin, Richard. "Estimates of Manufacturing Activity." In *Population Redistribution and Economic Growth.* Philadelphia: American Philosophical Society, 1957.

Easterlin, Richard. "Regional Income Trends, 1840–1950." *The Reinterpretation of American Economic History,* edited by Robert Fogel and Stanley Engerman. New York: Harper and Row, 1971, 38–49.

Eby, Frederick. *The Development of Education in Texas.* New York: Macmillan, 1925.

Edwards, Richard, *Contested Terrain: The Transformation of the Workplace in the Twentieth Century.* New York: Basic Books, 1979.

Edwards, T. J. "The Tenant System and Some Changes Since Emancipation." *Annals of the American Academy of Political and Social Science* 49 (September 1913): 38–46.

Elkins, Stanley, and Erik McKitrick. "A Meaning for Turner's Frontier." *Political Science Quarterly* 114 (September 1954): 321–353.

Eller, Ronald D. *Miners, Millhands, and Mountaineers: Industrialization of the Appalachian South 1880–1930.* Knoxville: University of Tennessee Press, 1982.

Elson, Ruth. *Guardians of Tradition: Schoolbooks in the Nineteenth Century.* Lincoln: University of Nebraska Press, 1964.

Entwistle, Harold. *Antonio Gramsci: Conservative Schooling for Radical Politics.* London: Routledge and Kegan Paul, 1979.

Entwistle, Harold. *Political Education in a Democracy.* London: Routledge and Kegan Paul, 1971.

Etzioni, Amatai. *The Active Society.* New York: Free Press, 1968.

Farish, Hunter D. *The Circuit Rider Dismounts: A Social History of Southern Methodism, 1865–1900.* Richmond, Va.: Dietz Press, 1938.

Farrell, Richard T. "The Content of Agricultural Newspapers, 1860–1890." *Agricultural History* 51 (January 1977): 209–217.

Faulkner, Ronnie W. "North Carolina Democrats and Silver Fusion Politics, 1892–1896." *North Carolina Historical Review* 59 (July 1982): 230–251.

Farmer, Hallie. "The Economic Background to Southern Populism." *South Atlantic Quarterly* 29 (January 1930): 77–91.

Feinberg, Walter. "On a New Direction for Educational History." *History of Education Quarterly* 21 (Summer 1981): 223–239.

Ferguson, James S. "The Grange and Farmer Education in Mississippi." *Journal of Southern History* 8 (November 1942): 497–512.

Ferkiss, Victor. "Populist Influences on American Facism." *Western Political Quarterly* 10 (June 1957): 350–373.

Fleming, Cynthia G. "The Plight of Black Education in Post-War Tennessee, 1865–1920." *Journal of Negro History* 64 (July 1979).

Fleming, W. L. "Pap Singleton, the Moses of the Colored Exodus." *American Journal of Sociology* 15 (July 1909): 61–82.

Flynt, Wayne. "Dissent in Zion: Alabama Baptists and Social Issues." *Journal of Southern History* 35 (November 1969): 523–542.

Flynt, Wayne. "One in the Spirit, Many in the Flesh: Southern Evangelicals." In *Varieties of Southern Evangelicalism,* edited by David E. Harrell. Macon, Ga.: Mercer University Press, 1981: 23–44.

Foner, Eric. "Reconstruction and the Crisis of Free Labor." In *Politics and Ideology in the Age of the Civil War.* New York: Oxford University Press, 1980.

Foner, Philip. *History of the Labor Movement in the United States,* vol. 2. New York: International Publishers, 1955.

Franklin, Vincent P., and James D. Anderson. *New Perspectives on Black Educational History.* Boston: G. K. Hall, 1978.

Freiberg, J. W., ed. *Critical Sociology.* New York: Irvington Publishers, 1979.

Friedman, Milton, and Anna Schwartz, *A Monetary History of the United States, 1867–1960.* Princeton: National Bureau of Economic Research, 1963.

Friesen, J. K. "The Wheat Pools Also Educate." *Food for Thought* (December 1950): 8–14.

Gaither, Gerald. *Blacks and the Populist Revolt.* University: University of Alabama Press, 1977.

Gallman, Robert. "Self-Sufficiency in the Cotton Economy of the Antebellum South." *Agricultural History* 44 (January 1970): 5–23.

Gaston, Paul. *The New South Creed: A Study in Southern Mythmaking.* Baton Rouge: Louisiana State University Press, 1970.

Gates, Paul W. *Landlords and Tenants on the Prairie Frontier.* Ithaca: Cornell University Press, 1973.

Gatewood, Willard B. "North Carolina and Federal Aid to Education: Public Reaction to the Blair Bill, 1881–1890." *North Carolina Historical Review* 40 (Autumn 1963): 645–648.

Genovese, Eugene. *In Red and Black.* New York: Pantheon, 1971.

Genovese, Eugene. *Roll, Jordan, Roll.* New York: Random House, 1972.

Genovese, Eugene. "Yeoman Farmers in a Slaveholder's Democracy." *Agricultural History* 49 (April 1975), pp. 331–342.

Gerster, Patrick, and Nicholas Cords, eds. *Myth and Southern History,* vol. 2, Chicago: Rand-McNally, 1974.

Gintis, Herbert. "Communication and Politics: Marxism and the 'Problem' of Liberal Democracy." *Socialist Review* 10 (March–June 1980).

Giroux, Henry A. *Ideology, Culture and the Process of Schooling.* Philadelphia: Temple University Press, 1981.

Going, Allen J. "The South and the Blair Education Bill." *Mississippi Valley Historical Review* 44 (September 1957): 267–290.

Goodenow, Ronald. *The Rise of Public Education in the New South.* Boston: G. K. Hall, 1981.

Goodwyn, Lawrence C. *Democratic Promise: The Populist Moment in America.* New York: Oxford University Press, 1976.

Goodwyn, Lawrence C. "Populist Dreams and Negro Rights: East Texas as a Case Study." *American Historical Review* 76 (December 1971): 1435–1436.

Goodwyn, Lawrence C. *The Populist Moment.* New York: Oxford University Press, 1978.

Grabiner, Gene. "Education, Colonialism, and the American Working Class." In *Education and Colonialism,* edited by Philip Altbach and Gail Kelly. New York: Longman, 1978.

Graham, Patricia A. *Community and Class in American Education, 1865–1918.* New York: John Wiley and Sons, 1974.

Green, James. *Grass Roots Socialism: Radical Movements in the Southwest, 1895–1943.* Baton Rouge: Louisiana State University Press, 1978.

Green, James. "Planter-Merchant Conflict in Reconstruction Alabama." *Past and Present* 68 (August 1975): 73–94.

Green, James. "Populism, Socialism, and the Promise of Democracy." *Radical History Review* 24 (Fall 1980): 7–40.

Green, James. "Tenant Farmer Discontent and Socialist Protest in Texas, 1901–1917." *Southern History Quarterly* 81.

Grubb, W. Norton, and Marvin Lazerson. "Rally Round the Workplace." *Harvard Educational Review* 45 (November 1975): 451–474.

Gurr, Ted. R. *Why Men Rebel.* Princeton: Princeton University Press, 1970.

Gutman, Herbert. "Protestantism and the American Labor Movement: The Christian Spirit in the Gilded Age." In *Work, Culture, and Society in Industrializing America.* New York: Vintage Books, 1977.

Hackney, Sheldon. *Populism to Progressivism in Alabama.* Princeton: Princeton University Press, 1969.

Hahn, Steven. "Common Right and Commonwealth: The Stock-Law Struggle and the Roots of Southern Populism." In *Region, Race, and Reconstruction: Essays in Honor of C. Vann Woodward,* edited by J. M. Kousser and James McPherson. New York: Oxford University Press, 1982.

Hahn, Steven. *The Roots of Southern Populism, Yeoman Farmers and the Transformation of the Georgia Upcountry, 1850–1890.* New York: Oxford University Press, 1985.

Handlin, Oscar. "American Views of Jews at the Turn of the Twentieth Century." *Publications of the American Jewish Historical Society* 40 (June 1951). 323–344.

Handlin, Oscar. "Reconsidering the Populists." *Agricultural History* 39 (April 1965): 68–74.

Handy, Robert T. *The Social Gospel in America.* New York: Oxford University Press, 1966.

Harlan, Louis. *Separate and Unequal.* New York: Atheneum, 1969.

Harlan, Louis. "The Southern Education Board and the Race Issue in Public Education." *Journal of Southern History* 23 (April 1957): 189–202.

Harrell, David E., Jr., ed. *Varieties of Southern Evangelicalism.* Macon, Ga.: Mercer University Press, 1981.

Harris, Kevin. *Education and Knowledge.* London: Routledge and Kegan Paul, 1979.

Hays, Samuel P. *The Response to Industrial America.* Chicago: University of Chicago Press, 1957.

Hendrick, Burton J. *The Training of an American: The Earlier Life and Letters of Walter Hines Page.* Boston: Houghton Mifflin, 1928.

Henretta, James. "Families and Farms: Mentalite' in Pre-Industrial America." *William and Mary Quarterly* 35, 3rd series (January 1978): 3–32.

Hicks, John. *The Populist Revolt.* Minneapolis: University of Minnesota Press, 1931.

Higgs, Robert. *Competition and Coercion.* Cambridge: Harvard University Press, 1977.

Higgs, Robert. "Patterns of Farm Rental in the Georgia Cotton Belt, 1880–1900." *Journal of Economic History* 34 (June 1974): 468–482.

Higgs, Robert. "Railroad Rates and the Populist Uprising." *Agricultural History* 44 (July 1970): 291–297.

Hill, Samuel, Jr. *Southern Churches in Crisis.* Boston: Beacon Press, 1968.

Hill, Samuel, Jr. *The South and the North in American Religion.* Athens: University of Georgia Press, 1980.

Hindness, Barry. *The Decline of Working Class Politics.* London: MacGibbon & Kee, 1971.

Hirschman, A. O. *Exit, Voice, and Loyalty.* Cambridge: Harvard University Press, 1970.

Hobsbawm, Eric J. "Class Consciousness in History." In *Aspects of History and Class Consciousness,* edited by Istvan Mezaros. London: Routledge and Kegan Paul, 1971.

Hobsbawm, Eric J. "Custom, Wages, and, Work Load." In *Labouring Men.* London: Weidenfeld and Nicolson, 1976.

Hobsbawm, Eric J. "The Labor Aristocracy in 19th-Century Britain." In *Labouring Men.* London: Weidenfeld and Nicolson, 1976.

Hobsbawm, Eric J. *Primitive Rebels.* New York: Norton, 1959.

Hofstadter, Richard. *The Age of Reform.* New York: Vintage Books, 1955.

Hofstadter, Rchard. *The Progressive Historians.* New York: Alfred A. Knopf, 1968.

Hogan, David. "Making it in America: Work, Education, and Social Structure." In *Work, Youth, and Schooling,* edited by Harvy Kantor and David Tyack. Stanford: Stanford University Press, 1982, pp. 142–179.

Holley, Donald. "Aspects of Southern Farm Life." *Agricultural History* 53, no. 1 (January 1979): 203–205.

Holliday, Carl. *History of Southern Literature.* New York: Neace Publishing Co., 1906.

Hollingsworth, J. Rogers. "Populism: The Problem of Rhetoric and Reality." *Agricultural History* 39 (April 1965).

Holmes, George K. "The Peons of the South." *Annals of the American Academy of Political Science,* 4 (September 1893).

Holmes, William F. "The Arkansas Cotton Pickers Strike of 1891 and the Demise of the Colored Farmers' Alliance." *Arkansas Historical Quarterly* 32, no. 2 (1973): 107–119.

Holmes, William F. "The Demise of the Colored Farmers' Alliance." *Journal of Southern History* 41, May 1975: 187–200.

Holmes, William F. "The Southern Farmers' Alliance and the Georgia Senatorial Election of 1890." *Journal of Southern History* 50 (May 1984: 197–224.

Hopkins, Charles. *The Rise of the Social Gospel in American Protestantism, 1865–1915.* New Haven: Yale University Press, 1940.

Hudson, Winthrop S. *Religion in America.* New York: Scribners, 1973.

Hunt, Robert L. *A History of Farmer Movements in the Southwest 1873–1925.* College Station, Tex.: Texas State University Press, 1935.

James, John A. "Financial Underdevelopment in the Post-Bellum South." *Journal of Interdisciplinary History* 11 Winter 1981.

James, John A. *Money and Capital Markets in Post-Bellum America.* Princeton: Princeton University Press, 1978.

Johnson, Richard. "Educational Policy and Social Control in Early Victorian England." *Past and Present* 49 (1970).

Johnson, Richard. "Really Useful Knowledge: Radical Education and Working Class Culture, 1790-1848." In *Working Class Culture,* edited by J. Clarke et al. New York: St. Martin's Press, 1979.

Jones, Jacqueline. *Soldiers of Light and Love: Northern Teachers and Georgia Blacks.* Chapel Hill: University of North Carolina Press, 1981.

Jones, Lance. *The Jeanes Teacher in the United States.* Chapel Hill: University of North Carolina Press, 1937.

Kaufman, Stuart B. *Samuel Gompers and the Origins of the American Federation of Labor, 1848-1898.* Westport, Conn.: Greenwood Press, 1973.

Katz, Michael B. "An Apology for American Educational History." *Harvard Educational Review* 49 (May 1979): 256–266.

Katz, Michael B. *Class, Bureaucracy, and Schools: The Illusion of Educational Change in America.* New York: Praeger, 1971.

Katz, Michael B. *The Irony of Early School Reform.* Boston: Beacon Press, 1968.

Katz, Michael B. "Origins of the Institutional State." *Marxist Perspectives* 1 (Winter 1978): 6–22.

Katz, Michael B. "The Origins of Public Education: A Reassessment." *History of Education Quarterly* 16 (Winter 1976): 381–407.

Katznelson, Ira, et al. "Public Schooling and Working Class Formation: The Case of the United States." *American Journal of Education* 90 (February 1982): 111–143.

Kendrick, B. B. "The Colonial Status of the South." *Journal of Southern History* 8 (1942): 3–22.

Kennedy, David, ed. *Progressivism: The Critical Issues.* Boston: Little Brown, 1971.

King, Kenneth J. *Pan-Africanism and Education.* New York: Oxford University Press, 1971.

Kirwan, Albert D. *Revolt of the Rednecks.* Lexington: University of Kentucky Press, 1951.

Klotter, James. "The Black South as White Appalachia." *Journal of American History* 66 (March 1980): 832–849.

Knapp, Joseph. *The Rise of American Cooperative Enterprise.* Danville, Ill.: Interstate Printers and Publishers, 1969.

Knight, Edgar W. *The Influence of Reconstruction on Education in the South.* New York: Teachers College Press, 1913.

Kolakowski, Leszeck. *Main Currents of Marxism,* 3 vols. London: Oxford University Press, 1978.

Kolko, Gabriel. *The Triumph of Conservatism.* New York: Free Press, 1963.

Kousser, J. Morgan, and James McPherson, eds. *Region, Race, and Reconstruction: Essays in Honor of C. Vann Woodward.* New York: Oxford University Press, 1982.

Kraditor, A. "American Radical Historians on Their Heritage." *Past and Present* 56 (August 1972): 136–153.

Laclau, Ernesto. *Politics and Ideology in Marxist Thought.* London: New Left Books, 1977.

Laird, William, and James Rinehart. "Deflation, Agriculture, and Southern Development." *Agricultural History* 42 (April 1968): 115–124.

Lane, J. J. *History of Education in Texas.* Washington, D.C.: Government Printing Office, 1903.

Landes, William, and Lewis Solomon. "Compulsory School Legislation: An Economic Analysis of Law and Social Change." *Journal of Economic History* 32 (March 1972).

Larson, M. S. *The Rise of Professionalism.* Berkeley: University of California Press, 1977.

Layer, Robert. *Earnings of Cotton Mill Operatives, 1825–1914.* Cambridge: Harvard University Press, 1955.

Lazerson, Marvin, and Norton Grubb. *American Education and Vocationalism.* New York: Teachers College Press, 1979.

Legergott, Stanley. "Labor Force and Employment, 1800–1860." In *National Bureau of Economic Research, Output, Employment, and Productivity in the U.S. after 1800.* New York: Columbia University Press, 1966.

Lears, T. J. "The Concept of Cultural Hegemony: Problems and Possibilities." *American Historical Review* 90 (June 1985).

Leidecker, Kurt F. *Yankee Teacher: The Life of William Torrey Harris.* New York: Philosophical Library, 1946.

Lerner, Eugene. "Southern Output and Agricultural Income, 1860–1880." *Agricultural History* 33 (July 1959): 117–125.

Lipset, S. M. *Political Man: The Social Basis of Politics.* New York: Doubleday, 1959.

Lukács, G. *History and Class Consciousness.* Cambridge: MIT Press, 1971.

McCardell, John. *The Idea of a Southern Nation, 1830–1860.* New York: W. W. Norton, 1979.

McConnell, Grant. *The Decline of Agrarian Democracy.* Berkeley: University of California Press, 1959.

McLaurin, Melton A. *The Knights of Labor in the South.* Westport, Conn.: Greenwood Press, 1978.

McLear, Patrick. "The Agrarian Revolt in the South: A Historiographical Essay." *Louisiana Studies* 12 (Summer 1973).

McMath, Robert. "Agrarian Protest at the Forks of the Creek: Three Sub-Alliances in North Carolina." *North Carolina Historical Review* 51 (Winter 1974): 41–63.

McMath, Robert. *Populist Vanguard.* Chapel Hill: University of North Carolina Press, 1975.

McMath, Robert. "Southern White Farmers and the Organization of Black Farm Workers." *Labor History* 18 (1977): 115–119.

McMath, Robert, and Vernon Burton, eds. *Class, Conflict, and Consensus.* Westport, Conn.: Greenwood Press, 1982.

MacPherson, C. B. *Democratic Theory: Essays in Retrieval.* Oxford: Clarendon Press, 1973.

McVey, Frank L. *The Gates Open Slowly: A History of Education in Kentucky.* Lexington: University of Kentucky Press, 1949.

Magdol, Edward, and Jon Wakelyn, eds. *The Southern Common People.* Westport, Conn.: Greenwood Press, 1980.

Malin, James C. "The Farmers' Alliance Subtreasury Plan and European Precedents." *Mississippi Valley Historical Review* 21 (September 1944).

Mandel, Jay. *The Roots of Black Poverty: The Southern Plantation Economy After the Civil War.* Durham: Duke University Press, 1977.

Marti, Donald B. "Women's Work in the Grange." *Agricultural History,* 56 (April 1982): 439–452.

Martin, Roscoe C. *The People's Party in Texas: A Study in Third Party Politics.* Austin: University of Texas Press, 1933.

Marty, Martin E. *Righteous Empire: The Protestant Experience in America.* New York: Dial Press, 1970.

May, Henry. *Protestant Churches and Industrial America.* New York: Harper & Bros., 1949.

Meier, August. *Negro Thought in America.* Ann Arbor: University of Michigan Press, 1973.

Merrill, Michael. "Cash is Good to Eat: Self-Sufficiency and Exchange in the Rural Economy of the United States." *Radical History Review* 3 (Winter 1977).

Meyer, John. "The Effects of Education as an Institution." *American Journal of Sociology* 83 (July 1977): 55–77.

Miller, Marc S., ed. *Working Lives: The Southern Exposure History of Labor*

Mitchell, Broadus. *The Rise of Cotton Mills in the South.* Baltimore: Johns Hopkins Press, 1921.

Montgonery, David. *Beyond Equality.* Urbana: University of Illinois Press, 1981.

Montgomery, David. "Goodwyn's Populists." *Marxist Perspectives* 1 (1978): 166–173.

Montgomery, David. *Worker Control in America.* New York: Cambridge University Press, 1979.

Montgomery, David. "Workers' Control of Machine Production in the Nineteenth Century." *Labor History* 17 (Fall 1976): 485–509.

Moore, Barrington, Jr. *Injustice: The Social Basis of Obedience and Revolt.* White Plains: M. E. Sharpe, 1978.

Moore, Barrington, Jr. *Social Origins of Dictatorship and Democracy.* Boston: Beacon Press, 1966.

Nixon, H. C. "The Cleavage Within the Farmers' Alliance Movement." *Mississippi Valley Historical Review* 15 (June 1949): 22–33.

Noble, David. *America by Design.* New York: Alfred A. Knopf, 1979.

Noble, David. *The Paradox of Progressive Thought.* Minneapolis: University of Minnesota Press, 1958.

North, Douglass C. *Growth and Welfare in the American Past.* Englewood Cliffs, N.J.: Prentice-Hall, 1974.

Nugent, Walter K. *The Tolerant Populists: Kansas Populism and Nativism.* Chicago: University of Chicago Press, 1963.

Oakes, James. *The Ruling Race.* New York: Knopf, 1982.

Oberschall, Anthony. *Social Conflict and Social Movements.* Englewood Cliffs, N.J.: Prentice-Hall, 1973.

Olsen, Otto. *Carpetbagger's Crusade: The Life of Albion Winegar Tourgee.* Baltimore: Johns Hopkins University Press, 1965.

Olson, Mancur, Jr. *The Logic of Collective Action.* Cambridge: Harvard University Press, 1965.

Orr, Dorothy. *A History of Education in Georgia.* Chapel Hill: University of North Carolina Press, 1950.

Painter, Nell I. *Exodusters: Black Migration to Kansas after Reconstruction.* New York: W. W. Norton, 1976.

Palmer, Bruce. *"Man Over Money."* Chapel Hill: University of North Carolina Press, 1980.

Parsons, Stanley, Karen T. Parsons, Walter Killilate, and Beverly Borgers. "The Role of Cooperatives in the Development of the Movement Culture of Populism." *Journal of American History* 69, no. 4 (March 1983): 866–885.

Patrick, M. E. "The Selection and Adoption of Textbooks: Texas, a Case Study." Unpublished Ph.D. dissertation, Stanford University, 1949.

Paulson, Rolland, and Gregory LeRoy. "Strategies for Non-Formal Education." *Teachers College Record* 76 (May 1975).

Pawa, Jay M. "Workingmen and Free Schools in the Nineteenth Century." *History of Education Quarterly* 11 (Fall 1971): 287–302.

Pessen, Edward. "The Workingmen's Movement in the Jacksonian Era." *Mississippi Valley Historical Review* 43 (December 1956): 428–443.

Piven, Frances Fox, and Richard Cloward. *Poor People's Movements.* New York: Vintage Books, 1979.

Pollack, Norman. "Fear of Man: Populism, Authoritarianism, and the Historian." *Agricultural History* 39 (April 1965): 59–67.

Pollack, Norman. "Hofstadter on Populism." *Journal of Southern History* 26 (November 1960): 478–500.

Pollack, Norman. "The Myth of Populist Anti-Semitism." *American Historical Review* 68 (October 1962): 76–80.

Pollack, Norman. *The Populist Response to Industrial America.* New York: W. W. Norton, 1962.

Porter, Jane M. "Experiment Stations in the South, 1877–1940." *Agricultural History* 53, no. 1 (January 1979): 84–101.

Poulantzas, Nicos. "The Political Crisis and the Crisis of the State." In *Critical Sociology,* edited by J. W. Freiberg. New York: Irvington Publishers, 1979.

Poulantzas, Nicos. "Toward a Democratic Socialism." In *State, Power and Socialism.* London: New Left Books, 1978.

Pugh, Patricia. *Educate, Agitate, Organize: One Hundred Years of Fabian Socialism.* London and New York: Methuen, 1984.

Rabinowitz, Howard. "From Reconstruction to Redemption in the Urban South." *Journal of Urban History* 2 (February 1976): 169–194.

Rabinowtiz, Howard. "Half a Loaf: The Shift from White to Black Teachers in the Negro Schools of the Urban South." *Journal of Southern History* 40 (November 1976): 565–594.

Rabinowitz, Howard. *Race Relations in the Urban South, 1865–1890.* Urbana: University of Illinois Press, 1980.

Ransom, Roger, and Richard Sutch. "Debt Peonage in the Cotton South after the Civil War." *Journal of Economic History* 32 (September 1972): 641–669.

Ransom, Roger, and Richard Sutch. "The 'Lock-In Mechanism' and Overproduction of Cotton in the Post-Bellum South." *Agricultural History* 49, no. 2 (April 1975): 405–425.

Ransom, Roger, and Richard Sutch. *One Kind of Freedom.* New York: Cambridge University Press, 1977.

Reid, J. D., Jr. "Antebellum Share Rental Contracts." *Explorations in Economic History* 13 (January 1977): 69–83.

Reid, J. D., Jr. "Sharecropping and Tenancy in American History." In *Risk and Uncertainty in Agriculture,* edited by James Roumasset. Berkeley: University of California Press, 1980.

Reid, J. D., Jr. Sharecropping as an Understandable Market Response to the Post-Bellum South." *Journal of Economic History* 33 (March 1973): 106–130.

Rice, Jessie P. *J. L. M. Curry: Southerner, Statesman, and Educator.* New York: Kings Crown Press, Columbia University, 1949.

Rice, Lawrence. *The Negro in Texas, 1874–1900.* Baton Rouge: Louisiana State University Press, 1971.

Rodgers, Daniel T. *The Work Ethic in Industrializing America, 1850–1920.* Chicago: University of Chicago Press, 1978.

Rogers, William W. "Alabama's Reform Press." *Agricultural History* 34 (April 1960): 62–70.

Rogers, William W. "The Negro Alliance in Alabama." *Journal of Negro History* 45 (January 1960): 38–44.

Rogers, William W. *The One-Gallused Rebellion: Agrarianism in Alabama.* Baton Rouge: Louisiana State University Press, 1970.

Rogers, William W. "Reuben F. Kolb: Agricultural Leader of the New South." *Agricultural History* 32 (April 1958): 109–119.

Rogin, Michael. *The Intellectuals and McCarthy: The Radical Spectre.* Cambridge: MIT Press, 1967.

Rosen, F. Bruce. "The Influence of the Peabody Fund on Education in Reconstruction Florida." *Florida Historical Quarterly* 55 (Fall 1977): 310–320.

Rubin, Julius. "The Limits of Agricultural Progress in the 19th Century South." *Agricultural History* 49, no. 2 (April 1975).

Rude, George. *The Crowd in the French Revolution.* London: Oxford University Press, 1969.

Rude, George. *Ideology and Popular Protest.* New York: Pantheon, 1981.

Saluotos, Theodore. *Farmer Movements in the South, 1865–1933.* Berkeley: University of California Publications in History, vol. 64, 1960.

Samuel, Raphael, ed. *People's History and Socialist Theory.* London: Routledge and Kegan Paul, 1981.

Sarup, Madan. *Marxism and Education.* London: Routledge and Kegan Paul, 1978.

Saunders, Robert. "Southern Populism and the Negro." *Journal of Negro History* 54 (July 1969): 240–261.

Schwartz, Michael. "An Estimate of the Size of the Southern Farmers' Alliance, 1884–1890." *Agricultural History* 51, no. 4 (December 1977): 759–769.

Schwartz, Michael. *Radical Protest and Social Structure: The Southern Farmers' Alliance and Cotton Tenancy, 1880–1890.* San Francisco: Academic Press, 1976.

Scott, Roy V. "Railroads and Farmers: Educational Trains in Missouri." *Agricultural History* 36 (January 1962): 3–15.

Scruggs, C. G. and S. W. Moseley. "The Role of Agricultural Journalism." *Agricultural History* 53 (January 1979): 22–29.

Seagrave, Charles. "The Southern Negro Agricultural Worker." Unpublished Ph.D. dissertation, Stanford University, 1971.

Shade, William G. "The Working-Class and Educational Reform in Early America." *Historian* 39 (November 1976): 1–23.

Shannon, Fred. "C. W. Macune and the Farmers' Alliance." *Current History* 28 (June 1955): 330–335.

Shannon, Fred. *The Farmers' Last Frontier.* New York: Reinhart, 1945.

Shaw, Barton. *The Wool Hat Boys, Georgia's Populist Party* (Baton Rouge: Louisiana State University Press, 1984.

Sheldon, William. *Populism in the Old Dominion.* Princeton: Princeton University Press, 1935.

Shils, Edward. *The Torment of Secrecy.* Glencoe, Ill.: Free Press, 1956.

Shugg, Roger. "Survival of the Plantation System in Louisiana." *Journal of Southern History* 3 (August 1937): 311–325.

Shurter, Edwin Dubois. *Oratory of the South.* New York: Neale Publishing Co., 1908.

Silver, Harold. *English Education and the Radicals.* London: Routledge and Kegan Paul, 1975.

Simkins, Francis B. *Pitchfork Ben Tillman: South Carolinian.* Baton Rouge: Louisiana State University Press, 1944.

Simkins, Francis B., and Robert Woody. *South Carolina During Reconstruction.* Chapel Hill: University of North Carolina Press, 1932.

Simon, Brian. *The Radical Tradition in Education in Britain.* London: Lawrence and Wishart, 1972.

Simon, Walter B. "Democracy in the Shadow of Imposed Sovereignty: The First Republic in Austria." In *Breakdown of Democratic Regimes,* edited by J. Linz and A Stepan. Baltimore: Johns Hopkins University Press, 1978.

Simons, A. M. *Social Forces in American History.* New York: Macmillan, 1915.

Smelser, Neil. *The Theory of Collective Behavior.* New York: Free Press, 1963.

Smith, Ralph A. " 'Macunism' or the Farmers of Texas in Business." *Journal of Southern History* 13 (May 1947): 220–244.

Smith, Travis E. *The History of Education in Monroe County, Georgia.* Forsyth, Ga.: Monroe Advertiser, 1934.

Solomon, Lewis. "Opportunity Costs and Models of Schooling in the Nineteenth Century." *Southern Economic Journal* (July 1970): 66–83.

Spivey, D. *Schooling for the New Slavery: Black Industrial Education, 1868–1915.* Westport, Conn.: Greenwood Press, 1978.

Spriggs, William E. "The Virginia Farmers' Alliance: A Case Study of Race and Class Identity." *Journal of Negro History* 64 (Summer 1979): 191–204.

Spring, Joel. *Educating the Worker Citizen.* New York: Longman, 1980.

Spring, Joel. *Education and the Rise of the Corporate State.* Boston: Beacon Press, 1972.

Stampp, Kenneth, and Leon Litwack, eds. *Reconstruction.* Baton Rouge. Louisiana State University Press, 1969.

Steelman, Lala Carr. "The Role of Elias Carr in the North Carolina Farmers' Alliance." *North Carolina Historical Review* 57, no. 2 (April 1980): 133–158.

Street, James, H. *The New Revolution in the Cotton Economy.* Chapel Hill: University of North Carolina Press, 1957.

Sweet, W. W. "Methodist Church Influence in Southern Politics." *Mississippi Valley Historical Review* 1 (March 1915).

Taylor, Carl Cleveland. *The Farmers' Movement, 1820–1920.* New York: American Book Company, 1953.

Taylor, J. H. "Populists and Disenfranchisement in Alabama." *Journal of Negro History* 34 (October 1949): 410–427.

Teitelbaum, Kenneth, and William Reese. "American Socialist Pedagogy and Experimentation in the Progressive Era: The Socialist Sunday School." *History of Education Quarterly* (Winter 1983): 429–454.

Therborn, Goran. *What Does the Ruling Class Do When it Rules?* London: New Left Books, 1978.

Tholfsen, Trygve R. *Working Class Radicalism in Mid-Victorian England.* New York: Columbia University Press, 1977.

Thompson, Edward Palmer. "Eighteenth Century English Society: Class Struggle Without Class." *Social History* 3 (May 1978).

Thompson, Edward Palmer. *The Making of the English Working Class.* New York: Vintage Books, 1966.

Thompson, Edward Palmer. "The Moral Economy of the English Crowd in the Eighteenth Century." *Past and Present* 50 (February 1971): 76–136.

Thompson, Edward Palmer. "Patrician Society: Plebian Culture." *Journal of Social History* 3 (Summer 1976.

Thompson, Edward Palmer. *The Poverty of Theory and Other Essays.* New York: Monthly Review Press, 1978.

Thornton, J. Mills, III. "Fiscal Policy and the Failure of Radical Reconstruction in the Lower South." In *Region, Race, and Reconstruction,* edited by J. Kousser and James McPherson. New York: Oxford University Press, 1982.

Tilly, Charles. *From Mobilization to Revolution.* Menlo Park, Calif.: Addison-Wesley, 1978.

Tindall, George B. *The Emergence of the New South, 1913–1945.* Baton Rouge: Louisiana State University Press, 1967.

Tindall, George B. *A Populist Reader.* New York: Harper Torchbooks, 1966.

Turner, James. "Understanding the Populists." *Journal of American History* 67 (September 1980): 354–373.

Tyack, David B. *The One Best System.* Cambridge: University Press, 1974.

Tyack, David, and Theodore Mitchell. "A Review of Lawrence Cremin's American Education the National Experience, 1783–1876." *American Journal of Education* 92 (February 1982).

Unger, Irwin. "Critique of Norman Pollack's 'Fear of Man.'" *Agricultural History* 39 (April 1965): 75–80.

Unger, Irwin. *The Greenback Era: A Social and Political History of American Finance 1865–1879.* Princeton: Princeton University Press, 1964.

Vance, J. Q. "Contributions of Teacher Training Agencies in Tennessee." *Peabody Journal of Education* 7 (March 1930): 272–280.

Viereck, Peter. "The Revolt Against the Elite." *The Radical Right,* edited by D. Bell. New York: Criterion, 1954.

Viereck, Peter. *The Unadjusted Man.* Boston: Beacon Press, 1956.

Violas, Paul. *The Training of the Urban Working Class.* Chicago: University of Chicago Press, 1978.

Watson, Alan D. "Society and Economy in Colonial Edgecombe County." *North Carolina Historical Review* 50, no. 3 (July 1973): 231–255.

Webber, Thomas. *Deep Like the Rivers.* New York: W. W. Norton, 1978.

Weinstein, James. *The Corporate Ideal and the Liberal State.* Boston: Beacon Press, 1968.

Welter, Rush. *The Mind of America, 1820–1860.* New York: Columbia University Press, 1975.

Welter, Rush. *Popular Education and Democratic Thought in America.* New York: Columbia University Press, 1962.

Wheeler, John T. *Two Hundred Years of Agricultural Education in Georgia.* Danville, Ill.: Interstate, 1948.

White, Ronald Cedrick, and Charles Hopkins. *The Social Gospel: Religion and Reform in Changing America.* Philadelphia: Temple University Press, 1976.

Wiebe, Robert. *The Search for Order.* New York: Hill and Wange, 1967.

Wieman, David. "Petty Production in the Cotton South: A Study of Upcountry Georgia 1840–1880." Unpublished Ph.D. dissertation, Stanford University, 1983.

Wiener, Jonathan. "Class Structure and the Economic Development of the American South, 1865–1955." *American Historical Review* 84 (October 1979): 970–992.

Wiener, Jonathan. *Social Origins of the New South: Alabama, 1860–1885.* Baton Rouge: Louisiana State University Press, 1978.

Williams, Raymond. "Base and Superstructure in Marxist Cultural Theory." *New Left Review* 83 (1973).

Williams, Raymond. *The Long Revolution.* New York: Columbia University Press, 1961.

Williams, Raymond, *Marxism and Literature.* New York: Oxford University Press, 1977.

Williams, Raymond. *Sociology of Culture.* New York: Schocken, 1981.

Willis, Paul. *Learning to Labor.* New York: Columbia University Press, 1981.

Wilson, Charles R. *Baptized in Blood: The Religion of the Lost Cause, 1865–1920.* Athens: University of Georgia Press, 1980.

Woodman, Harold D. *King Cotton and His Retainers.* Lexington: University of Kentucky Press, 1968.

Woodman, Harold D. "New Perspectives in Southern Economic Development." *Agricultural History* 49, no. 2 (April 1975): 374–381.

Woodman, Harold D. "Post Civil War Agriculture and the Law." *Agricultural History* 53, no. 1 (January 1979): 319–337.

Woodward, C. Vann. *The Origins of the New South, 1877–1913.* Baton Rouge: Louisiana State University Press, 1971.

Woodward, C. Vann. "The Populist Heritage and the Intellectual." *American Scholar* 29 (1959–60): 55–72.

Woodard, C. Vann. *The Strange Career of Jim Crow.* 3d edition, revised. New York: Oxford University Press, 1974.

Woodward, C. Vann. *Tom Watson: Agrarian Rebel.* New York: Oxford University Press, 1979.

Woodward, C. Vann. "Tom Watson and the Negro." *Journal of Southern History* 4 (February 1938): 14–33.

Wright, Gavin. *The Political Economy of the Cotton South.* New York: W. W. Norton, 1978.

GOVERNMENT DOCUMENTS

U.S. Department of Agriculture. "Causes of Southern Rural Conditions and the Small Farms as an Important Remedy," by Seaman A. Knapp. *Yearbook,* 1908.

U.S. Department of Agriculture. "Popular Education for the Farmers in the United States," by Alfred C. True. *Yearbook,* 1897.

U.S. Department of Agriculture. "The Grange: Its Origin, Progress, and Educational Purposes." *Special Report* 55, 1883.

U.S. Department of Agriculture. "A History of Agricultural Extension Work in the U.S.," by A. C. True. *Miscellaneous Publications* 15, 1923.

U.S. Department of Agriculture. "Services in Cotton Marketing." *Bulletin* 1445, 1926.

U.S. Department of Agriculture, Office of Experiment Stations. "The American System of Agricultural Education." *Circular* 106, 1911.

U.S. Department of the Interior, Bureau of the Census. *Compendium of the Eleventh Census,* 1890.

U.S. Department of the Interior, Bureau of the Census. *Compendium of the Tenth Census,* 1880.

U.S. Department of the Interior, Bureau of the Census. *Compendium of the Twelfth Census,* 1900.

U.S. Department of the Interior, Bureau of the Census. *Farm Population of the United States,* by Leon Truesdell. *Census Monograph* 4, 1920.

U.S. Department of the Interior, Bureau of the Census. *Farm Tenancy in the United States,* by E. A. Goldenweiser and Leon Truesdell. *Census Monograph* 5, 1924.

U.S. Department of the Interior, Bureau of the Census. *Report on Cotton Production of the State of Mississippi,* by E. W. Hilgard, 1884.

U.S. Department of the Interior, Bureau of the Census. *Report on Cotton Production in the United States at the Tenth Census,* 2 pts., 1884.

U.S. Department of the Interior, Bureau of the Census. *Report on Farms and Homes: Property and Indebtedness at the Eleventh Census,* 1890.

U.S. Department of the Interior, Bureau of the Census. *Report on Population at the Eleventh Census,* vol. 1, pt. 1, 1893.

U.S. Department of the Interior, Bureau of the Census. *Statistics of Agriculture in the United States at the Eleventh Census,* 1892.

U.S. Department of the Interior, Bureau of Education. *Annual Report of the Commissioner of Education 1880–1905.*

U.S. Department of the Interior, Bureau of Education. "Commissioner's Annual Statement," by N. H. R. Dawson. *Report of the Commissioner of Education, 1887–8.*

U.S. Department of the Interior, Bureau of Education. "Education in the South," by W. R. Garrett. *Circular of Information 2, 1889.*

U.S. Department of the Interior, Bureau of Education. "The Educational Movement in the South," by W. T. Harris. *Report of the Commissioner of Education, 1903.*

U.S. Department of the Interior, Bureau of Education. "Educational Periodicals During the Nineteenth Century." *U.S. Office of Education Bulletin 28, 1919.*

U.S. Department of the Interior, Bureau of Education. "The Educational Needs and Status of the New South," by Robert Bingham. *Miscellaneous Papers 1884–1893.*

U.S. Department of the Interior, Bureau of Education. "Educational Problems in the Several States Since the Organization of the Southern Education Board." *Report of the Commissioner of Education, pt. 1, 1907.*

U.S. Department of the Interior, Bureau of Education. "History of Education in Alabama," by Willis Clark. *Circular of Information 3, 1889.*

U.S. Department of the Interior, Bureau of Education. "History of Education in Florida," by G. G. Bush. *Circular of Information 7, 1888.*

U.S. Department of the Interior, Bureau of Education. "History of Education in Georgia," by C. E. Jones. *Circular of Information 4, 1888.*

U.S. Department of the Interior, Bureau of Education. "Higher Education and the Negro," by E. C. Mitchell. *Report of the Commissioner of Education, 1894–5.*

U.S. Department of the Interior, Bureau of Education. "Industrial Education of Blacks," by B. T. Washington. *Report of the Commissioner of Education, 1895.*

U.S. Department of the Interior, Bureau of Education. "Industrial Education in the New South," by George Winston. *Report of the Commissioner of Education, 1900–1.*

U.S. Department of the Interior, Bureau of Education. "A Letter Concerning the Establishment of a Normal School for the Women of Virginia." *Report of the Commissioner of Education, 1901.*

U.S. Department of the Interior, Bureau of Education. "The New Plan of the Peabody Fund," by W. T. Harris. *Report of the Commissioner of Education, 1888–9.*

U.S. Department of the Interior, Bureau of Labor Statistics. "History of Wages in the U.S. From Colonial Times to 1925." *Bulletin 499, 1926.*

U.S. Congress, Senate. *Report on the Condition of Cotton Growers in the United States.* S.Rept. 986. 53d Congress, 3d session, 1895.

U.S. Congress, Senate. *Proceedings of the Select Committee of the U.S. Senate to Investigate the Causes of the Removal of the Negroes from the Southern States.* S. Rept. 693. 46th Congress, 2d session, 1880.

U.S. Congress, Senate. *Report of the Senate Committee on Education and Labor.* 48th Congress, 2d session, 1885.

U.S. Industrial Commission. *Report of the Industrial Commission.* Government Printing Office: 1901.

Index

DATE DUE

DEMCO NO. 38-298